Macroeconomic Policy, Growth and Poverty Reduction

Macroeconomic Policy, Growth and Poverty Reduction

Edited by

Terry McKinley
Human Development Economist
United Nations Development Programme
New York

First published 2001 by
PALGRAVE
Houndmills, Basingstoke, Hampshire RG21 6XS and
175 Fifth Avenue, New York, N. Y. 10010
Companies and representatives throughout the world

PALGRAVE is the new global academic imprint of
St. Martin's Press LLC Scholarly and Reference Division and
Palgrave Publishers Ltd (formerly Macmillan Press Ltd).

ISBN 0–333–92897–0

This book is printed on paper suitable for recycling and made from fully managed and sustained forest sources.

A catalogue record for this book is available from the British Library.

Library of Congress Cataloging-in-Publication Data
Macroeconomic policy, growth, and poverty reduction /
edited by Terry McKinley.
    p. cm.
Includes bibliographical references and index.
ISBN 0–333–92897–0
    1. Structural adjustment (Economic policy)—Developing countries. 2. Economic stabilization—Developing countries. 3. Poor—Developing countries. 4. Investments—Developing countries. I. McKinley, Terry.
    HC59.7 .M2392 2001
    339.5'09172'4—dc21

                        00–054950

10	9	8	7	6	5	4	3	2	1
10	09	08	07	06	05	04	03	02	01

Printed and bound in Great Britain by
Antony Rowe Ltd, Chippenham, Wiltshire

Contents

v

Acknowledgements

I wish to thank Thierry Lemaresquier, formerly the Director of the Social Development and Poverty Elimination Division of UNDP for his continuing support for this book, and for his direct support for three of the chapters that constitute it. Also, I want to thank for their support Anders Wijkman and Eimi Watanabe, consecutive Assistant Administrators and Directors of the Bureau for Development Policy of UNDP during the time that this book was being produced.

Special thanks go to Elizabeth Satow, a fellow professional in the Social Development and Poverty Elimination Division of UNDP, without whose invaluable work this book could never have been completed.

Thanks also go to UNDP's Regional Bureau for Africa, Regional Bureau for Asia and the Pacific and Regional Bureau for Latin America and the Caribbean for their support of a number of the chapters. Thanks are also in order for Samir Radwan, Director of the ILO's Development Policies Department, who was responsible for commissioning the chapter by Keith Griffin, and for Franklyn Lisk, Chief of the ILO's Entrepreneurship and Management Development Branch, who was responsible for commissioning the chapter by Keith Griffin and Mark D. Brenner.

Thanks also go to the International Labour Office for granting publication of the following three chapters:

Chapter 2, 'Macroeconomic Reform and Employment: An Investment-Led Strategy of Structural Adjustment in Sub-Saharan Africa', by Keith Griffin (Copyright, International Labour Organization 1997).

Chapter 3 by John Weeks, 'Macroeconomic Policy for Growth, with Reference to Africa South of the Sahara', is a substantially revised version of a paper originally written for the ILO's Development Policies Department.

Chapter 4, 'Domestic Resource Mobilization and Enterprise Development in Sub-Saharan Africa', by Keith Griffin and Mark D. Brenner. The chapter in this volume is an edited version of an unpublished paper prepared for the International Labour Office, Entrepreneurship and Management Development Branch (Copyright, International Labour Organization 1997).

Chapter 5, 'Macroeconomic Policies and Poverty', by Azizur Rahman Khan. This paper was part of the Papers and Proceedings of the Regional

Tripartite Workshop on Policies for Poverty Alleviation, Bangkok, 5–7 February 1997 (Copyright, International Labour Organization 1997). Following is a list of the chapters in this book commissioned by UNDP: Chapter 6 by Albert Berry, 'The Macroeconomic Context to Promote Social Development and Combat Poverty in Latin America and the Caribbean', is a shortened version of a paper written in 1996 for the UNDP project 'Poverty Alleviation and Social Development' (Copyright, United Nations Development Programme 1996).

Chapter 7 by Diana Alarcón, 'National Poverty Reduction Strategies of Chile, Costa Rica and Mexico: Summary of Findings', was written in 1997 for the Social Development and Poverty Elimination Division of UNDP (Copyright, United Nations Development Programme 1997).

Chapter 8 by Terry McKinley, 'The Macroeconomic Implications of Focusing on Poverty Reduction', was written in 1997 as a Technical Support Document for the Social Development and Poverty Elimination Division of UNDP (Copyright, United Nations Development Programme 1997).

Chapter 9 by Keith Griffin and Amy Ickowitz, 'The Distribution of Wealth and the Pace of Development', was written in 1997 for the Social Development and Poverty Elimination Division of UNDP (Copyright, United Nations Development Programme 1997).

Although the United Nations Development Programme retains the copyright to these chapters, it is not responsible for the views expressed in them or for the views in the other four chapters in this volume.

Notes on the Contributors

Diana Alarcón, Social Development Specialist, Interamerican Development Bank, Washington, DC.

Albert Berry, Professor of Economics, University of Toronto and Centre for International Studies, Toronto.

Mark D. Brenner, Research Fellow, Political Economy Research Institute, University of Massachusetts–Amherst.

Keith Griffin, Professor of Economics, Department of Economics, University of California–Riverside.

Amy Ickowitz, PhD student, Department of Economics, University of California–Riverside.

Azizur Rahman Khan, Professor of Economics, Department of Economics, University of California–Riverside.

Terry McKinley, Human Development Economist, Social Development and Poverty Elimination Division, United Nations Development Programme, New York.

John Weeks, Professor of Economics and Director, Centre for Development Policy and Research, School of Oriental and African Studies, University of London.

1 Introduction to Macroeconomic Policy, Growth and Poverty Reduction

Terry McKinley

Lively controversies continue on the effect of orthodox structural adjustment policies on growth and poverty reduction. Critics argue that the macroeconomic policies associated with structural adjustment have produced neither significant growth nor poverty reduction. Often the poor are directly harmed by such policies, as severe slumps in output and employment follow. Even when growth occurs, it is frequently slow and its impact mitigated by rising inequality.

Much of the recent debate in development circles has centred on the relationship between growth and inequality. The traditional position – now widely questioned – has been that some degree of inequality is a spur to growth because it motivates greater work effort, savings and investment. A more recent position argues exactly the opposite: inequality impedes growth by restricting access to such productive assets as land and human capital and lowering productivity. Most recently, the traditionalists have mounted a counter-attack, contending that 'growth is good for the poor' because, in part, growth does not worsen inequality: the poor benefit as much as the rich.

No doubt, the nature of this debate clouds some of the policy issues involved – especially by positing some necessary connection between 'growth in general' and 'inequality in general'. The real issue is determining the set of policies that each country should implement in order to achieve both growth and greater equity. The set might contain some policies that are more conducive to growth and others that are more conducive to lowering inequality. The challenge is to construct a policy package that achieves the optimal impact in terms of reducing poverty.

The chapters in this volume explore this issue in the context of determining the relationship between macroeconomic policies, on the one hand, and growth and poverty reduction, on the other. As noted in the acknowledgements, either the United Nations Development Programme or the International Labour Office has commissioned each chapter in the volume. Together, the chapters cover a number of regions in the world: those by Griffin, Griffin and Brenner, and Weeks examine sub-Saharan Africa; those by Alarcón and Berry examine Latin America and the Caribbean; and Khan's chapter examines Asia and the Pacific. The chapters by Griffin and Ickowitz and by McKinley explore some of the same themes as the others but from a more general perspective.

The chapters take similar approaches to determining the relationships among macroeconomic policies, growth and poverty reduction and come to many of the same conclusions. In comparison to the positions of the so-called 'Washington Consensus',[1] they are noteworthy for taking a more critical or independent view of conventional wisdom. Many of the points they have raised are now more widely endorsed and are similar to those associated with what has been labelled a new 'Post-Washington Consensus'.[2] The issues raised by this volume remain timely and relevant since the positions comprising the 'Post-Washington Consensus' have come under sharp attack and have yet to consolidate themselves as any kind of broad 'consensus'.

A Critique of Structural Adjustment

A number of the chapters take an explicitly heterodox approach to restructuring economies. Their orientation is more growth-oriented and more employment-intensive than is customary. Many of them are critical, explicitly or implicitly, of the standard policy package for structural adjustment. Instead of favouring reliance on the liberalization of prices, they emphasize the importance of boosting investment, that is, increasing public investment that is complementary to private investment, and stimulating private investment further through a more efficient allocation of credit.

This implies a more favourable attitude toward expansionary fiscal policies and greater acceptance of fiscal deficits, as long as they are sustainable, and of inflation, as long as it is kept moderate. In reforming state-led economies to provide greater scope to market forces, the heterodox position focuses less on privatization of state-owned enterprises than on encouraging the growth of new private-sector enterprises – particularly those that are small-scale and employment-intensive.

Emphasizing Investment

In order to finance greater investment, many of the chapters advocate reliance primarily on domestic resource mobilization. Depending on official development assistance or inflows of private capital to jump-start growth is considered ill-advised. Some resources can be mobilized by tilting public expenditures more towards productive investment – in human capital as well as in physical and natural capital. Public policies can also create an environment more conducive to broad-based private investment, through either more favourable macroeconomic policies or more equitable redistribution of assets. With greater opportunities for investment, people save more and/or work more to expand their asset base.

Several chapters emphasize the importance of fostering such investment opportunities among the poor. This is based on the unconventional view that the poor are fully capable of saving – and also of building up their productive assets through greater application of labour – if they are afforded the profitable opportunities to do so. A major theme of many of the chapters is that given the correct mix of public policies, there need be no inherent trade-off between equity and growth. As a result of an examination of the development experience of East Asian economies and the findings of a number of recent research efforts, this formerly heterodox view is now becoming more widely accepted. In fact, it is now more generally believed that a high degree of inequality – particularly in the distribution of assets – in fact impedes growth.

Macroeconomics and Redistribution

Some of the chapters in this volume extend the standard analysis by linking inequality with human development instead of merely with growth. The evidence for a positive relationship between greater equality in the distribution of wealth and more human development is found to be compelling. Particular stress is placed on greater equity in the distribution of land and housing, both of which are critically important productive assets for the poor. More research work is needed, however, to demonstrate that poverty reduction – a more specific objective than achieving equity – can be made consistent with increased growth and human development.

Most of the chapters agree that a rise in inequality can pose a serious impediment to poverty reduction, and some present evidence that in a number of cases sharply rising inequality – often coupled with slow growth – has accompanied structural adjustment policies. Of particular concern is a worsening of inequality that is brought about by the declining share of income of poor households.

Such a trend of rising inequality indicates that unless a country's growth is exceedingly rapid, its development strategy and macroeconomic policies will tend to reproduce poverty rather than reduce it. The character of its growth, in other words, is likely to be 'anti-poor' rather than 'pro-poor'. Most of the chapters agree that 'macro' policies can have as much impact as – if not more than – targeted anti-poverty programmes. But what do they claim is needed to make growth more pro-poor?

The general answer given by most of the chapters is that three conditions should be created: a concentration of growth in economic sectors that can directly benefit the poor, an enabling environment that promotes their employment and real incomes and enhancement of their basic human capabilities. The chapters generally agree that macroeconomic policies can influence whether growth is pro-poor, but that such policies cannot be a substitute for an equitable distribution of productive assets. Provided that measures are taken to help secure the poor's access to productive assets, such as land, housing and equipment for microenterprises, then employing macroeconomic policies to help raise the returns to these assets is considered the most useful approach.

Macroeconomic Reform and Employment

In 'Macroeconomic Reform and Employment: An Investment-Led Strategy of Structural Adjustment in Sub-Saharan Africa', Keith Griffin offers a critical evaluation of the standard approach to stabilization and structural adjustment.

He points out that there are three distinct paths of achieving structural adjustment of an economy. The first path, which is the route often recommended by conventional policies, is to allow market-determined relative prices to rapidly reallocate the existing stock of productive resources. Getting relative prices right is the central prescription of such a policy package.

This approach assumes that resources can remain fully employed and output can be maintained at the same level during restructuring, but Griffin argues that such a scenario is unlikely unless there is a significant increase in investment in expanding profitable sectors – an increase that more than compensates for the loss of productive resources in contracting unprofitable sectors. Thus, structural adjustment requires a growth strategy in order to succeed, and for this, getting prices right is inadequate.

The reality of structural adjustment in sub-Saharan Africa has been associated with a drastic drop in production instead of stability of production. Despite rhetoric to the contrary, a second path has, in effect, been followed, which Griffin calls 'structural adjustment through contraction'. This path has led to widespread economic contraction, high unemployment and massive poverty.

According to Griffin, a third path should have been followed – 'structural adjustment through investment'. Such an investment-led path is based on simultaneous expansion of all sectors of the economy, but at differing rates. Hence, restructuring has to be based on a growth process, not on contraction of the economy. Griffin points to China and Vietnam as examples of such an approach.

The key is to implement policies that boost investment and allocate it efficiently. Griffin identifies two broad areas where improvements can be made. The first is public investment, which is poorly allocated in sub-Saharan Africa. He advocates its reallocation to building up rural and urban infrastructure and human capital – forms of investment that are complementary to private investment instead of being competitive. The second area for reforms is private investment, which is inefficiently allocated mainly because of poorly functioning capital markets. The pricing of credit is not the major problem, but rather most people's lack of access to credit, at any price. The emphasis, Griffin believes, should be on channelling credit to encourage the emergence of new small and medium-sized private sector enterprises.

Macroeconomic Policy for Growth

The chapter by John Weeks, 'Macroeconomic Policy for Growth, with Reference to Africa South of the Sahara', concurs with Griffin in advocating an investment-led growth strategy and tries to determine what macroeconomic policies are best suited to promote it. Through testing various assumptions in a macro model, Weeks advances a set of heterodox, but pragmatic, policy recommendations that contrast with the orthodox package customarily proposed by multilateral financial institutions.

Whereas the orthodox approach stresses the role of relative prices in achieving optimal allocative efficiency, the heterodox approach maintains that most markets in sub-Saharan Africa do not operate efficiently. If left unregulated, markets are therefore unlikely to generate 'appropriate' price signals and even if they did, structural obstacles would prevent private agents from responding to them.

By testing the heterodox position on macroeconomic data for Africa, Weeks reaches a number of counter-conventional conclusions. He claims that investment is the driving force of growth, but that investment responds only weakly to relative price changes, such as in the real rate of interest. The most important determinant of investment is growth itself. Exports are found to stimulate growth, but neither exports nor imports respond strongly to changes in the real exchange rate. In fact, a real devaluation tends to have a contractionary effect on African economies by lowering essential imports. A rise in the government deficit does indeed tend to raise the real rate of interest, but because private investment does not respond robustly to the interest rate, it is not 'crowded out' by the government deficit. In addition, when the interest rate is raised, domestic saving does not necessarily increase. Moreover, instead of stimulating growth by contributing additional resources, foreign assistance is found to depress it by lowering domestic savings and investment.

All of the above findings run counter to the policy conclusions usually derived from the orthodox macroeconomic model. For the typical African economy – characterized by low growth, moderate inflation and substantial trade and fiscal deficits – the heterodox model would recommend a pragmatic policy mix of monetary restraint, fiscal expansion (instead of fiscal restraint) and controlled devaluation (instead of exchange rate liberalization).

In order to reduce the inflation rate, the government would be advised by the heterodox model to lower the rate of growth of the money supply (that is, practise monetary restraint) and use a 'crawling peg' mechanism to carefully regulate devaluation (that is, controlled devaluation). These two policies would have a contractionary impact on the economy that would have to be counteracted with a drop in the real rate of interest (instead of the usual recommendation to raise it) and, most importantly, with an increase in public investment (that is, fiscal expansion).

The heterodox policy package assumes that if fiscal expansion generates government deficits, these do not necessarily have a strong impact on increasing inflation and that inflation does not necessarily dampen growth. What is critical is that growth be stimulated so that it can, in turn, boost private investment. Public investment plays a leading role in stimulating growth by inducing greater private investment, both domestic and foreign, and by counteracting the contractionary effects of such policies as import-depressing devaluation. If properly designed, public investment, such as labour-intensive public works, can in fact help lower the need for capital imports. Growth also serves to raise the share of savings in gross domestic product, which can then be used to finance additional investment.

The crucial contrast between the orthodox and heterodox approach is that whereas the orthodox approach places priority on reduction of the fiscal deficit as a primary means to stabilize prices, and is concerned about public investment crowding out private investment, the heterodox approach subordinates deficit reduction to achieving the growth-inducing impact of increased public investment and is willing therefore to accommodate moderate levels of fiscal deficit and inflation. Consequently, the heterodox approach criticizes the conventional policy package of deficit cutting, exchange rate liberalization and high real interest rates as anti-growth.

Domestic Resource Mobilization and Enterprise Development

Chapter 4, 'Domestic Resource Mobilization and Enterprise Development in Sub-Saharan Africa', by Keith Griffin and Mark D. Brenner, expands on the theme of investment-led structural adjustment introduced in Griffin's earlier chapter 'Macroeconomic Reform and Employment' by focusing on how resources can be mobilized for such a growth strategy.

The chapter maintains that although official development assistance to sub-Saharan Africa has been substantial, it has been ineffectual in accelerating investment. Moreover, foreign direct investment's contribution of resources has been negligible and is expected to remain so. Hence, the financing of an investment-led strategy has to come from domestic resources.

These resources can be mobilized in part by altering the composition of government expenditures to promote what is conventionally regarded as current consumption – such as expenditures on health and education services – but what in fact is human capital accumulation. A significant portion of investment can also be undertaken by mobilizing under-utilized labour for public works projects.

Most importantly, public policy can indirectly promote greater domestic resource mobilization by fostering a more favourable climate for private investment. This assumes that people tend to save more if profitable investment opportunities are made available to them, and also save more if they possess productive assets, such as land or a house, in which they can invest. Hence, public policy should encourage broad, equitable ownership of productive assets. In this context, the chapter proposes that small businesses, most of which are in Africa's large informal sector, can play a critical role in an investment-led growth strategy.

The state has an important role to play in fostering growth by making credit accessible to small enterprises and informal producers. On their own, credit markets cannot be expected to allocate resources efficiently. Therefore, targeted credit programmes in particular have a useful role to play: they have demonstrated the ability to reach disadvantaged groups, such as women and the poor, while at the same time remaining economically viable.

The chapter also calls on public policy to recognize the important role of home-based enterprises. In this regard, the paper maintains that housing should be regarded as a productive asset, and credit supplied to housing construction in order to both enhance people's productive capacities and satisfy their material needs. Targeted credit programmes for housing should thus be reconceptualized as entrepreneurial development programmes.

Public investment in human capital is vitally important for creating investment opportunities since the market for human capital does not operate efficiently. According to Griffin and Brenner, such investment and the expansion of small enterprises go hand in hand. Credit programmes are most effective, for example, when borrowers have some basic level of education that enables them to be literate and numerate.

The chapter puts particular emphasis on launching nation-wide public works projects to boost the overall rate of investment. Guaranteed employment programmes should be directed, they maintain, as much as possible at the poor. The chapter goes further in advocating that such capital formation be combined with progressive wealth redistribution by turning over to the poor the ownership of the assets that they have created.

Finally, the chapter maintains that resource mobilization can be aided by commercializing state enterprises. While agreeing that such enterprises often incur substantial losses and thereby drain public finances, the chapter argues for reforming rather than privatizing them. If the enterprises cannot be successfully reformed, they should then be declared bankrupt and closed down.

The thrust of all these policy recommendations is to mobilize more domestic resources to increase the level of both public and private investment and improve their composition. By stimulating growth, such domestic investment can then begin attracting and successfully utilizing significant inflows of foreign capital.

Macroeconomic Policies and Poverty

Chapter 5 by Azizur Rahman Khan, 'Macroeconomic Policies and Poverty', goes further than the chapters by Griffin and Weeks in focusing on the linkages between macroeconomic policies, growth and poverty reduction instead of primarily on the linkages between macroeconomic policies and growth. The context is an analysis of the experience of ten Asian countries.

Khan's chapter contends that the success of economic growth in reducing poverty cannot be taken for granted but depends on a number of factors, such as the sectoral composition of growth, the translation of growth into increases in personal income and progressive changes in the distribution of personal income. Moreover, the interaction of macro-economic policies and the circumstances of each country vitally affects the efficacy of these factors in reducing poverty.

The chapter maintains that the impact on poverty of the same macroeconomic policy can vary depending on the specific circumstances of each country and it therefore cautions against drawing universally applicable lessons. It also contends that general sweeping statements about the growth of per capita GDP and changes in distribution are not helpful in identifying what specifically causes reductions in poverty. In Asia, where most of the poor are located in rural areas, growth of rural per capita personal income is a better predictor, for instance, of reductions in poverty than the growth of per capita GDP for the whole country.

Similarly, a general increase in income inequality does not necessarily worsen the condition of the poor unless the relative loss of income is concentrated among them instead of among households higher up in the distribution. It is possible for inequality to increase at the same time that poverty is reduced, but poverty could be curtailed much more quickly if inequality were diminished by channelling more resources to the poor.

Khan asserts that macroeconomic policies can have an important effect on reducing inequality, but it is unwise to rely on them alone to carry out redistributive measures. Much of the impact of policies depends, for instance, on social institutions such as the system of land holdings or corporate ownership.

The ten country case studies provide a number of illustrations of how growth in GDP might not translate into poverty reduction. A frequent reason is stagnation in rural incomes. Also, in some cases, rapid growth can be accompanied by an increase in poverty when there is a sharp deterioration in inequality that directly immiserates the poor. Sometimes the pursuit of rapid capital accumulation to fuel future economic growth can work against the current interests of the poor by forcing them to lower their own consumption in the name of supplying more funds for investment. In such a case, increases in personal incomes are likely to lag behind increases in GDP.

A general rule is that a high rate of GDP growth may be necessary for poverty reduction, but it is not necessarily sufficient. Such growth must be translated into increases in personal income in sectors of the economy where the poor are concentrated.

The chapter reviews the effects on poverty of various macroeconomic policies that are associated with rising food prices, reform of the trade regime, increases in public expenditures, price stability and integration with the global economy. One of Khan's major points is that the impact of policies can vary depending on the structure of the economy and on who the poor are. For example, if the poor are net buyers of food – which is likely to be the case for the urban poor – then rising food prices are bound to adversely affect them; if, however, the poor are agriculturists who are net producers of food, they are likely to gain.

The Macroeconomic Context of Poverty Reduction in Latin America and the Caribbean

In similar vein to Khan, Albert Berry, in 'The Macroeconomic Context to Promote Social Development and Combat Poverty in Latin America and the Caribbean', examines the effect of economic reforms on growth and inequality and identifies on this basis the most important policy initiatives that can contribute to poverty reduction. According to Berry, what are crucial are not only growth that is more rapid, but also growth that is translated into productive employment and wage increases among low-income workers.

The economic reforms in the region have led to more outward-oriented and less interventionist models of development, but the impact has been only moderate rates of economic growth and marked deteriorations of income distribution. The biggest beneficiaries of reforms have been the richest 5–10 per cent of the population. As a consequence, little progress has been achieved in reducing poverty.

Greater export orientation has not contributed to more employment because exports have not been particularly labour-intensive while import liberalization has contributed to worsening income distribution. Contrary to expectations, the dismantling of protectionist systems and the opening up of trade have done little to benefit poorer agricultural workers. As a result of trade liberalization, real wages among workers have fallen and earnings differentials between unskilled and skilled workers have widened markedly.

The factors that have caused growing inequality in the distribution of income are technological change, more open trade regimes, the dismantling of labour institutions and the 'socialization' of private debts by the state. Berry identifies trade and labour market reforms as the factors most clearly linked to rising inequality.

Given the disappointing record in terms of growth and distribution, Berry maintains that carefully planned public policies are needed to counteract this situation. He attaches a great deal of importance to improving the distribution of education and human capital since problems in this area have been the single most important source of inequality in the region. He also argues that governments need to exercise more direct control over the process and the effects of technological change and to provide greater support to small and medium enterprises as an important means to generate employment and reduce poverty. One of the most controversial areas of reform has been labour-market institutions. In Latin America and the Caribbean, unions have been an important line of defence for workers and have contributed to counter-acting sharply rising inequality. But Berry agrees that strong unions have been associated with some labour market inefficiencies and that some regulations, such as provisions for severance pay and strict protection against worker dismissals, might have been prejudicial to employment and the growth of small and medium enterprises. However, many labour market regulations, he believes, have continued to have a beneficial effect and should be maintained. This appears to have been the case with regard to minimum wage legislation, for example. One of the more successful policies to reduce poverty has been emergency employment policies, which have been implemented in a number of countries and have been relatively low-cost and well targeted.

National Poverty Reduction Strategies in Latin America and the Caribbean

A complement to Berry's chapter, 'National Poverty Reduction Strategies of Chile, Costa Rica and Mexico: Summary of Findings', by Diana Alarcón, examines the development experiences of the three countries in order to document the inter-relations among three types of policy interventions against poverty: the basic development strategy of a country, its macroeconomic policies and its targeted programmes.

The chapter emphasizes that a country's strategy of development and its associated macroeconomic policies can have as much effect as – and in many cases more effect than – targeted interventions. In fact, if the country's development strategy and macroeconomic policies continu-ously reproduce poverty, targeted interventions can do little to reverse the situation.

Like other writers in this volume, Alarcón stresses that for growth to substantially reduce poverty, it should have a pro-poor character. This has implications for sectoral growth: the sectors in which the poor are concentrated need to grow, either through their own dynamic or through strong links with other expanding sectors. This happened to some extent in Costa Rica because its export crops were produced on small-scale units and in Chile because its manufactured exports were relatively labour-intensive.

In addition to pro-poor sectoral growth, what is needed is a favourable enabling environment that generates employment opportunities for the poor, increases their access to productive assets and, particularly for the self-employed, expands their access to credit and support services.

A third critical condition for poverty reduction is building up the human capabilities of the poor through provision of such basic social services as primary health care, primary education, nutrition and family planning. This was a strong tradition in Chile and Costa Rica even before the mid-1970s. But in the 1970s and 1980s, the military government in Chile altered this strategy through more restrictive targeting of benefits and greater decentralization of service provision.

A fourth condition for poverty reduction that Alarcón mentions is success by a country in inserting itself into the global economy and managing its external indebtedness – a point that has gained greater relevance in recent years because of increased international financial instability. In this regard, Costa Rica and Chile have appeared to fare better than Mexico.

Inequality has traditionally been high in Latin America. In accord with Berry, Alarcón points out that economic reforms in recent years in Chile and Mexico have been associated with rising inequality. She asserts that increased growth rates can help reduce poverty in spite of rising inequality, but a growth pattern that is associated with low or declining inequality would be much more effective.

Alarcón examines the targeted poverty-reduction programmes of the three Latin American countries and concludes that the most effective programmes have attempted to incorporate the poor into the economic mainstream rather than rely on income transfers. Efficient targeting of benefits is always a problem but the more successful cases appear to rely on self-targeting or targeting of resources to economic groups, such as the producers of non-traditional export crops in Costa Rica, or to specific economic activities. Moreover, successful targeting to particular groups seems to occur on the basis of the prior achievement of universal coverage of basic social services – a strength in both Chile and Costa Rica.

Reforming Macroeconomic Policies to Promote Poverty Reduction

The chapter by Terry McKinley, 'The Macroeconomic Implications of Focusing on Poverty Reduction', examines whether macroeconomic policies should be geared specifically to promote poverty reduction – namely, whether they should be used to influence the character of growth so as to channel a disproportionate share of resources to the poor.

McKinley criticizes the conventional approach to macroeconomic policies on a number of points: focusing inordinately on short-term stabilization, undercutting the long-term basis for economic growth and ignoring the redistributive effects of growth policies. But he argues further that even economic growth is not a meaningful end in itself. What is important is whether growth is translated into human development – and into the reduction of poverty in particular.

He contends that, in general, there has been an over-emphasis on economic growth as the main determinant of poverty reduction. This approach has assumed that the functioning of market mechanisms, undistorted and unfettered by governmental intervention, would solve the poverty problem. But such an approach ignores the constraints imposed by inequality in the distribution of income, wealth and human development. Inequality not only makes it more difficult to reduce poverty, but, according to recent evidence, also reduces economic growth itself.

McKinley contends that under certain circumstances there need be no trade-off between greater equity and growth. Boosting the current consumption of the poor at the expense of investment might restrict growth, but investing in the poor, he believes, need not do so. Therefore, a central policy issue becomes how to ensure that investment in the poor is growth enhancing or at least growth-compatible. The conclusion is that two general inter-related sets of policies are needed:

(i)   redistributing assets to the poor, such as land and human capital, and
(ii) using macroeconomic policies to help raise the returns to these assets.

This implies an activist pro-poor public policy that is geared to redirecting investment to the poor and explicitly evaluating macro-economic policies in terms of their impact on poverty. Such a pro-poor strategy would favour channelling resources, in the short term, to the relatively low-productivity economic activities in which the poor are currently engaged. But the long-term solution would be to enhance the ability of the poor to find employment in the higher-productivity growth sectors of the economy.

Inequality, Growth and Human Development

The main assertion of the chapter by Keith Griffin and Amy Ickowitz, 'The Distribution of Wealth and the Pace of Development', is that a more equal distribution of wealth tends to accelerate the pace of human development rather than retard it. It thus supports the position of a number of recent papers – including some in this volume – that have contested the traditional view of a trade-off between equality and growth and have pointed to the development experience of East Asian countries as historical evidence.

An important difference is that whereas the traditional view examines the relationship between income inequality and growth, the Griffin and Ickowitz chapter focuses on the relationship between wealth inequality and human development. This they do because they regard i) productive wealth as the basis for generating income and ii) an increase in income as a means to human development, not an end in itself. An additional point is that because there are diminishing marginal returns to human development from increases in income, a more equal distribution of income can enhance overall human development. When Griffin and Ickowitz focus on the relationship between wealth inequality and human development, they find the evidence even weaker for a trade-off between equality and development than is found by the conventional analysis.

The two authors examine the political reasons for why inequality might impede growth but find the economic reasons more compelling. They agree with recent research findings, for example, that the higher the initial inequality in the distribution of land, the slower the economic growth. A more equal distribution of land gives people collateral with which to borrow for productive purposes, particularly for investing in the human capital of their children. The authors also agree with the well-documented position that greater and more equal investment in human capital increases growth.

Griffin and Ickowitz emphasize an additional point: having land gives people greater motivation to supply labour, save and invest, and this also stimulates growth. Because of surplus labour in many agrarian economies, the poor are capable of supplying more labour but need a productive outlet to motivate greater work. Griffin and Ickowitz also counter the traditional view that because greater savings is the basis for growth, income should be channelled to rich people because they allegedly save more than poor people. The poor are fully capable of saving more, they assert, but need a productive asset in which to invest their savings. Land is such an asset. Moreover, land's more equal distribution can increase growth because smallholdings in developing countries are often more productive than large ones. The authors also assert that it is easier and quicker to redistribute natural capital such as land than to redistribute physical capital.

Evidence is less abundant to document a positive relationship between greater equality in the distribution of physical capital and growth than between the distribution of natural capital and growth. However, Griffin and Ickowitz point out that small and medium enterprises can create more employment per unit of capital and can have higher productivity of capital than large enterprises. Their greater labour intensity can contribute to a more equal distribution of income. If redistributing physical capital proves difficult, government policies can still help, they believe, by promoting broader access to financial capital, removing restrictions on the growth of small and medium enterprises and providing incentives for employment-intensive patterns of growth.

Notes

1. John Williamson, 'What Washington Means by Policy Reform', in John Williamson (ed.), *Latin American Adjustment: How Much Has Happened?* (Washington, DC: Institute for International Economics, 1990).
2. Joseph Stiglitz, 'More Instruments and Broader Goals: Moving toward the Post-Washington Consensus', WIDER Annual Lectures 2 (Helsinki: World Institute for Development Economics Research, 1998).

2 Macroeconomic Reform and Employment: An Investment-Led Strategy of Structural Adjustment in Sub-Saharan Africa

Keith Griffin

There are 50 countries in sub-Saharan Africa.[1] These countries, containing over 600 million people, are among the poorest in the world. Indeed the World Bank classifies 74 per cent of the countries of sub-Saharan Africa as 'low-income economies' and the United Nations Development Programme classifies 79 per cent as being 'low human development' countries.

Macroeconomic performance in sub-Saharan Africa since 1980 thus has been remarkably bad. The rate of growth has been slow, output per head has declined, average incomes have fallen, inequality probably has increased and the proportion of the population living in poverty has risen. The outcome has not been uniformly bad, some countries have performed better than others and in a few countries performance has been good, but, seen as a whole, the economies of sub-Saharan Africa compare unfavourably with the rest of the world – with the possible exception since 1989 of the economies of the former Soviet Union.

Those concerned about the acute and increasing hardship in Africa, particularly external advisors and international financial agencies, have recommended policies of 'stabilization' and 'structural adjustment'.[2] The meaning of these phrases is not unambiguous and it is useful to examine them with some care. This we do in the next two sections.

Stabilization

The purpose of stabilization policies is to restore macroeconomic balance. In the African context severe imbalances are reflected in high and possibly accelerating rates of inflation, a large and possibly increasing balance of payments deficit and perhaps, too, in a large public sector deficit, including deficits of public sector enterprises. The general policy recommendation in such a situation is to reduce the level of aggregate demand so that it corresponds more closely to the economy's production potential and to lower inflationary expectations by establishing the 'credibility' of strong anti-inflation measures by the government.

Specific policies recommended usually include a reduction in the supply of money and an increase in nominal interest rates; a reduction in government expenditure and, less frequently, an increase in tax revenues; privatization of state-owned enterprises or, again less frequently, reform of state enterprises to reduce losses or increase profits; and unification of exchange rates and devaluation of the currency. The primary purpose of the policies is to stabilize the price level and, secondarily, to restore balance to the external trading account and to the public sector's income and expenditure accounts. In fact, most countries in sub-Saharan Africa (35 according to the latest count) have introduced stabilization and structural adjustment programmes and it is now possible in general terms to evaluate the outcomes.

Before doing so, however, it is necessary to be specific about the standard of evaluation. High rates of inflation undoubtedly are harmful to an economy. First, they lead to inefficiencies in the allocation of resources and consequently to a lower level of output and income than would otherwise be possible. Second, high rates of inflation also make it more difficult to make long term investment decisions and this leads to a lower rate of capital formation and to a pattern of investment biased in favour of projects with a quick pay-off. The result is a lower rate of growth of output, incomes and employment. Third, rapid inflation usually is accompanied by large and arbitrary changes in the distribution of income and this damages economic incentives and leads to a widespread sense of injustice.

It does not follow from this, however, that 'stabilization' should be taken literally, that is that the objective of policy should be to stabilize the price level and achieve a zero rate of inflation. Such an objective, if attained, probably would increase inefficiency and reduce the rate of growth. The reason for this is that a well functioning price system depends for its success on the flexibility of relative prices, and these are likely to be more flexible if the rate of inflation is positive but moderate.

An illustration may clarify the point. If the demand for bicycles diminishes while that for radios increases, the price of bicycles should fall and the price of radios should rise, that is, relative prices should move against bicycles. Similarly, if the demand for carpenters declines while the demand for electricians increases, relative wages should shift against carpenters. The problem is that many prices (for example in the manufacturing sector) and many wages (notably in the urban formal sector) are 'sticky' downwards; a nominal cut in some prices and wages is difficult to achieve. Yet if the aggregate level of prices is stable, that is, there is zero inflation, a change in relative prices implies that for every price rise there must be a compensating price fall elsewhere. Sticky prices and wages may make this impossible unless stabilization measures are pushed to such an extreme that the level of effective aggregate demand falls below the potential level of production of the economy.

Rather than allow that to happen, it would be better to tolerate mild inflation so that relative prices can adjust, with some prices rising faster than others but without the necessity of some prices falling absolutely while others rise. Exactly how much inflation should be tolerated on grounds of economic efficiency and growth is impossible to say, but the answer presumably depends on the degree of downward stickiness of prices and on the extent of relative price adjustments that are necessary. That is, the more sticky are prices and the greater the required changes in relative prices, the higher the rate of inflation that should be tolerated. Given the highly 'distorted' structures of prices in many sub-Saharan countries, an upper limit of the rate of inflation of 20 per cent a year might be a reasonable objective of a 'stabilization' programme.[3]

This would allow the government some margin to run a modest fiscal deficit. This margin of flexibility should be used to finance public investment, not to cover the deficits of state enterprises or to finance current operating expenditure. Higher public investment, as emphasized below, should raise incomes and accelerate growth directly and, in addition, stimulate investment and growth in the private sector. Government borrowing, in moderation and if used for the right purposes, thus could play a constructive role.

Table 2.1 contains data on the rate of inflation (as measured by the GDP deflator) in the 33 countries of sub-Saharan Africa for which information is available. The data cover three periods, namely, the decade of the 1980s, the first four years of the 1990s and the entire period 1980–1994. One possible test of the success of stabilization efforts would be whether the rate of inflation has diminished over time, regardless of the initial or terminal rate of inflation. That is, non-accelerating inflation might well be an objective of macroeconomic policy.

Unfortunately, sub-Saharan Africa has not done particularly well by this test. The rate of inflation actually accelerated between the first and second periods in 18 of the 33 countries. In the remaining 15 countries the rate of inflation did indeed diminish. In most of the countries where inflation accelerated, there is little cause for concern because even after the acceleration the rate of inflation was well below our cut-off point of

Table 2.1 Indicators of Stabilization

Country	GDP Deflator (av. annual percentage rate of growth)			Nominal Lending Rate of Banks, 1994 (% per annum)
	1980–90	1990–94	1980–94	
Angola	n.a.	n.a.	n.a.	n.a.
Benin	1.6	7.9	3.8	16.8
Botswana	13.1	8.4	11.7	13.9
Burkina Faso	3.1	4.0	3.4	16.8
Burundi	4.4	7.1	5.2	n.a.
Cameroon	5.7	2.7	4.8	17.5
Cape Verde	n.a.	n.a.	n.a.	n.a.
Central Africa Republic	5.6	6.2	5.8	17.5
Chad	1.1	6.6	2.7	17.5
Comoros	n.a.	n.a.	n.a.	n.a.
Congo	0.3	2.1	0.8	17.5
Côte d'Ivoire	3.1	6.8	4.2	16.8
Djibouti	n.a.	n.a.	n.a.	n.a.
Equatorial Guinea	n.a.	n.a.	n.a.	n.a.
Eritrea	n.a.	n.a.	n.a.	n.a.
Ethiopia	n.a.	n.a.	n.a.	14.3
Gabon	1.9	10.5	4.4	17.5
Gambia	8.7	5.6	14.9	25.0
Ghana	42.4	20.7	36.1	n.a.
Guinea	n.a.	11.7	n.a.	22.0
Guinea-Bissau	56.1	53.4	55.3	36.3
Kenya	9.0	17.7	11.5	n.a.
Lesotho	13.6	11.9	13.1	14.3
Liberia	n.a.	n.a.	n.a.	n.a.
Madagascar	17.1	16.8	17.0	n.a.
Malawi	14.6	22.8	17.0	31.0
Mali	5.6	8.0	6.3	16.8
Mauritania	8.6	7.6	8.3	10.0
Mauritius	8.7	7.2	8.3	18.9
Mayotte	n.a.	n.a.	n.a.	n.a.
Mozambique	38.4	49.3	41.6	n.a.
Namibia	13.6	9.5	12.4	17.1
Niger	2.9	4.7	3.4	16.8
Nigeria	16.6	37.4	22.6	20.5
Reunion	n.a.	n.a.	n.a.	n.a.
Rwanda	3.3	9.7	5.2	15.0
São Tomé and Principe	n.a.	n.a.	n.a.	n.a.
Senegal	6.4	7.1	6.6	16.8
Seychelles	n.a.	n.a.	n.a.	n.a.
Sierra Leone	56.0	55.9	56.0	27.3
Somalia	n.a.	n.a.	n.a.	n.a.
South Africa	14.8	11.9	14.0	15.6
Sudan	n.a.	n.a.	n.a.	n.a.
Swaziland	n.a.	n.a.	n.a.	n.a.

Table 2.1 (continued)

Country	GDP Deflator (av. annual percentage rate of growth)			Nominal Lending Rate of Banks, 1994 (% per annum)
	1980–90	1990–94	1980–94	
Tanzania	35.7	20.4	31.3	39.0
Togo	4.7	5.7	5.0	17.5
Uganda	125.6	28.8	97.5	n.a.
Zaire	n.a.	n.a.	n.a.	n.a.
Zambia	42.4	124.2	66.1	113.3
Zimbabwe	11.5	27.0	16.0	34.9

Source: Calculated from data in World Bank, *World Development Report 1996* (New York: Oxford University Press, 1996), Tables 2 and 11.

20 per cent a year. In only three countries (Malawi, Nigeria and Zimbabwe) did the acceleration in inflation move the country from below the threshold level to above it, and in only one country (Mozambique) was inflation initially above the threshold level and then accelerated further. Thus one can safely say that, in general, accelerating inflation is not a major problem in Africa, at least in those countries where data are available.

A second test of the success of stabilization efforts would be whether the rate of inflation during the second period (the 1990s) is below the threshold level of 20 per cent a year. The results of this test are quite encouraging: 23 out of the 33 countries for which data are available are below the threshold and only 10 are above it. Half of the 10 countries above the threshold (Ghana, Malawi, Tanzania, Uganda and Zimbabwe) have rates of inflation below 30 per cent a year and hence the extent of price instability may not be alarming; the remaining 5 countries however (Guinea-Bissau, Mozambique, Nigeria, Sierra Leone and Zambia) clearly do have serious inflationary problems and require further stabilization efforts in order to improve their macroeconomic performance.

So far we have used the word 'stabilization' to refer to changes in the general level of prices, that is, to the rate of inflation. We have argued that 'stabilization' ought to imply a rate of inflation no higher than 20 per cent per annum and have used this standard to evaluate performance in Africa. There is, however, a second sense in which the word 'stabilization' could be used, namely, stability of certain strategic or key prices. The word is seldom used in this second sense, but a case can be made that stability in this second sense is even more important than stability in the first sense of moderate inflation.

Two obvious candidates for strategic prices that ought to be kept stable are the real rate of interest and the real exchange rate. Let us consider each in turn.

The real rate of interest is the nominal (or market) rate of interest adjusted for expected or anticipated inflation. Since anticipated inflation is hard to measure, in practice the real rate of interest usually is calculated as the nominal rate of interest minus the current rate of inflation. Thus if the nominal rate of interest is 8 per cent a year and the rate of inflation is 10 per cent, the real rate of interest is a negative 2 per cent. In most discussions of macroeconomic policy emphasis is placed on the role of interest rates (that is, the deposit rate of interest) in providing an incentive to save (particularly through formal sector financial institutions) and in reducing aggregate consumption demand (and hence contributing to price stabilization). Negative or low but positive real deposit rates of interest are criticized for discouraging savings. Given the low (and even negative[4]) savings rates in many sub-Saharan countries, this criticism is not without merit. The problem with this argument, however, is that most of the empirical evidence suggests that savings are not very sensitive to changes in interest rates.

More significant in our view is the effect of interest rates on the efficiency of investment. That is, the strategic price is the real lending rate of interest. If the rate of interest charged by banks to their customers is negative in real terms, the risk to the borrower disappears and the demand for credit will greatly exceed the available funds. Price (that is, interest rates) will play no role in allocating credit and the banks will have to rely on credit rationing devices to distribute funds among enthusiastic would-be borrowers. The temptation for bankers to lend to their friends or to those with political influence or to engage in corrupt practices will be very great. Since the banks will not run a risk of default on their loans, bankers will have no incentive to select the best projects (those with the highest rates of return) and to weed out the worst projects (those with a high likelihood of failure). The result is that the composition of investment will be adversely affected and the return on investment will be reduced. This, in turn, will lower the average rate of growth.

It is thus important that the real lending rate of interest should be positive, moderately high and stable. While it is true that gross domestic investment in sub-Saharan Africa has been lower than in other developing regions, and in addition the rate of investment has fallen substantially (from 23 per cent of GDP in 1980 to 17 per cent in 1994), the most serious problem is the low return on investment as reflected in the large number of 'white elephants', economically non-viable projects, and a poor project mix.

The real lending rate of interest influences not only what projects will be undertaken but also the degree of labour intensity of production. A low real rate of interest introduces a bias against the employment of labour, a factor in relative abundance in Africa, and instead creates incentives for producers to adopt relatively capital intensive methods of production. Given that the great majority of countries in sub-Saharan Africa obtain their capital goods from abroad, low real rates of interest in effect represent a subsidy by Africa to employment in the capital goods industries of the rest of the world. This is hardly a desirable macroeconomic policy.

As a rough rule of thumb, a sensible policy in sub-Saharan Africa might be a real lending rate of interest of a minimum of 10 per cent per annum. This would not reduce demand for investment below the available funding but it would increase the incentive to allocate funds for investment more efficiently. How well have our countries done according to this test? In the last column of Table 2.1 (p. 19) there is information on the nominal lending rate of banks in 1994. This nominal rate of interest can be compared with the actual rate of inflation in 1990–94 as reported in the second column of the table. This comparison will give us a crude approximation to the real lending rate of interest and is the best that can be done in the absence of detailed country studies.

A comparison of nominal lending rates with the actual rate of inflation is possible in 28 countries. In 24 of the 28 countries the real rate of interest is positive; only in Guinea-Bissau, Nigeria and Sierra Leone is it negative. This is encouraging. On the other hand, in only 12 countries is the real rate of interest at least 10 per cent a year. In other words, 16 out of 28 countries fail to pass the test. This implies that throughout much of sub-Saharan Africa 'stabilization' is being hampered by less than optimal interest rate policies.

A second strategic price that ought to be kept stable is the real rate of exchange. The real rate of exchange is the nominal rate of exchange adjusted for rates of inflation in the domestic economy and in the country's trading partners. In effect the nominal exchange rate is adjusted to take into account the difference between the domestic and foreign rates of inflation. A stable real exchange rate means that the structure of incentives as regards importing and exporting is held constant.

Once a unified 'equilibrium' exchange rate is established which brings the balance of payments deficit to a level which can be sustained by long term inflows of foreign capital, both public and private, the rate of exchange should be stabilized, that is, the real rate of exchange should remain roughly constant until fundamental economic conditions change.

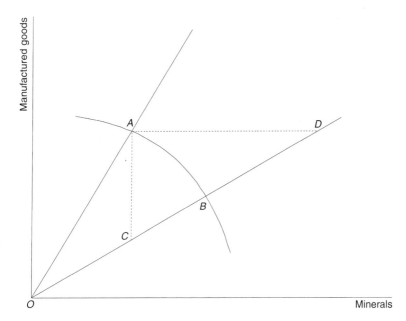

Figure 2.1 Alternative Paths of Structural Adjustment (from *A* to *B*, *C* or *D*)

This is especially important in small countries where dependence on foreign trade is high. Unfortunately, there is no evidence on the evolution over time in the real exchange rate in the sub-Saharan countries, but, as we shall see below, the behaviour of exports suggests that real exchange rates in many countries have been allowed to appreciate, to the detriment of the countries' balance of payments position.[5]

The argument in favour of stabilizing strategic prices such as the real rate of exchange and the real borrowing rate of interest can be extended to the policy regime as a whole. Investment is inherently a risky undertaking: it requires a commitment of funds 'today' in the expectation of rewards 'tomorrow', sometimes in a rather distant tomorrow. If risks are high and uncertainty is great, the volume of investment will diminish and the time horizon of investors will shrink: investors will be unwilling to commit large sums of money over long periods of time. Volatile government policies – and arbitrary changes in policies – increase risk and harm investment whereas stable policies and a 'credible' policy regime, by reducing uncertainty, create a more favourable economic environment and can help to stimulate private investment and growth.

Structural Adjustment

Structural adjustment policies have three major purposes. First, they are designed to effect a substantial change in the composition of output, primarily through a radical alteration in the structure of relative prices. The intention is to reform the market mechanism so that prices reflect marginal costs and benefits, in the expectation that this in turn would induce a change in the pattern of production in favour of products in which the country has or can rapidly acquire a comparative advantage. An improvement in the internal terms of trade of the rural sector, for example, would be expected to reverse the decline in per capita agricultural production. Second, structural adjustment is intended to integrate the countries of sub-Saharan Africa more closely into the global economy. Exports were expected to grow rapidly and to increase their share of GDP. Foreign trade was expected to become a leading sector, reversing the import substituting industrialization strategy adopted in the early post-independence period. Third, structural adjustment is intended to raise the rate of investment and improve the allocation of investment thereby increasing the rate of growth of output, incomes and employment. Poverty would decline as average incomes rose. The ultimate consequence of the economic reforms thus would be a fundamental restructuring of the economy and a marked improvement in its performance.

There are, however, three very distinct ways of bringing about structural adjustment – of radically changing the composition of output – and these three ways or paths have markedly different consequences for the people concerned. The first path is the one that is usually implicit in conventional policy advice given to sub-Saharan African countries. It is assumed that changes in the composition of output occur as a result of a reallocation of the existing stocks of productive assets. That is, physical, human and natural capital can be reassigned and combined in different proportions to produce a new mix of products from the set of feasible alternatives. Movement occurs along a given 'production possibilities frontier' in response to changes in relative product prices. This movement is assumed to be frictionless and rapid and consequently full utilization of resources is ensured and structural adjustment is achieved without significant lags.

This first path is illustrated in Figure 2.1 as a movement from point *A* to point *B*. The initial composition of output at *A* reflects a development strategy which gives priority to manufacturing and promotes growth along an expansion path represented by the ray *OA*. Structural adjustment entails a new development strategy – one that gives higher priority, say, to the minerals sector – and an attempt to move along a different expansion path represented by the ray *OD*. This expansion path is intersected by a segment of the production possibilities frontier at *B* and the purpose of the economic reforms is to effect a shift from *A* to *B* by reallocating existing resources.

This story is not implausible. Assume, for instance, that the price of millet falls relative to the price of maize. Farmers are likely to reallocate their land, labour power and mechanical equipment from the production of millet to that of maize. The output of millet will decline and the output of maize will increase and, moreover, this change in the cropping pattern will occur quickly (namely, within one crop season) and without a decline in the degree of utilization of land, physical capital or labour. A change in relative crop prices is sufficient in this case to bring about a change in the composition of output.

Consider another example: a fall in the price of cocoa relative to alternative crops. In this case there may be no supply response, that is, a fall in cocoa production and a corresponding rise in the output of alternative crops. That is, there may be no reallocation of resources, no structural adjustment. The reason for this is that once the heavy investment in cocoa trees has occurred, the marginal cost of harvesting the output may be very low and hence even if prices fall sharply it may pay the farmer to maintain production. The failure to respond to the price disincentive may persist indefinitely, or until it is necessary to replace the old cocoa trees by replanting young ones.

Consider, finally, the opposite case of a rise in the price of a tree crop (say, coffee) relative to the price of an annual crop (say, beans). It is not possible merely to reallocate the land and labour used to grow beans in order to increase coffee production. Considerable investment is needed: the farmer must purchase and plant coffee saplings and then wait several years for the trees to mature to a fruit bearing age. This investment will not occur unless: (a) the farmer expects the relatively favourable price of coffee to be semi-permanent and (b) the farmer is able to finance the investment, including the consumption needs of himself and his family while waiting for the coffee trees to yield their first harvest. That is, structural adjustment in this case is heavily dependent upon the rate of investment.

We have deliberately selected examples from agriculture to illustrate the first path of structural adjustment – namely, adjustment through reallocation – because conditions in agriculture more closely approximate the assumptions that lie behind the conventional view. Even so, it is evident that once specific capital is introduced, as was the case with cocoa and coffee trees, the conventional story becomes much more complicated.

Let us turn now to the second path of structural adjustment. This is the path that comes closest to describing the path actually followed in much of sub-Saharan Africa and this path can be called structural adjustment through contraction. Imagine, as in Figure 2.1, that structural adjustment is interpreted to mean a shift in the composition of output away from manufactured goods and in favour of minerals (petroleum, natural gas, copper, diamonds, platinum, gold, and so on). How might this shift occur within a context of decreased aggregate demand and price stabilization and of a radical change in relative prices?

Clearly both the demand effects and the relative price effects would reduce the profitability of the manufacturing sector. Labour would be discharged, idle manufacturing capacity would increase, unwanted capital equipment would be released for use elsewhere or sold as scrap, output of manufactured goods would decline. So far so good: production in the low priority sector would contract and the resources used in that sector would in principle become available to facilitate the expansion of the minerals sector, the high priority sector. But could the resources formerly used in manufacturing profitably be re-absorbed in the minerals sector? There is reason for doubt, and the doubt centres on the specificity of much physical and human capital.

The physical capital used in a brewery or a textile mill or a food processing plant cannot rapidly be converted for use down a mine shaft, to cut a seam of coal, to sift diamonds, to transport ores on a conveyor belt or to separate the economically valuable minerals from the surrounding rock. Each economic activity requires specific types of capital equipment, specific tools, even sometimes specific buildings and this physical capital cannot readily be reallocated for other purposes.

The same is true of much human capital. Indeed the existence of firm-specific human capital is one reason why industrial enterprises often pay their experienced and skilled employees more than a 'market clearing' wage. It is worthwhile for firms to pay a premium in order to retain their human capital. The worker on an electronics assembly line (who could well be female) cannot be transformed into an underground miner (where physical strength is important). The worker in a furniture factory does not possess the skills needed on an oil rig. The worker in a pharmaceutical company, the salesperson in a kitchen utensils factory or the quality control inspector in a meat processing plant can only with difficulty be absorbed in a totally different occupation. Resources, in other words, cannot normally be reallocated quickly and without friction. Expansion of newly profitable activities (minerals in our example) usually requires investment both in plant and equipment (physical capital) and in the education and training of the labour force (human capital). Moreover, the greater the desired transformation of the economy, the more essential it is to achieve a high rate of investment in physical and human capital.

Structural adjustment can still occur, but it occurs through contraction of unprofitable activities combined with stagnation of output in the profitable activities. This is depicted in Figure 2.1 as a movement from *A* to *C*. Note that *C* is on the same expansion path as *B* (namely, the ray *OD*) and hence the proportion of manufactured goods and minerals is the same as at point *B*, but the level of production of both manufactured goods and minerals is much lower. Structural adjustment is purchased at the price of economic contraction, high unemployment and massive poverty. This essentially is what has happened in large parts of sub-Saharan Africa.

The response of well meaning advisors and aid donors has been to advocate the construction of a 'safety net' to alleviate the worst forms of hardship. This advocacy however is based on a misconception about the nature of the problem. A safety net would be appropriate if the increased unemployment and poverty were temporary and constituted a small deviation from the path of structural adjustment through resource allocation, that is, a movement from *A* to *B*. In fact, sub-Saharan Africa is on a quite different path – a path of structural adjustment through contraction – and the human distress associated with this path is neither of short duration nor small in magnitude. The resources required to construct an effective safety net would consequently be enormous and such an undertaking is not feasible given the sharp decline in available resources. What is needed is not so much a safety net as policies that put the economy on a different path of adjustment.

Here, too, well-meaning advisors and aid donors have an inkling of what is required, namely, a sharp acceleration in the rate of growth of investment. There has been a proliferation of so-called structural adjustment loans and, indeed, the amount of foreign aid received in sub-Saharan Africa, when expressed as a proportion of GDP, is relatively high in many countries.[6] The problem is that foreign capital inflows have not been used to increase the level of investment but instead they have been used to finance current public and private expenditure. This reflects not the foolishness of donors but inappropriate government policies during the transition.

This brings us to the third path of structural adjustment – namely, adjustment through investment. In Figure 2.1 this is illustrated by the movement from *A* to *D*. Point *D* is on the ray *OD* and hence the expansion path and the composition of output are the same as at points *B* and *C*. The

Table 2.2 Investment Performance in 31 Countries of Sub-Saharan Africa, 1980–1994 (number of countries)

	Yes	No	Total
$Gi < 0$	14	17	31
$Gi \leq Gpop$	22	9	31
$Gi \leq Ggdp$	20	11	31

difference is that the movement to *D*, that is, the path to structural adjustment, occurs without any reallocation of pre-existing resources and without any decline in the level of output in the manufacturing sector. Structural adjustment along this path is part of a growth strategy, a strategy designed to increase investment in physical, human and natural capital and to channel that investment into economic activities which have become highly profitable as a result of changes in the structure of incentives.

The third path – structural adjustment through investment – does not result in a rise in unemployment, a fall in average real incomes or an increase in poverty. On the contrary, the rate of growth of GDP accelerates and average incomes rise rapidly. Moreover, as the experiences of China and Vietnam illustrate during their transition from central planning to a more market-oriented economic system, an investment dominated path of structural adjustment is compatible with a simultaneous expansion of all sectors of the economy, but of course expansion at different rates. In terms of our diagram, this implies a movement in a north-easterly direction from *A* rather than the movement due east from *A* to *D*. Far too much attention has been devoted to adjustment through reallocation in sub-Saharan Africa; much more attention should in future be devoted to adjustment through investment.

Investment: The Neglected Path to Adjustment

This brings us closer to the heart of the matter, the urgent need to increase investment and improve its allocation among sectors and projects. This should be the primary task of macroeconomic policy in sub-Saharan Africa.[7] Indeed, unless this can be achieved, structural adjustment will fail. The task is formidable.

Data are available on the annual rate of growth of investment in 31 countries during the period 1980–1994. The simple average for these 31 countries is a miserable 0.3 per cent a year. Even this low figure probably overstates the true rate of growth of investment in sub-Saharan Africa as a whole since many of the countries for which data are lacking have been wracked by civil wars and have suffered considerable destruction of and damage to the stock of physical capital.

As usual in so large and diverse a group of countries, there are several which have performed much better than average and several which are much worse than average. Uganda, Namibia and Lesotho have experienced rates of growth of investment in excess of 7.0 per cent a year and in Mauritius investment has grown 10 per cent a year. If these rates can be sustained in the decades ahead, these countries have a good chance of achieving structural adjustment through investment. At the other extreme are five countries – Zambia, Côte d'Ivoire, Togo, Nigeria and Congo – where investment has declined between 6.8 and 10.4 per cent a year. These are classic cases of structural adjustment through contraction.

In Table 2.2 we ask and answer questions about investment performance. In the first row of Table 2.2 we ask whether the rate of growth of investment (Gi) was negative. The answer, surprisingly, is that in 14 out of the 31 countries for which we have data the rate of growth was indeed negative. That is, in those countries the stock of physical capital assets was smaller in 1994 than it was in 1980. There was an absolute decline in the value of such things as the number of dwellings and commercial buildings, the stock of machinery and transport equipment, the quality and length of the road and railroad networks, the size of inventories, and so on. The productive potential of the economy, in other words, was slowly shrinking. In the other 17 countries, fortunately, the stock of capital assets was increasing, even if the rate of growth in most cases was rather low.

In the second row of Table 2.2 we ask whether investment was growing less rapidly than the population ($Gpop$). In more than two-thirds of the cases (22 countries) the per capita rate of growth of investment was negative. In the remaining nine countries it was positive. The implication is that the amount of physical capital per person was declining in most of sub-Saharan Africa. Assuming that in the long run average incomes are closely correlated with the amount of capital available per person, the data suggest that even the currently low levels of income in sub-Saharan Africa are not sustainable unless trends in population growth and investment are reversed.

Finally, in the third row of Table 2.2 we address an issue that is central to structural adjustment through investment. Is the rate of growth of investment less rapid than the rate of growth of GDP ($Ggdp$)? In 20 out of 31 countries it turns out that investment is growing less rapidly than total

Table 2.3 The Labour Force

Country	Growth of the Labour Force, 1980–1994 (% per annum)	Percentage of the Labour Force in Agriculture, 1990
Angola	n.a.	n.a.
Benin	2.6	64
Botswana	3.3	46
Burkina Faso	2.0	92
Burundi	2.8	92
Cameroon	2.6	70
Cape Verde	n.a.	31
Central Africa Republic	1.8	80
Chad	2.1	83
Comoros	n.a.	77
Congo	2.8	49
Côte d'Ivoire	3.0	60
Djibouti	n.a.	n.a.
Equatorial Guinea	n.a.	77
Eritrea	n.a.	n.a.
Ethiopia	2.6	86
Gabon	2.4	52
Gambia	3.4	82
Ghana	3.1	59
Guinea	2.3	87
Guinea-Bissau	1.6	85
Kenya	3.6	80
Lesotho	2.6	40
Liberia	n.a.	72
Madagascar	3.0	78
Malawi	3.5	87
Mali	2.7	86
Mauritania	2.2	55
Mauritius	2.1	17
Mayotte	n.a.	n.a.
Mozambique	1.6	83
Namibia	2.4	49
Niger	3.0	90
Nigeria	2.6	43
Reunion	n.a.	n.a.
Rwanda	3.1	92
Sâo Tomé and Principe	n.a.	n.a.
Senegal	2.5	77
Seychelles	n.a.	n.a.
Sierra Leone	1.9	67
Somalia	n.a.	75
South Africa	2.6	14
Sudan	n.a.	69
Swaziland	n.a.	39

Table 2.3 (continued)

Country	Growth of the Labour Force, 1980–1994 (% per annum)	Percentage of the Labour Force in Agriculture, 1990
Tanzania	3.2	84
Togo	2.7	66
Uganda	2.9	85
Zaire	n.a.	68
Zambia	3.4	75
Zimbabwe	3.3	68

Sources: World Bank, *World Development Report 1996* (New York: Oxford University Press, 1996) and UNDP, *Human Development Report 1996* (New York: Oxford University Press, 1996).

output, implying that the investment ratio is declining in about two-thirds of the countries of sub- Saharan Africa. In 11 countries the investment ratio is rising.

A falling investment ratio would not matter if the ratio were high at the beginning of the period of structural adjustment and per capita incomes were growing rapidly. But in most of sub-Saharan Africa the investment ratio is low and per capita incomes are falling. In these circumstances it is essential to increase the rate of growth of investment and raise the proportion of output that is devoted to capital formation. Only thus can employment be generated and the long slide in living standards be halted and reversed.

Labour and Adjustment through Contraction

The three paths to structural adjustment obviously have very different implications for employment and the remuneration of labour. The path followed in most of sub-Saharan Africa, unlike the other two possible paths, is highly disadvantageous. Those who were working in 1980 suffered the consequences of a decline in output per head; those who entered the work force between 1980 and 1994 found it more difficult than

Table 2.4 Changes in the Capital–Labour Ratio and the Productivity of Labour, 1980–1994 (number of countries)

	Rising	Constant	Falling	Total
Capital–labour ratio	8	2	23	33
Productivity of labour	12	0	21	33

their predecessors to obtain full time employment and, when employed, they found that on average they were less well rewarded for their efforts than the previous generation.

The labour force in sub-Saharan Africa is growing exceptionally fast. Indeed only in the Middle East and North Africa is the labour force increasing more rapidly. Between 1980 and 1994 the simple average annual rate of growth of the labour force in 35 countries of sub-Saharan Africa for which we have data was 2.7 per cent. The lowest rate of growth was in Guinea-Bissau and Mozambique (1.6 per cent a year) and the highest was in Kenya (3.6 per cent). (See Table 2.3.) In 12 countries the work force increased 3.0 per cent a year or more.

Rapid growth in the numbers of those seeking employment combined with slow growth of investment has resulted in a fall in the capital-labour ratio in most countries. This has undermined the ability of the economy to sustain production at previously attained levels. As can be seen in Table 2.4, the capital–labour ratio was constant in two countries and rose in 8; in the other 23 countries for which we have data, it fell. That is, in two-thirds of the countries of sub-Saharan Africa the amount of capital available to equip each member of the labour force actually declined over a 14-year period.

This negative trend in capital–labour ratios is reflected in trends in the productivity of labour and hence in the income received by working people. If the labour force rises more rapidly than output, the average productivity of labour will fall and, in fact, this is what occurred in much of sub-Saharan Africa. In 12 of the 33 countries for which we have data, the average productivity of labour increased, but in the remaining 21 countries it fell. This downward trend in productivity, extending over 14 years in 21 countries, means that it was impossible to maintain the real incomes of workers and, primarily because of this, poverty increased.

Structural adjustment through contraction, in other words, resulted in a contraction of employment opportunities and real incomes. This contraction of the labour market took various forms which differed in urban and rural areas. In the urban areas the formal sector declined absolutely in terms of output and employment.[8] This is especially true of public sector activities. Those who remained in formal sector employment usually experienced a fall in real wages,[9] demonstrating that wage rates may be sticky but that they are not rigidly fixed.[10]

Some of those who lost formal sector jobs became openly unemployed and some of the new entrants into the labour market who were unable to obtain formal sector jobs continued to search and meanwhile joined the ranks of the openly unemployed. Rates of open unemployment however have not risen dramatically in sub-Saharan Africa. Instead there has been a large increase in part-time employment and a rapid 'informalization' of the urban economy in response to the contraction of formal sector activities. Indeed the 'informalization' of the economy is the most notable, or at least the most visible, consequence of the prolonged economic crisis. Finally, unable to find productive employment, some workers became discouraged and withdrew from the labour force; they simply dropped out.

The implication is that although there is not much idle labour in Africa's cities, there is an enormous amount of slack in the labour market. That is, there is a great deal of labour that potentially could be employed in more productive activities, including of course investment activities. We shall argue below that this potential should be exploited by organizing investment projects in the public sector.

Although the rate of urbanization in Africa is the most rapid in the world, the proportion of the labour force engaged in agriculture also is the highest in the world. The second column of Table 2.3 (pp. 30–1) contains information for 43 countries. On average, 68 per cent of the labour force in these countries obtains a livelihood from agriculture. The range is very wide. At the top end of the distribution, three countries (Burkina Faso, Burundi and Rwanda) employ 92 per cent of the labour force in agriculture whereas at the lower end of the distribution only 14 per cent of the working population is engaged in agriculture in South Africa. In 34 out of the 43 countries however more than 50 per cent of the labour force is in the agricultural sector. The economies of sub-Saharan Africa, in other words, still are predominantly rural.

Worsening labour market conditions in the rural areas were in large part a manifestation of a fall in labour productivity in agriculture – and of a decline in food output per capita. Small farmers, tenants and wage workers experienced a fall in real incomes because of a fall in output per worker per year. Structural adjustment policies, contrary to the expectations of many, have been associated with a decline in the rate of growth of agricultural output. In the decade of the 1980s, agriculture in sub-Saharan Africa grew 1.8 per cent a year on average, but in the period 1990–1994 the rate of growth declined by more than half, to 0.7 per cent a year.

Structural adjustment brought about a change in relative prices which favoured agriculture (as opposed to manufacturing) and, within agriculture, export crops (as opposed to food crops). Careful studies of Sierra Leone, Tanzania and Zambia, however, indicate that the change in relative prices was not sufficient to induce:

(i)   an acceleration of agricultural output as a whole, or
(ii) a switch from food production to export crops, or
(iii) a reverse flow of labour from urban to rural areas.[11]

The failure of changes in relative prices to reallocate resources in the predicated direction could of course be attributed to the presence of long lags in the system, but a more natural interpretation of the evidence, consistent with the view presented above, would be that reallocation of resources is extremely difficult in the absence of high rates of investment.[12] Getting prices right is not enough.

The Structure of Incentives

Structural adjustment through reallocation places primary emphasis on improving the structure of incentives by reforming and liberalizing prices. Specific policies advocated include the removal of price controls and government subsidies, removal of quotas and other non-tariff barriers to international trade combined with a reduction of tariffs to a uniform modest level, and unification and liberalization of the foreign exchange rate. The broad purpose is to eliminate 'distortions' so that prices accurately reflect social costs and benefits. We have no quarrel with this broad objective, but we would make three qualifications.

First, if one supports a programme of structural adjustment through investment, then the most important aspect of the structure of incentives is its effect on the efficiency of investment. The challenge of economic reform is to produce a set of price signals that channel new investments into the socially most profitable sectors and projects. Had the allocation of investment in sub-Saharan Africa been better, the rates of growth of output and incomes would have been much higher, even if the level of investment had remained relatively low. The primary objective of a new structure of incentives should be to correct this glaring deficiency.

Second, it would be a serious mistake to equate price liberalization with *laissez faire*. Prices convey information. When markets work well they convey accurate information about social costs and social benefits, but markets often do not work well – they convey misleading information – and when this occurs there is a possible argument for government intervention. For example, strong cases can be made to tax the consumption of tobacco products (to protect public health), or to tax the consumption of alcoholic beverages (to prevent injury or death to others in automobile accidents) or to tax the use of hydrocarbon fuels (to reduce damage to the environment). These are examples of negative 'externalities' which result in market failure.

Most important from our perspective are market failures that lead to a severe misallocation of investment. Consider education. It is widely recognized that expenditure on education is a form of investment in human capital that confers substantial benefits both on the person being educated and on society at large. That is, there are large positive 'externalities' associated with education which are not taken into account by a free market. Hence there is a good reason, on grounds of efficiency in investment allocation, for governments to subsidize the cost of education. The same is true of some types of vocational training. Governments which reduce expenditure on primary and secondary education, either on grounds that they are reducing subsidies and thereby improving the structure of incentives or on grounds that they are reducing the fiscal deficit and thereby promoting stabilization, are implicitly turning their backs on structural adjustment through investment and following a path of structural adjustment through contraction.[13]

A similar argument can be made for government expenditure on public health and nutrition programmes. The benefits of measures to prevent the spread of communicable diseases (cholera, yellow fever, typhoid, malaria and, above all, AIDS) are reaped by the community as a whole and not just by the individual receiving treatment. There is thus a case for collective provision of disease prevention and eradication services; if left to the market these services will be underprovided. More generally, well nourished children and a healthy working population will absorb knowledge more quickly and be more innovative and productive. This will raise the average productivity of labour and benefit directly the workers concerned and indirectly their dependants, co-workers and fellow citizens.

Thus public subsidy of certain types of expenditure on education, training, nutrition and health should be seen as improving the allocation of investment. These are investments in human capital with potentially high rates of return. The experience of East Asia demonstrates that this form of market intervention contributes to faster, more sustainable and equitable growth. The same almost certainly would be true in sub-Saharan Africa. Where there are major market failures (as in education and health) selective government intervention can improve the structure of incentives.

The third qualification to more conventional ways of thinking about incentives is to note that there is much more to the structure of incentives than relative prices.[14] The price structure is only a part, albeit an important part, of the structure of incentives. Equally important are barriers which exclude people from participating in some markets, as happens with licensing regulations which restrict a number of informal sector activities in many cities in sub-Saharan Africa; or features of an economy which restrict the ease of access of some people to markets, such as the restricted access of small farmers and small businesspeople to formal sector credit markets; or overt discrimination, which reduces occupational mobility and income-enhancing opportunities of some people because of their gender, ethnic or other characteristics. There are also many cases of missing markets in sub-Saharan Africa, where economic activity occurs without market mediation and consequently the output that is produced is not explicitly valued. Important examples include food produced for household consumption, in urban as well as rural areas, by unpaid female labour and, more generally, labour performed by female labour within a household economy in a wide range of activities that include food preparation, child raising, assistance to the elderly and provision of medical services.[15]

The structure of incentives includes all activities, whether mediated by the market or not, and in the case of market-mediated activities, it includes discrimination, barriers to entry, market access and, of course, relative prices. The essential point, however, is that even if one is a believer in structural adjustment through reallocation, and hence focuses on changing incentives, 'getting prices right' will not suffice. Particularly in sub-Saharan Africa the phenomenon of missing markets is widespread. Unpaid women producing unpriced goods and services account for a high proportion of productive labour. The price system – the structure of incentives narrowly defined – often is biased against the crops grown by women (and other goods and services they produce) as well as against innovations which reduce the time and effort spent by women in crop cultivation (and other activities), since the labour of women is not valued by the market. It is hardly surprising that an incentive system, broadly defined, that is strongly biased against half the population has produced such unsatisfactory outcomes.

Consistent with our theme of giving high priority to a better allocation of investment, there are two areas where substantial improvements are possible.[16] First, public sector investment often is poorly allocated. It is excessively capital intensive and hence creates less employment than it could; there is enormous scope for labour intensive public investment programmes, as we shall see below. In addition, public investment is excessively concentrated in the capital and hence rural–urban and regional inequalities are accentuated. Further, public investment often is directed to projects that have low rates of return and hence produces less income than it should. Fresh thinking is needed on the role of the state in domestic resource mobilization and the financing of investment, on project selection and evaluation, and on the objectives and management of state enterprises. The 'commercialization' of state-owned enterprises may be more important, for example, than the 'privatization' of state enterprises.

Second, private sector investment also is poorly allocated in sub-Saharan Africa. The reason for this is the underdevelopment of capital markets and the concentration of the banking system. The problem is partly a matter of inappropriate pricing, namely, low real borrowing rates of interest, as discussed above. In addition there is a problem about the sectoral allocation of credit. Most people in Africa do not in fact have access to formal sector credit at any price and large sectors of the economy are starved of finance. Small and medium sized urban businesses have great difficulty in obtaining credit; agriculture and livestock are under-supplied, apart from large plantations and ranches, and small farmers obtain virtually no credit from banks. Fishermen and rural artisans cannot obtain loans from commercial banks; the informal sector as a whole has little access to credit; and new enterprises in any sector are rarely able to obtain start-up capital. The great majority of people in Africa either are self-financed or use the informal credit market supplied by traders, money lenders, friends and relatives. Most formal sector credit, in effect, is reserved for large, well established urban enterprises. The consequence of this massive defect in the structure of incentives is that many highly profitable private sector enterprises fail to get established and many small but established enterprises are unable to grow rapidly for lack of credit.

The pace and efficacy of structural adjustment would be much increased by improvements in the functioning of capital markets in Africa – by institutional innovation, by improved regulation of the banking sector, by supporting credit programmes targeted at specific groups such as women, informal sector entrepreneurs and small farmers and by increasing the supply of 'venture capital'. The emphasis should be on encouraging new private sector enterprises to emerge (particularly those which are small in scale and labour intensive) and on enabling small private sector enterprises to expand, innovate and penetrate new markets, including of course export markets. Changing the structure of incentives, in other words, is about accelerating growth by creating new productive assets; a more efficient allocation of the existing stock of resources, while not unimportant, is of secondary significance.

Investment and the Role of the State

The obvious question to ask of an investment-led strategy of structural adjustment in sub-Saharan Africa is how an acceleration of investment can be financed. There are three possible sources we shall examine: (1) foreign financing, (2) private sector saving and investment and (3) the public sector. Let us consider each of these in turn.

It is always tempting to look abroad for a solution to financial problems. In the case of sub-Saharan Africa, however, it is unlikely that a solution will be found there. Foreign direct investment in the region is negligible and is likely to remain so. A few countries with rich mineral deposits to exploit may be able to attract private foreign capital and South Africa's relatively large urban market may attract some foreign investors, but most countries with small markets, falling incomes and poorly educated workers will be avoided by foreign capital. The evidence from China and the market economies of East and Southeast Asia is that foreign capital flows to a country in large volume only after the country has succeeded in attaining rapid rates of growth. That is, inflows of private foreign capital are a consequence of successful development, not a cause of it.

There is of course foreign aid, but total aid allocations have been falling rapidly and it is perhaps improbable that the trend will be reversed in the near future. In principle Africa's share of a declining total could increase, so that aid inflows actually rose or at least remained constant, but it would seem unwise to plan on this when designing a strategy for structural adjustment. If foreign aid is available, and it is thought to be useful,[17] it would be a welcome addition to domestic resources, but when it comes to financing national development, governments in sub-Saharan Africa should make conservative assumptions and choose self-reliance.

Foreign debt is a major problem in many countries of the region. In sub-Saharan Africa as a whole total external indebtedness increased by 153 per cent between 1980 and 1994 and external debt as a percentage of GNP rose during the same period from 30.6 to 78.7 per cent. Debt servicing in some countries (Côte d'Ivoire, Congo, Burundi, Uganda, Kenya) absorbs well over 30 per cent of export earnings and a combination of debt forgiveness, a moratorium on repayment and unilateral default could release large sums of foreign exchange to help finance an investment-led structural adjustment programme.[18] Countries contemplating unilateral action, however, should consider carefully the possible consequences, namely, termination of aid programmes and a reduction in the already meagre inflows of private foreign capital.

Despite the low and even negative savings rates that characterize sub-Saharan Africa, the private domestic sector could under the right conditions finance a much higher level of investment. A change in the structure of incentives along the lines suggested, including greatly widening access of potential investors to formal sector credit institutions, could increase the incentive to save and improve the allocation of savings. Because some saving by a would-be borrower almost always is required before obtaining a loan, widening access to lending institutions should increase the number of savers and the rate of savings.

It is customary to think of the savings decision as being separate from the investment decision. The two are guided by different incentives and are brought into balance by price adjustments in financial markets and variations in the level of national income. However, this is only a partial view of the savings process. In many sectors of a sub-Saharan economy the amount saved by an enterprise, household or individual depends upon the specific investment opportunities open to that enterprise or household. If those engaged in a small family-owned and family-operated firm, for example, see a promising opportunity for expansion, they may seize the opportunity by reinvesting some of the firm's profits rather than using them to increase current consumption. That is, it is the presence of a profit opportunity that determines simultaneously the amount of investment and saving that occurs. The saving and investment decisions merge into one. People restrict their consumption not in order to 'save' but in order to finance a desired investment. In such a situation, the role of government policy should not be to try to induce people to consume less (save more) but rather to create a development environment in which there are large numbers of profitable investment opportunities.

This way of examining the problem of how to finance investment in sub-Saharan Africa can be extended further. In many instances investment requires little more than the direct application of labour: digging an irrigation or drainage ditch; planting a tea garden, coffee bushes or fruit trees; clearing, levelling or terracing a field; constructing a wall, animal shelter or home out of earth bricks. Whether a household will expend labour on such tasks depends on whether it is worthwhile or profitable. If there is plenty of slack in the labour market, for example in the form of seasonal rural unemployment, potentially profitable investments can be 'financed' not by consuming less (that is saving) but by working longer. That is, surplus labour at the level of the household can be used to finance household level investment projects. The problem is not how to save more but how to create investment opportunities. If there is an abundance of investment opportunities, the savings problem will take care of itself.

The issue then is not savings in a narrow sense but domestic resource mobilization. This way of posing the problem sheds new light on the question of the right balance between public and private sector investment. Governments which have attempted to follow a path of structural adjustment through reallocation have regarded public sector investment, and indeed public spending in general, as competitive with private sector investment. Public spending is said to 'crowd out' private investment. This view, however, urgently needs to be reassessed.

In the conditions which prevail in sub-Saharan Africa, many types of public expenditure are likely to be complementary to private sector investment.[19] This is likely to be true of public investment in rural and urban infrastructure (transport, power, water and sewerage facilities) and of public expenditure on several kinds of human capital investment (primary and secondary education, certain types of vocational training, basic health and nutrition, applied agricultural research). Expenditure in these areas can increase investment opportunities in the private sector and raise, not lower, private sector 'savings'. That is, public investment can increase the profitability of private investment and this, in turn, will increase private savings and domestic resource mobilization more generally.

The state thus has a leading role to play. This presupposes of course that there is a functioning state that is able to evaluate policies, choose from among them and implement programmes that bear some resemblance to what was planned. Where the state has disintegrated (Liberia, Somalia) or is in rapid decay (Zaire, Sudan), development is impossible and the first order of business must be to reconstruct the state (as is happening in Uganda and Mozambique). Any strategy of adjustment, that is, any set of policies deliberately selected to achieve a specified objective, even *laissez faire*, requires a functioning state. The alternative is anarchy, not the spontaneous order of well functioning markets.

A strategy of structural adjustment through investment implies that the composition of government expenditure, at all levels, should be shifted as far as possible in the direction of investment in human, physical and natural capital. There has been much debate about whether the state in sub-Saharan Africa is 'too large' and should be reduced in size. A more fruitful debate would be over the role of the state, directly and indirectly, in promoting a rapid rate of growth of investment and ensuring an efficient allocation of investment funds. It is not sufficient that government spending be heavily biased toward capital formation, it is equally important that within each spending category, funds be allocated to achieve the highest possible rate of return.

Let us consider spending on human capital as an example. It is well established that investing in education yields a high return, often comparable to or higher than the returns from investing in physical capital. Within education, the rate of return is highest on expenditures on primary education, followed by secondary education. The returns on university and other forms of tertiary education tend to be lower than the returns on primary and secondary education. Yet when one examines the composition of public expenditure on education, it often turns out to be the case that funds are allocated in inverse proportion to the rate of return: university education receives the largest amount of funds, followed by secondary and then primary education. It follows from this that if budgetary priorities were reversed – some of the funds now allocated to universities being transferred to primary education – the rate of return on investment in education as a whole would rise and the overall efficiency of investment would increase. Similarly, if governments are forced to cut spending on education, for example because of the need to stabilize the economy, the damage minimizing strategy would be to cut university budgets first and leave spending on primary and secondary education intact.

The same arguments apply to public spending on health. Investing in the health of the people can be an excellent use of a country's resources, but not all forms of health expenditure are equally profitable. Some types of medical treatment are costly and produce modest results whereas other types are inexpensive and produce large benefits. Particularly in sub-Saharan Africa where resources are very scarce, it is important to allocate government expenditure on health services so as to maximize the returns. In general this implies favouring preventive health programmes, primary health care centres, mother and child nutrition programmes and pre- and post-natal maternity services and family planning programmes. In practice, however, government health expenditure pyramids often are inverted: most of the funds are allocated to the less beneficial activities while those with high returns are starved of resources. Large urban hospitals in particular absorb a disproportionate amount of the budget, to the neglect of primary health centres in the rural areas and preventive programmes in general. The overall impact of investments in health could be increased substantially if funds were better allocated.

Consider next government financed investment in physical capital. There is an enormous need in sub-Saharan Africa for investment in infrastructure, in both rural and urban areas. Much public investment at present, however, uses relatively capital intensive methods of production (which require imported equipment), relies on large, well established contractors (and thus excludes small and medium sized African-owned businesses) and even uses imported construction materials (which denies investment opportunities to local suppliers). The result is that public investment is costly and the returns are rather low. Numerous opportunities are overlooked to generate a large amount of employment for low skilled labour at very low wages, to encourage the emergence and growth of small local contractors by providing a bit of training and credit, and to foster a large, rapidly expanding local construction materials industry.

Notes

1. In the *World Bank, World Development Report 1996* (New York: Oxford University Press, 1996) 50 countries are listed. The UNDP, *Human Development Report 1996* (New York: Oxford University Press, 1996) contains 44 countries on its list. The six countries in the World Bank's list but not on the UNDP's list are Djibouti, Eritrea, Mayotte, Reunion, Somalia and Sudan. This study will use the World Bank's list.

2. The World Bank has published three major studies of sub-Saharan Africa in each of which analysis is followed by policy prescription. See World Bank, *Toward Sustained Development in Sub-Saharan Africa: A Joint Program of Action* (Washington, DC, 1984); World Bank, *Sub-Saharan Africa: From Crisis to Sustainable Growth* (Washington, DC, 1989); and World Bank, *A Continent in Transition: Sub-Saharan Africa in the Mid-1990s* (Washington, DC, 1995). Also see World Bank, *Adjustment in Africa: Reforms, Results and the Road Ahead* (New York: Oxford University Press, 1994) for the Bank's assessment of policy reforms in 29 countries. The World Bank tends to blame uneven implementation of reforms for the failure of structural adjustment rather than the choice of the reform strategy itself. In Ishrat Husain, *Why Do Some Economies Adjust More Successfully Than Others? Lessons From Seven African Countries* (World Bank: Washington, DC, Policy Research Working Paper 1364, October 1994), uneven implementation is attributed to lack of 'domestic ownership' and 'capacity'. The policies themselves, in other words, are assumed to be correct. World Bank and IMF policies, however, have been severely criticized by the Economic Commission for Africa. See ECA, *African Alternative Framework to Structural Adjustment Programmes for Socio-Economic Recovery and Transformation (AAF-SAP)*, E/ECA/CM.15/6/Rev 23, Addis Ababa, 1989 and Adebayo Adedeji, *Structural Adjustment for Socio-economic Recovery and Transformation: The African Alternative*, Addis Ababa: United Nations Economic Commission for Africa, 1990.

3. For a justification of an upper limit of 20 per cent see Michael Bruno, 'Does Inflation Really Lower Growth?,' *Finance and Development* 35, 8 (September 1995) and I.M.D. Little, Richard Cooper, W. Max Corden and Sarath Rajapatirana, *Boom, Crisis and Adjustment: The Macroeconomic Experience of Developing Countries* (New York: Oxford University Press, 1993).

4. In 1994 gross domestic savings were negative in Rwanda, Burundi, Malawi, Chad and Lesotho.

5. There is evidence that many countries in sub-Saharan Africa did adjust the real exchange rate to cushion the impact of the decline in the external terms of

trade on domestic economic activity. (See Michael Hadjimichael, Dhaneshwar Ghura, Martin Mükleisen, Roger Nord and E. Murat Uçer, *Sub-Saharan Africa: Growth, Savings and Investment, 1986–93* (Washington, DC: International Monetary Fund, January 1995). The question remains, however, whether nominal exchange rates were fully adjusted to compensate for inflation.

6. In 1993, official development assistance (ODA) was 10.5 per cent of GNP in sub-Saharan Africa. This was much higher than the proportion in all other developing regions apart from East Asia (excluding China), where it was 19.5 per cent. The average for all developing countries was 1.4 per cent. UNDP, *Human Development Report 1996* (New York: Oxford University Press, 1996) Table 47, p. 212.

7. See Jean-Marc Fontaine, 'Trading Off Investment for Exports: African Adjustment Experiences,' in Sunanda Sen (ed.), *Financial Fragility, Debt and Economic Reforms* (London: Macmillan, 1996).

8. For example, formal sector wage employment as a percentage of the total labour force declined in Kenya from 18 per cent in 1988 to 16.9 per cent in 1994; in Uganda from 17.2 per cent in 1991 to 12.7 per cent in 1995; in Zambia from 29.4 per cent in 1980 to 18.2 per cent in 1994; and in Zimbabwe from 34.1 per cent in 1980 to 25.3 per cent in 1995. (Rolph van der Hoeven, 'Labour Markets and Structural Adjustment', paper presented at a seminar on Policies for Economic Growth and Development in Southern Africa, Harare, Zimbabwe, 1–3 April 1996, Table 12. Also see Willem van der Geest and Ganeshan Wignaraja, *Adjustment, Employment and Labour Market Institutions in Sub-Saharan Africa in the 1990s: A Survey* (Geneva: International Labour Office, Employment Papers 10, 1996).

9. For example, real earnings in manufacturing in Kenya declined 30.5 per cent from 1987 to 1992 and in Zambia the decline was 23.6 per cent from 1987 to 1991. (Rolph van der Hoeven, *ibid.*, Table 15.)

10. Vali Jamal and John Weeks, *Africa Misunderstood or Whatever Happened to the Rural-Urban Gap?* (Geneva: International Labour Office, 1988).

11. Vali Jamal, (ed.), *Structural Adjustment and Rural Labour Markets in Africa*, (London: Macmillan, 1995).

12. In the case of internationally mobile resources, however, reallocation certainly is possible. There was a large exodus of human capital from Africa in the form of the emigration to Europe and North America of high skilled, professional, managerial and technical labour. There was also considerable capital flight. Both these scarce resources could in principle be repatriated under favourable conditions, such as those associated with an investment-led strategy of structural adjustment.

13. The implication of this argument is that in a context of economic decline and a fall in total government expenditure, public expenditure on human capital formation should be protected and hence the proportion of government expenditure devoted to education (and health) actually should rise.

14. See Keith Griffin and Terry McKinley, *Implementing a Human Development Strategy* (London: Macmillan, 1994), Ch. 2.

15. Ingrid Palmer has argued persuasively that the reduction in state provided health services that has accompanied structural adjustment has increased disproportionately the burden on women since it is they who must now provide substitutes for the lost services. (Ingrid Palmer, 'Public Finance from a Gender Perspective', *World Development* 23, 11 (November 1995).)

16. See the essay on 'Domestic Policies in Developing Countries and their Effects on Employment, Income Inequality and Poverty' in Keith Griffin, *Studies in Globalization and Economic Transitions* (London: Macmillan, 1996).
17. Large inflows of foreign aid can lean in an anti-development direction by (i) reducing real rates of interest, (ii) putting upward pressure on the exchange rate, (iii) increasing consumption at the expense of savings and (iv) distorting the composition of investment. (See the essay on 'Foreign Aid After the Cold War' in Keith Griffin, *ibid.*)
18. Rolph van der Hoeven recommends 'a moratorium on African debt for the next 10 years …' (Rolph van der Hoeven, 'External Dependence, Structural Adjustment and Development Aid in Sub-Saharan Africa', in Karel Jansen and Rob Vos (eds.), *External Finance and Adjustment, Failure and Success in the Developing World* (London: Macmillan, 1996.)
19. For evidence in support of the 'crowding in' hypothesis see Lance Taylor, *Varieties of Stabilization Experience* (Oxford: Clarendon Press, 1988); Lance Taylor (ed.), *The Rocky Road to Reform* (Cambridge: MIT Press, 1993); Helen Shapiro and Lance Tayor, 'The State and Industrial Strategy', *World Development* 18 (1990); and implicitly, World Bank, *World Development Report 1994* (New York:Oxford University Press, 1994).

References

Bruno, Michael (1995) 'Does Inflation Really Lower Growth?' *Finance and Development* 35, 8 (September).

Fontaine, Jean-Marc (1996) 'Trading Off Investment for Exports: African Adjustment Experiences.' *Financial Fragility, Debt and Economic Reforms*, ed Sunanda Sen (London: Macmillan).

Griffin, Keith and Terry McKinley (1994) *Implementing a Human Development Strategy* (London: Macmillan).

Griffin, Keith (1996) 'Domestic Policies in Developing Countries and their Effects on Employment, Income Inequality and Poverty.' *Studies in Globalization and Economic Transitions* (London: Macmillan).

Hadjimichael, Michael, Dhaneshwar Ghura, Martin Mükleisen, Roger Nord and E. Murat Uçer (1995) *Sub-Saharan Africa: Growth, Savings and Investment, 1986–93* (Washington, DC: International Monetary Fund).

Husain, Ishrat (1994) *Why Do Some Economies Adjust More Successfully Than Others? Lessons From Seven African Countries*. Policy Research Working Paper 1364 (October) (World Bank: Washington, DC).

Jamal, Vali and John Weeks (1988) *Africa Misunderstood or Whatever Happened to the Rural-Urban Gap?* (Geneva: International Labour Office).

Jamal, Vali (ed) (1995) *Structural Adjustment and Rural Labour Markets in Africa* (London: Macmillan).

Little, Richard Cooper, W. Max Corden and Sarath Rajapatirana (1993) *Boom, Crisis and Adjustment: The Macroeconomic Experience of Developing Countries* (New York: Oxford University Press).

Palmer, Ingrid (1995) 'Public Finance from a Gender Perspective' *World Development* 23, 11 (November).

Shapiro, Helen and Lance Tayor (1990) 'The State and Industrial Strategy', *World Development* 18.

Taylor, Lance (1988) *Varieties of Stabilization Experience* (Oxford: Clarendon Press).

Taylor, Lance (ed) (1993) *The Rocky Road to Reform* (Cambridge: MIT Press).

UNDP. (1996) *Human Development Report 1996* (New York: Oxford University Press).

Van der Geest, Willem and Ganeshan Wignaraja (1996) *Adjustment, Employment and Labour Market Institutions in Sub-Saharan Africa in the 1990s: A Survey.* Employment Papers 10 (Geneva: International Labour Office).

Van der Hoeven, Rolph (1996a) 'External Dependence, Structural Adjustment and Development Aid in Sub-Saharan Africa'. In *External Finance and Adjustment, Failure and Success in the Developing World*, ed Karel Jansen and Rob Vos (London: Macmillan).

Van der Hoeven, Rolph (1996b) 'Labour Markets and Structural Adjustment'. Paper presented at a seminar on Policies for Economic Growth and Development in Southern Africa, 1–3 April, at Harare, Zimbabwe.

World Bank (1984) *Toward Sustained Development in Sub-Saharan Africa: A Joint Program of Action* (Washington, DC).

World Bank (1989) *Sub-Saharan Africa: From Crisis to Sustainable Growth* (Washington, DC).

World Bank (1994) *Adjustment in Africa: Reforms, Results and the Road Ahead* (New York: Oxford University Press).

World Bank (1994) *World Development Report 1994* (New York: Oxford University Press).

World Bank (1995) *A Continent in Transition: Sub-Saharan Africa in the Mid-1990s* (Washington, DC).

World Bank (1996) *World Development Report 1996* (New York: Oxford University Press).

3 Macroeconomic Policy for Growth, with Reference to Africa South of the Sahara

John Weeks

I. Introduction

While the Asian and Latin American countries enjoyed rising per capita incomes during the 1970s, the sub-Saharan countries stagnated and in numerous cases their average incomes declined. In the 1980s most Asian countries continued to enjoy economic growth in excess of population increase, while virtually all Latin America plunged into debt-provoked depressions. However, by the early 1990s the consensus of experts was that Latin America had recovered, with a few distressing exceptions and with a notable reverse caused by the Mexican financial crisis in late 1994. For the sub-Saharan region recovery has been heralded but yet to arrive. Governments of the region entered into stabilization and structural adjustment programmes of the International Monetary Fund and the World Bank early and often the outcomes were disappointing.[1]

As a result, the debate over appropriate policy for the region has two characteristics either absent or of less prominence in other regions. First, the debate typically focuses upon the role and behaviour of the two multilaterals. One form that this takes is the allegation that the two multilaterals have imposed a particular (and, by implication, inappropriate) policy package on the region. Because of this, a World Bank report on adjustment lending placed heavy stress upon assigning 'ownership' of adjustment programmes to the contracting governments.[2]

Second, the extremely mixed growth performances of countries in the sub-Sahara opting for IMF and World Bank programmes contrast with the recovery of some 'adjusting' countries in other regions. Since Costa Rica, for example, recovered impressively, the debate as to whether structural adjustment helped or hindered is largely academic. Adjustment failures, on the other hand, call forth accusations of culpability. Especially in cases of countries that the multilaterals once heralded as success stories, failure is all the more spectacular and controversial. There are many such negative 'turnarounds' in the sub-Saharan region. The combination of these two characteristics of the region, the high profile of the multilaterals and the extremely mixed adjustment outcomes, make for a bitter and protracted policy debate, in which the contributions become increasingly stylized and predictable, even recycled.

II. Economic Characteristics of the Region

The central focus of economic policy in the sub-Saharan region should be to formulate policies to alleviate poverty and foster development, in which the gains from growth are equitably distributed. 'Employment generation' and 'labour market policies' are short-hand terms to summarize such a focus. One must use these terms cautiously in the context of sub-Saharan countries. While there are a few countries in Asia whose labour forces have a smaller portion of *formal* sector wage labour, in no other region of the world is this category as unimportant as in the sub-Saharan region. In 1990 less than 30 per cent of the region's population lived in urban areas and 70 per cent of the labour force earned all or part of its livelihood from agriculture.[3] While there is considerable wage employment in agriculture, this is largely of a seasonal nature. Further, much of rural wage employment is enmeshed in labour relations that are not easily incorporated into the neo-classical concept of a labour market, tied as they are to indebtedness and other non-wage obligations.

One indication of the relatively and absolutely small size of formal sector wage employment in most countries of the region is the lack of reliable estimates for this segment of the labour force.[4] Demographic statistics in general are extremely unreliable,[5] reflecting in part the administrative weakness of the state apparatus. The sub-Saharan countries are societies of small-scale agriculturists in rural areas,[6] and traders and petty commodity and service producers in towns and cities.[7] Therefore, 'generating (formal sector) employment' is a part, but a quantitatively small part of the problem of generating livelihoods, raising producer productivity and reducing poverty in the region.[8]

If formal sector wage earners in the region ever represented a relatively privileged elite in terms of standard of living, this was invalidated by rural–urban income trends in the late 1970s and 1980s.[9] Increasingly throughout the 1980s, economic decline and stagnation enrolled urban wage earners in increasing numbers into the ranks of the poor. Generating formal sector wage employment at earnings levels above subsistence must constitute part of social policy in the region, though this would address a minority part of the poverty problem. For the foreseeable future, the formal sector wage labour force is too small in most countries of the region for its expansion to effect a substantial relative transfer of labour from low-productivity and low-income rural and urban activities. Growth, and growth of agriculture in particular, is the necessary condition for a solution to the employment and livelihoods problem. In order to raise the incomes of the rural and urban poor, growth alone, however, is not enough: attention to the composition and distribution of growth is the necessary condition for poverty reduction. One should not leap to the simple view that agricultural growth is best fostered by overwhelmingly directing resources to the sector itself. Agricultural growth is part of a more general process of development, in which the various sectors interact. The task of policymaking is to devise a strategy in which agricultural policy and industrial policy are complementary, and the investments in each sector reinforcing.

III. Trickle-down South of the Sahara

From the late 1970s there began a shift in the bilateral and multilateral approach to development from an emphasis upon distributional concerns to an almost exclusive focus upon growth. The strategy for growth was one long-familiar in economics: liberalization of markets and restriction of state interventions with the purpose of fostering greater openness to international commodity and capital markets. This strategy has been encapsulated inaccurately by the vague and contra-dictory term 'export-led growth'.[10] As the 1980s progressed and many perceived that the liberalization strategy generated considerable social costs, pressure accumulated for the inclusion of distributional and poverty considerations within the policy packages of the multilateral organizations.[11]

The response of the major lending agencies proved marginal: the liberalization strategy was not altered in any significant way, but augmented by recommendations for 'targeting' the poor[12] and *a priori* arguments alleging that 'freer' markets would benefit the poor. This approach derives from the long-standing 'trickle-down' philosophy: growth as such, unadulterated by attempts to drive a wedge of equality between the primary and secondary distributions of income, will pass its benefits through the population via unregulated markets; those left out in the process can be reached by welfare programmes ('targeting') of limited scope.

While 'targeting' may have had some success in the middle-income countries,[13] both critics and defenders of the liberalization strategy now agree that it is largely irrelevant for the sub-Saharan region.[14] All but a few sub-Saharan countries lack effective systems for delivery of welfare programmes either to urban or rural areas.[15] The case for the liberalization version of the trickle-down approach rests solely upon *a priori* arguments and sweeping empirical generalizations. The argument begins with the uncontested observation that the majority of the poor in the sub-Saharan region live in rural areas.[16] To this is added that the poor in rural areas derive their incomes largely from agriculture, either from their own farms or as labourers on farms. While this is also correct, it excludes the rural non-farm poor, whose numbers have increased over the 1980s. The next step in the argument is to conclude that increases in agricultural incomes will directly help the poor who farm (though not necessarily the non-farming poor). If one then assumes that state interventions have depressed farm incomes, the inference is drawn that liberalization of markets, by raising farm incomes generally, will help the poor specifically.[17]

There is now general recognition that this line of argument reaches an unjustified conclusion.[18] Critics pointed out that the argument lacked both logical coherence and empirical support. There are two major problems with the argument: a) it is not possible *a priori* to predict relative price movements in response to liberalization except at the most general level (tradables versus non-tradables); and b) whether the poor benefit from relative increases in agricultural prices (should they occur) depends on factors which vary across countries, such as whether the rural poor are net food producers or consumers, and whether their income is primarily from tradable or non-tradable agricultural products. Available empirical evidence suggests that the poor in sub-Saharan countries do not for the most part produce tradables. This is almost certainly the case for workers in the urban informal sector, whose activities are primarily services. The same applies for rural non-farm activities, which involve transport, commerce and repair.

Evidence suggests that international traded commodities account for a minority of the income of the farming poor.[19] Indeed, the effect of trade liberalization on the farming poor can be negative. While one must be careful with generalizations, it would seem that in many countries the marketed produce of poor farm families is primarily foodstuffs.[20] To the extent that these are tradable, they are importables. Distorted world grain markets can result in cheap imports substituting for home production supplied by the poor. If liberalization programmes are combined with demand-reducing fiscal and monetary measures, marketed output can fall due to a constriction of consumer demand.[21]

Some would argue that the possible negative effects of liberalization might be off-set by the indirect benefits to the rural poor in their role as farm labourers, derivative from the increase in income of better-off farm households through a rise in the demand for labour to produce export crops. This is trickle-down with a vengeance: relative price changes may directly hurt the poor (they do not 'trickle-down'), but via the actions of those that gain the poor may enjoy indirect benefits. A recent World Bank report concedes that the importance of this mechanism is open to question.[22] If food prices as well as export prices rise and the poor are net buyers of food, it is difficult to construct a general equilibrium outcome in which the poor emerge better off from the process. There is also a theoretical problem with the two-stage trickle-down process. If devaluations shift relative prices in favour of tradables, it must be the case that those producing non-tradables lose relatively, no matter what the indirect demand effects on prices and incomes might be.

In many and perhaps a majority of sub-Saharan countries, a relative price shift from non-tradables to tradables at best has a weak positive effect on the poor, at the cost of a more unequal distribution of agricultural income.[23] At worst, the result depresses the incomes of the poor. If trade liberalization results in a more efficient allocation of resources, in many sub-Saharan countries this occurs in a context of a probable trade-off between efficiency and poverty reduction. The previous view, that protectionism taxed agriculture and free trade benefited it, derived from three false assumptions: that all agricultural output was tradable (indeed, exportable), that inequality in the distribution of land was not important and that any downward trend in border prices of agricultural products could be ignored as unimportant.

IV. Orthodox Adjustment Policies

To highlight the major issues in the debate over adjustment policies, it is useful to state the position of the World Bank on the application of the major instruments of macroeconomic policy:[24]

1. *a restrictive fiscal policy* which seeks to reduce overall public sector deficits towards zero;
2. *a tight monetary policy* which restricts money growth to close to the rate of economic growth and places emphasis upon the role of interest rates in stimulating saving; and

3. *free convertibility of the exchange rate* through a non-interventionist 'float'.[25]

The outcomes that these policies are supposed to foster are low inflation, increased saving and investment and a competitive exchange rate. These outcomes, in turn, are alleged to generate a satisfactory and sustainable rate of economic growth. The policies and outcomes are summarized in Table 3.1. One possible internal contradiction can be noted in this policy perspective. On the one hand, fiscal austerity has as one of its goals the reduction of the 'crowding out' phenomenon, that is the alleged tendency for private investment to be reduced as a result of government expenditure creating upward pressure on interest rates. This argument implies that fiscal austerity is beneficial by its downward effect on real interest rates. At the same time, a goal of monetary policy is to foster interest rates that would increase saving in the economy. Real interest rates cannot both rise and fall. In practice the orthodox approach places emphasis upon the need to increase real interest rates in the early stages of adjustment, since adjustment frequently follows a period of rather high inflation and negative real rates. While this emphasis may be sensible and pragmatic, it is not obviously consistent with an increase in investment during adjustment. Indeed, a universal finding of empirical studies is that stabilization and structural adjustment are associated with declines in investment.[26]

Thus, adjustment programmes have as their purpose several outcomes: a) a faster rate of growth of national income, b) lower inflation, c) increased 'open-ness', and d) an improved investment performance. Before considering these in a formal model, it is useful to review performance, shown in Figures 3.1–4. Each figure presents the deviation of the relevant variable from its mean for the period, with each value calculated from the cross-country average for the year in question.[27] If we take 1981 as separating pre-adjustment from adjustment years,[28] the average rate of growth before this date was 4 per cent per annum and 2.3 per cent subsequently (see Figure 3.1). For the fifteen years, 1982–1996, growth was below its long-term average for ten of the years, and above it for only four. If one takes the World Bank's preferred dating for the adjustment era, 1985 onwards,[29] performance is much the same (seven years out of ten with below-average growth rates). Whether the above-average growth rates in 1995 and 1996 will be sustained, or be temporary, as in 1988, remains to be seen. The evidence is at best ambiguous on whether the spread of adjustment programmes in the sub-Saharan region stimulated recovery.

Table 3.1 The WB-IMF Orthodox Policy Perspective

Type of Policy	Policy Characteristics	Instrument	Desired Outcome	Goal
Fiscal	low deficit	expenditure reduction frequently preferred to tax increases	low inflation, increased private investment (smaller public sector)	stimulate investment (including FDI)
Monetary	slow money growth, positive interest rates (in practice above the rate of economic growth)	deficit reduction (since deficits are usually monetized), administratively set interest rates	low inflation	stimulate saving
Exchange rate	convertible, deregulated foreign exchange market	deregulation	competitive exchange rate, balance of payments equilibrium	stimulate exports & 'efficient' import substitution
				To yield: rapid, sustained growth

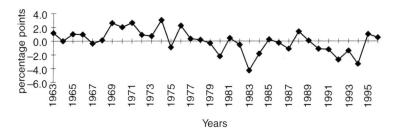

Figure 3.1 Sub-Saharan Africa: Deviations from the Cross-Country Average of GDP Growth, 1963–1996

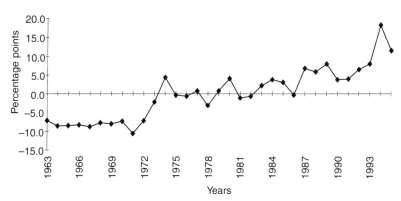

Figure 3.2 Sub-Saharan Africa: Deviations from the Cross-Country Average for Inflation, 1963–1995

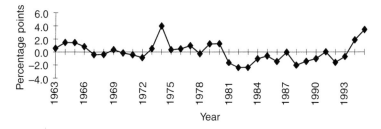

Figure 3.3 Sub-Saharan Africa: Deviations from the Cross-Country Average for the Export Share (*X/GDP*), 1963–1995

With regard to inflation (Figure 3.2), the evidence is clear: the adjustment period has been associated with a substantial and statistically significant increase in inflation across countries. Whether this represents a problem which requires solution is in part a question of

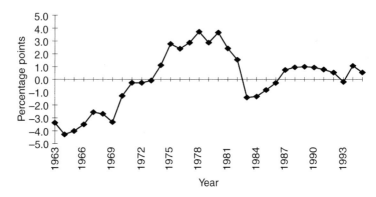

Figure 3.4 Sub-Saharan Africa: Deviations from the Cross-Country Average for the Investment Share (I/GDP), 1963–1995

theoretical perspective; however, it is contrary to the explicit goal of adjustment programmes. During the adjustment period there has been little evidence of a sustained increase in export performance, as measured by the share of exports in GDP. From 1982 through 1993, the export share across countries was at or below its long-term mean for every year. The last two years, 1994 and 1995, brought increases, which may or may not be sustained. Also ambiguous has been the movement in the investment share. After a continuous rise in the 1970s, the investment share declined sharply, to below its long-term mean, reaching its lowest point in 1983. Subsequently, the ratio rose, but stayed close to the mean before declining again after 1990. As for exports, 1994 brought a recovery, followed by a decline in 1995.

On balance, the movements in these key variables suggest that adjustment programmes at best have been associated with limited improvement in economic performance,[30] with a possible recovery in the second half of the 1990s. In the absence of evidence of adjustment generating sustained improvement, it is relevant to consider alternative policies for growth and poverty reduction.

V. Empirical Evidence on Macreconomic Policies

The debate over what would be the appropriate macroeconomic strategy for sub-Saharan countries can be clarified by use of a growth model. The equations are estimated across countries and over time.[31] From the perspective of the orthodox approach, growth is derivative from relative prices, which, if they approach the general equilibrium set that implies optimal allocative efficiency, will foster the rate of growth implied by an economy's productive potential. On the other hand, the heterodox approach stresses quantity adjustments: relative prices are important, but most markets in sub-Saharan countries do not operate efficiently. Therefore, 1) unregulated markets are unlikely to generate the 'appropriate' price signals (prices conforming to allocative efficiency) and 2) should the signals be 'appropriate', structural obstacles can prevent private agents from responding to them. For example, it may or may not be true that a 'floating' exchange rate would move to a level implying a sustainable balance of payments; if it did so, rigidities in credit, product and input markets might prevent the quantity responses required for sustainability.

These two perspectives can be investigated by use of a model based upon the Harrod-Domar framework, in which the aggregate rate of growth is determined primarily by the rate of investment. If y_w is the warranted (potential) rate of growth, then:

(1) $y_w = \alpha\beta$

where α is the output-capital ratio ($\Delta Y/\Delta K$) and β is the investment rate. (I/Y). The actual investment rate is determined by the desired or target rate:

(2) $\beta_{(t)} = \beta_{(t-1)}) + \gamma[\beta^*_{(t)} - \beta_{(t-1)}]$

In this formulation, producers select the desired investment rate, then make a partial adjustment to bring the rate in the previous period to the desired level (if γ is unity, the adjustment is complete in each period). The desired rate is the output-weighted average of private and public sector producers, with the former basing their target on profitability calculations, and the latter on a policy-identified rate of growth. To specify the desired rate of investment, it is assumed that in both sectors increases in the capital stock are import dependent and, therefore, influenced by the availability of foreign exchange, with this approximated by the rate of growth of exports. The rate of growth of exports can be decomposed into the rate of growth of volume (x) and the terms of trade (TT). It is also assumed that inflation has a negative effect on private investment, by discouraging projects with a long gestation period. Thus,

(3) $\beta^*_{(t)} = \beta^*_{(t)}(x_t, TT_t, p_t)$

Substituting, the actual rate of growth, y_t, determined by the ex-post investment rate, is:

(3a) $y_t = \alpha\{\beta_{(t-1)}) + \gamma\{[\beta^*_{(t)}(x_t, TT_t, p_t)] - \beta_{(t-1)}\}$

This can be simplified to:

(3b) $y_t = \alpha\{[1 - \gamma][\beta_{(t-1)}] + \gamma\{[\beta^*_{(t)}(x_t, TT_t)]\}$

In the orthodox approach, the quantity adjustments (β and x) and the inflation rate result from changes in relative prices and the rate of money expansion. These are substituted for the quantities they allegedly determine to achieve a 'reduced form' equation. To make the model conform more closely to that estimated in a World Bank report on adjustment policies in Africa, the fiscal deficit as a portion of GDP is included as an argument.[32] The justification for inclusion is the 'crowding out' mechanism: allegedly, increases in the public sector deficit reduce private sector investment. Therefore,

(4) $y_t = \alpha\{[1 - \gamma][\beta_{(t-1)}] + \gamma\{[\beta^*_{(t)}(e_t, r_t, Df/GDP, m_t)]$

The variables e_t, r_t, Df/GDP, and m_t are the real exchange rate, the real rate of interest, the fiscal deficit, and the growth of the money supply. For the last variable, a World Bank report uses the rate of growth of the money supply in excess of the rate of growth of output (which it is fashionable to call 'seigniorage').[33] Table 3.2 reports the result of the orthodox

Table 3.2 OLS-Estimated Growth Model, *'Orthodox'* (aka World Bank) across Sub-Saharan Countries, 1971–1995 [dependent variable: growth of GDP]

Variable	Coefficient	T-statistic	Significance
Constant	0.05153	1.582	0.115
[*Fiscal deficit/GDP*]t	0.0035	0.049	0.961
Δ[*real exchange rate*]t	0.0322	1.630	0.104
[*Seigniorage* $(m - y)$]t	−0.1042	−4.276	0.000
[*Real interest rate*]t	−0.0066	−0.014	0.851
Adjusted R^2	0.1343		
F-statistic	2.25		
	(@ 0.001)		
Degrees of freedom	283		
Countries with significant shift coefficients (0.10 or less): *two*			
(Omitted, Benin; no complete observations for Angola, Madagascar, Mozambique, Zaire)			

Note: All variables in logarithmic form.

specification, estimated using ordinary least squares, across sub-Saharan countries for 1960–1995, with incomplete observations omitted. The performance of the model is unimpressive, not because of the low correlation coefficient, but because of the insignificance of the allegedly explanatory variables. Using the standard 10 per cent rule,[34] only 'seigniorage' is significant (and of the predicted sign). This variable should be viewed with some suspicion, because it is a composite variable derivative from the simple quantity theory of money. Despite its use in a World Bank report along with the other price variables, its inclusion over-determines the equation. Thus, it is not surprising that the others are non-significant.[35]

The Heterodox Model

A heterodox perspective does not conclude that the non-significant variables necessarily imply that the hypothesized causal links are invalid. They may be invalid, but it is also possible that their links to the quantity variables (for example, the investment share) are so tenuous and inelastic that the correlations are lost by the conversion to 'reduced form'. To evaluate the possibility of lost causality, equation (3b) is estimated directly, in modified form. A specifically heterodox mechanism is specified: the possibility that the economies might be growth-constrained by restrictive monetary and fiscal policy. Many critics of orthodox stabilization and adjustment have argued that theory predicts that the emphasis of these programmes on reduction of fiscal deficits and on monetary restraint is excessive, constraining economies from their potential growth. This hypothesis is difficult to test empirically outside a general-equilibrium simulation model. The approach here is to take the real interest rate, lagged one period, as a proxy for demand compression. It is assumed that the nominal interest rate is an administered price (by Central Banks), used to constrain credit growth. Lower aggregate demand, in turn, depresses the desired rate of investment of the private sector.[36] Equation (3a) can be re-written as:

$$(5) \quad y_t = \alpha\{[1 - \gamma][\beta_{(t-1)}] + \gamma\{r(r_{t-1})[\beta^*_{(t)}(x_t, TT_t)]\}$$

The results of the heterodox estimation are given in Table 3.3 and indicate a considerably better outcome than for the orthodox model. The improvement is not due to the correlation coefficient (which is almost the same as in Table 3.2), but to the performance of the explanatory variables, all of which are significant and of the predicted sign. The results prompt three important points of interpretation. First, growth appears to be directly quantity constrained, by the rate of growth of exports and the

Table 3.3 OLS-Estimated Growth Model, '*Heterodox*' across Sub-Saharan Countries, 1971–1995 [dependent variable: growth of GDP]

Variable	Coefficient	T-statistic	Significance
Constant	–0.0581	–3.748	0.000
[Investment/GDP]t	0.0291	5.509	0.000
Δ[Export volume]t	0.0252	2.573	0.010
Δ[Terms of Trade]t	0.0610	3.865	0.000
[Real Interest Rate] (t – 1)	–0.0627	–3.661	0.000
Adjusted R²	0.1306		
F-statistic	14.76		
	(@ 0.000)		
Degrees of freedom	532		
Without country dummies			

Note: All variables in logarithmic form.

terms of trade (which determine imports).[37] Second, the economies can be interpreted as demand constrained, as approximated by the lagged interest rate.[38] Therefore, a pragmatic macroeconomic policy is required, one that keeps real interest rates moderate without provoking excessive inflation. The erstwhile Golden Rule of real interest rates should guide policy: short-term real interest rates should be managed such that the long-run rate is close to the rate of growth of per capita income. This point is developed below.

Of the four variables in the heterodox model, two are subject to direct policy influence, the real interest rate (via the nominal interest rate) and the rate of investment (via public sector investment). These move in reaction to other influences. To construct a model useful for policy assessment, the next step is to expand the model to include all the basic macro relationships: investment, saving, imports, exports, inflation and the real interest rate.

For the investment equation, a modified accelerator model is used. Consistent with the growth equation, investment is assumed to respond to changes in output in the previous period, constrained by current import availability. It is further assumed that inflation has a negative effect on the private sector element of investment, by fostering a short-term preference for non-productive investments with a rapid turnover.

(6) $(I/Y)_t = i(y_{t-1}, N/Y_t, p_t)$

Saving as a portion of GDP is specified as a function of prevailing interest rates, the rate of income growth and foreign assistance. It is anticipated that the impact of the interest rate will be relatively weak. A large part of saving in sub-Saharan countries is non-monetized and implicit in the act of investment, such as improvement of agricultural land by smallholders. The rate of growth of GDP is included as an argument because of the low absolute level of per capita income in the sub-Saharan countries. Thus, a function non-homogeneous with respect to the level of income is assumed. The inclusion of external assistance is to test for the possibility that aid decreases saving by reducing the pressure for governments to increase public sector revenues (a hypothesis which is confirmed).

(7) $(S/Y)_t = s(y_{t-1}, r_t, A/Y_t)$

The shares of imports and exports in GDP are assumed to be functions of the real exchange rate (measured such that an increase reflects devaluation). It is further assumed that the import share increases with the rate of growth, and, holding the exchange rate constant, exports rise with an improvement in the terms of trade.

(8) $(N/Y)_t = n(y_{t-1}, rer_t)$

(9) $(X/Y)_t = x(rer_{t-1}, TT_t)$

Inflation is specified as implied by the quantity theory of money: $PY = vM$, with a two period adjustment to changes in both output and the money supply. From the total derivative of the quantity equation, with all variables in rates of change, one obtains:[39]

(10) $p_t = p(y_t, y_{t-1}, m_t, m_{t-1})$

Finally, the real interest rate, in the absence of administrative intervention, is a function of the fiscal deficit before external grants and changes in the money supply (with the deficit defined as negative when expenditure exceeds revenue).

(11) $r_t = r([Df/GDP]_t, m_{t-1})$

The model is summarized in Table 3.4, where shaded boxes indicate the variables used in the simulation exercise below. The coefficients and test statistics are given in Table 3.5. In addition to the heterodox specifications, other variables were tested for their impact. When these were significant, the relevant cell is bordered, but not shaded. The implications of the model can be summarized as follows. Growth of GDP is quantity-driven (by investment and exports) and demand constrained (implied by the negative coefficient on the interest rate). Further, growth receives a one-off boost from an improvement in the terms of trade. Investment is also quantity-driven, not determined by relative prices (the interest term

Table 3.4 Summary of OLS Modelling Results, sub-Saharan Countries

Dependent: Independent:	GDP Growth (y)	Investment/ GDP (I/Y)	Imports/ GDP (N/Y)	Exports/ GDP (X/Y)	Saving/ GDP (S/Y)
Real (quantity) variables:					
GDP growth (y)		positive & significant (t − 1)	positive & significant (t − 1)		positive & significant (t − 1)
Investment/GDP (I/Y)	positive & significant (t)				
Export growth (X)	positive & significant (t)				
Imports/GDP (N/Y)		positive & significant (t)			
Aid/GDP (A/Y)	non-significant	negative & significant (t)	positive & significant, correlated with *rer*		negative & significant (t − 1)
Relative prices & money variables					
Terms of trade (TT)	first difference, positive & significant (t)			positive & significant	
Real interest rate (r)	negative & significant (t − 1)	non-significant (t − 1)			positive & significant (3 yr aver)
Real exchange rate (rer)	non-significant		negative & significant (t)	positive & significant (t − 1)	
Inflation (p)	non-significant	negative & significant (t)			
Money growth (m)	positive & significant				
Seignorage (seign)	negative and significant (t)				
Fiscal deficit (Df/Y)	non-significant	negative & significant (correlated with p)			
Interpretation	Growth is demand constrained, not relative price constrained	Investment is stimulated by growth, constrained by imports	imports determined by growth, relatively inelastic with respect to exchange rate	exports determined by relative, prices, terms of trade more important than exchange rate	saving determined by growth, inelastic with respect to interest rate

Table 3.4 (*continued*)

Dependent: Independent:	Inflation (*p*)	Real Interest Rate (*r*)	(X–N)/ GDP	Money Growth (*m*)
Real (quantity) variables: GDP growth (*y*)	negative & significant (*t, t* − 1)		negative & significant (*t* − 1)	
Investment/GDP (*I/Y*)				
Export growth (*x*)				
Imports/GDP (*N/Y*)				
Aid/GDP (*A/Y*)	positive & significant (*t*)		negative & significant (*t* − 1)	non-significant
Relative prices & money variables Terms of trade (*TT*)			positive & significant (*t*)	
Real interest rate (*r*)	negative & significant (*t*)			negative & significant (*t*-1)
Real exchange rate (*rer*)			positive & significant (*t*)	
Inflation (*p*)				
Money growth (*m*)	positive & significant (*t, t* − 1)	positive & significant (*t*)		
Seignorage (*seign*)	positive & significant (*t*)			
Fiscal deficit (*Df/Y*)	positive & significant, but inferior specification	positive & significant (*t* − 1)		non-significant
Interpretation:	money is not neutral	not 'crowding out' because *I/Y = f(r)* not statistically significant	aid worsens the trade balance (equation not used in simulation)	money growth is not correlated with the fiscal deficit

Note: Shaded boxes indicate relationships used in simulations.

Table 3.5 Summary of Macroeconomic Model for the Sub-Saharan Countries, 1970–1995 (all variables in logarithmic form)

Dependent Variable	Constant	Independent Variables:			
GDP growth	-0.0581 (0.000)	+0.0291 $(Y/I)_t$ (0.000)	+0.0252$(x)_t$ (0.010)	+0.0610$(\Delta TTd)_t$ (0.000)	-0.0627 $(r)_{t-1}$ (0.000) $R^2 = 0.1306$ $F = 14.76$ $DF = 532$
Inv/ GDP	1.5116 (0.000)	+1.2080$(y)_{t-1}$ (0.000)	+0.3999$(M/Y)_t$ (0.000)	-0.2234$(p)_t$ (0.051)	-0.0556$(A/Y)_t$ (0.023) $R^2 = 0.6844$ $F = 25.98$ $DF = 491$
Saving/ GDP	0.2071 (0.000)	+0.2605$(y)_{t-1}$ (0.002)	+0.0911$(r)_{t3}$ (0.023)	-0.0537$(A/Y)_t$ (0.000)	$R^2 = 0.3062$ $F = 68.56$ $DF = 466$
Imports/ GDP	3.5884 (0.000)	+0.4251 $(y)_{t-1}$ (0.003)	-0.1012$(RER)_t$ (0.000)		$R^2 = 0.7252$ $F = 75.29$ $DF = 1136$
Exports/ GDP	0.3217 (0.175)	+0.0530$(RER)_{t-1}$ (0.021)	0.3033 $(TT)_t$ (0.000)		$R^2 = 0.7376$ $F = 74.00$ $DF = 999$

Table 3.5 (continued)

Dependent Variable	Constant	Independent Variables:			
Inflation	0.0238 (0.000)	−0.3994(y)$_t$ (0.000)	−0.2888(y)$_{t-1}$ (0.000)	+0.4034(m)$_t$ (0.000)	+0.3315(m)$_{t-1}$ (0.000) $R^2 = 0.5024$ $F = 254.63$ $DF = 1001$
Real Interest Rate	0.0431 (0.000)	+0.2340(Df/Y)$_{t-1}$ (0.009)	−0.4723(m)$_{t-1}$ (0.000)		$R^2 = 0.3996$ $F = 110.79$ $DF = 333$

Notes:

1. Model closure condition is: [(I/Y) − (S/Y)] + [(X/Y) − (M/Y)] = 0.
2. Numbers in parenthesis give the probability that the coefficient might be zero.
3. The correlation coefficients are adjusted for degrees of freedom.

is non-significant). The most important influence on investment is the rate of growth itself (lagged), as the accelerator theory predicts.

Two factors have a negative impact on investment: inflation (affecting expectations) and external assistance. As with saving, there appears to be a trade-off between the motivation to invest and external assistance. This might be explained by the shift in much donor assistance from project aid to balance of payments support. The important result for the external sector is that both imports and exports are relatively inelastic with respect to the real exchange rate: a devaluation of the real exchange rate of 100 per cent would decrease the import share by 10 per cent, and increase the export share by only 5 per cent.

Inflation conforms to the quantity equation, but money is not neutral. The predicted coefficients for changes in output and the money supply are minus one and plus one, respectively. When the coefficients for years t and $t-1$ are combined, the elasticity of inflation with respect to output is minus 0.68, and with respect to the money supply 0.73. This implies that at full capacity ($y = 0$), a 10 per cent increase in the money supply increases inflation by just over 7 per cent. An alternative specification, in which the fiscal deficit is used in place of changes in the money supply (which assumes the deficit is monetized), yields an inferior result on the basis of theoretical criteria.[40] This judgement is supported by a simple regression that shows the deficit and money growth not to be significantly correlated. The non-neutrality of money is manifested in the real interest rate. Were money neutral, the real interest rate should not be correlated with changes in the nominal stock of money. The positive coefficient on the deficit supports the orthodox view that increased government borrowing pushes up interest rates. However, since investment is not significantly correlated with the real interest rate, 'crowding out' is not implied.

Policy Implications

To pursue policy implications, we first consider elasticities between growth and the trade balance, on the one hand, and between key prices and quantities, on the other. Because investment is a function of changes in GDP, the model maintains a constant rate of growth only for a value of zero. Thus, one cannot calculate equilibrium elasticities as such, from one stable growth rate to another. In place of this, Table 3.6 presents elasticities after the lagged variables have imparted their impact, on the macroeconomic condition that the internal and external balances are equal ($[X - M] = [I - S]$). In what follows, *we assume a 10 per cent increase in each variable in turn*. As expected, a *ceterius paribus* increase in the money supply raises the rate of growth, via a decrease in the real interest rate, by a

Table 3.6 OLS Implied Elasticities between Variables for the Sub-Saharan Region (direct and indirect effects included)

Change in: with respect to:	GDP Growth Rate	Partial	Trade Balance	Comments:
Money supply	0.113		–0.030	
Investment/GDP	1.052		–0.054	
Real interest rate	–0.128		0.004	
Real exchange rate	–0.194		0.671	
Deficit	–0.001		0.001	
Terms of trade	0.277	2.167	1.105	<<[Partial: after one period, ΔTT zero in 2nd period]
Foreign aid	–0.059			
GDP growth rate			–0.268	
	saving			
real interest rate	0.062			
	Inflation			
money supply	0.897	0.734		Partial: output constant

Notes: A trade surplus and a fiscal surplus as defined as positive. An increase in the exchange rate indicates a devaluation. Consistent with closure rule, $(I - S) = (X - M)$.

meagre 1 per cent, and it also causes a minor increase in the trade deficit. By contrast, an increase in the investment share (for example, via more public sector investment) increases growth by a matching 10 per cent. With regard to relative prices, a rise in the real interest rate reduces growth by slightly over 1 per cent, reflecting demand compression.

One of most important implications of the model for policy purposes is that a real devaluation is contractionary, by 2 per cent for a 10 per cent devaluation. While devaluation increases the export share in GDP (imparting a growth stimulus through the rate of growth of exports), this is more than cancelled by its depressing effect on imports. The reduction in imports lowers the investment share, and thus the GDP growth rate.[41] At the same time, devaluation has a strong effect on improving the trade balance (by 7 per cent). The effect on growth of a change in the fiscal deficit, implied by an increase in government investment, is virtually nil. The terms of trade, over which the government has no control, have a strong growth-enhancing effect. A 10 per cent improvement results in a 20 per cent increase in the growth rate in the initial period, then a 3 per cent increase subsequently (when the terms of trade remain at the higher level, but the change is zero). Finally, foreign assistance has a small negative impact on growth, through its depressing effect on both saving and investment.

Other important elasticities are given in the lower part of the table. A *ceterius paribus* increase in the growth rate (an upward, parallel shift in the growth equation) of 10 per cent (for example, from 3.0 to 3.3) results in a 3 per cent deterioration in the trade balance, threatening the sustainability of the increase. When all feedbacks are considered, saving is highly inelastic with respect to the interest rate (an elasticity of 0.06). Taking the inflation equation alone, a 10 per cent change in the money supply results in a 7.3 per cent increase in the price level. However, because changes in the money supply affect the rate of growth (through the interest rate), the elasticity with all feedbacks is almost unity.

The Heterodox Policy Package

These feedback elasticities imply a heterodox policy package for growth. Let the analysis begin with a 'typical' sub-Saharan country with a GDP growth rate of 3 per cent, trade deficit of 6 per cent of GDP, a fiscal deficit of 5 per cent, and an inflation rate of 12 per cent.[42] The policy goals are to increase the growth rate, reduce the trade deficit and lower the rate of inflation. Table 3.7 presents the relevant policy mix. To reduce the rate of inflation, the government acts to lower the rate of money growth. This will be associated with an elasticity close to unity with all feedbacks, with little effect on output. To reduce the trade deficit, the exchange rate is devalued, using a 'crawling peg'. These two effects together result in a contraction of the economy.

To offset the contraction, the Central Bank administers a low, but positive real interest rate, of 2–3 per cent. A low real interest rate would have little effect on the saving rate. More important for increasing saving would be to increase the growth rate. Simultaneously with these three policy measures, the central government would increase public investment to stimulate growth directly. The coefficients of the model predict that a combined 10 per cent change in money growth (decrease), the share of public investment in GDP (increase) and the real exchange rate (devaluation) would increase the growth rate by 7 per cent (from 3 to 3.2 per cent), reduce inflation by 9 per cent (to below 11 per cent), and narrow the trade gap by 8 per cent (to 5.5 per cent of GDP). In summary, the packages involve monetary restraint, fiscal expansion and purposeful and controlled devaluations.

Orthodox objections to such a policy combination might focus on the fiscal deficit (which increases from 5 to 5.5 per cent of GDP) because of its alleged impact on inflation or its 'crowding out' effect. With regard to the inflation impact, the model indicates that the deficit is not correlated with money growth, casting doubt upon the inflation mechanism. If the change in the money supply is replaced by the fiscal deficit in the inflation equation (see Annex), it proves to be correlated with changes in the price

Table 3.7 An Expansionary Policy Mix for Sub-Saharan Countries (based on OLS coefficients)

Policy Measure	First Round Impact	Lagged Impact & Net Effect	Commentary
Reduce money supply	Lowers inflation Raises real interest rate	Stimulates investment (via inflation), lowers growth (via interest rate) Net GDP effect: *negative* ($\varepsilon_y = 0.113$)	Effective if goal is to reduce inflation ($\varepsilon_{p,m} = 0.897$) *Inflation policy*
Devalue	Increases export share Lowers import share	Stimulates growth (via exports), Lowers trade deficit, reduces investment (via imports), Net GDP effect: *negative* ($\varepsilon_y = -0.194$)	Effective if goal is to reduce trade deficit ($\varepsilon_{td.rer} = 0.671$) *Trade policy* (crawling peg)
Fix a low real interest rate (e.g., 2–3%)	Reduces demand constraint on the economy (assuming the rate is lowered)	If lowered, negative effect on saving, Net GDP effect: *positive* ($\varepsilon_y = -0.128$)	Effective if goal is to increase growth, *Growth policy*
Increase government investment	Directly increases growth rate, Increases deficit	Increases interest rate (lowers growth) Net GDP effect: *strongly positive* ($\varepsilon_y = 1.052$)	Effective if goal is to increase growth, *Growth policy*

level. However, the elasticity is low, and the deficit is inter-correlated with changes in output. This indicates that the relevant causality is from growth to the deficit, with the former generating an increase in public sector revenues. As for the 'crowding out' effect, while deficits do promote higher real interest rates, the impact of these on investment is non-significant.

These relationships do not contradict orthodox theory; rather, they indicate that policy should be formulated upon an empirical evaluation of their practical importance. It may be that deficits foster inflation, but the mechanism is weak, and the impact of inflation on growth minor, as demonstrated in recent World Bank research.[43] Indeed, several of the orthodox parables contain a grain of truth: devaluation reduces the trade deficit (but is contractionary); expansion of the money supply generates inflationary pressures (but high real interest rates reduce GDP growth); and deficits increase interest rates (but the impact on investment is non-significant). The problem with the orthodox parables is that they tend to be presented *ceterius paribus*, with their feedback effects neglected.

The Pragmatic Application in Sub-Saharan Africa

A pragmatic application of macroeconomic principles should be based upon the characteristics of sub-Saharan economies. The relevant characteristics for policy making are several. First, infrastructure investment is of considerably greater importance in these economies than in more developed middle-income countries. As a result, public sector investment plays a leading role in stimulating growth. Private sector investment, both domestic and foreign, is sensitive to the growth rate, so growth-enhancing policies are simultaneously investment-enhancing. Second, due to the low per capita income of the countries, saving as a share of GDP rises with increases in the growth rate. Much of saving is unresponsive to interest rates, especially in the household sector, where it is identical with the act of investment.

Second, for the trade sector, imports and exports tend to be insensitive in the short run to exchange rates. For imports this results from the low level of industrialization, implying a limited scope for substitution of domestic for imported inputs and capital goods. As a result, the negative income effect of devaluation tends to overwhelm the positive substitution effect. The net effect is to discourage investment. This provides a further argument for a leading role for public sector investment, which can be administratively designed to be import-saving (for example, labour-intensive public works).

Third, financial markets remain at a relatively primitive stage of development. In particular, governments typically lack the financial instruments to 'sterilize' foreign exchange flows. As a result, the movement of unregulated exchange rates can go contrary to the goal of export promotion, especially if there are substantial inflows of development assistance and foreign investment.[44] The underdevelopment of financial markets also implies that interest rates tend to be administered, by the private sector if not by the Central Bank. If public sector bonds are a poor substitute for foreign bonds, and if the private banking sector is relatively concentrated, then interest rates will tend to reflect market power rather than allocative efficiency. In this circumstance, it would be appropriate for the government, through the Central Bank, to administer interest rates consistent with its growth policy.

The Two Models

To complete the discussion of the two policy frameworks, Table 3.8 presents the orthodox and heterodox applications of the basic policy measures. With regard to money growth, the two approaches agree: money growth should be constrained to reduce inflationary pressures. However, this is easier to recommend than to implement. If domestic and foreign capital flows are deregulated, and if the monetary authorities lack the instruments of effective control (for example, a market for public sector bonds), the scope for directly managing the money supply is limited. For the orthodox framework, interest rates should be used in place of open market-type operations for restriction of money growth, but the heterodox package rejects this. In the latter, interest rates should be consistent with the government's growth objective, not an instrument of

Table 3.8 Summary of Policy Packages

Policy Measure	Orthodox (WB/IMF)	Heterodox
Reduce money supply	*Yes*	*Yes*
Fix a low real interest rate (e.g., 2–3%)	*No*	*Yes*
Devalue	Yes in principle, in practice accept the result of a float	*Yes*, through administered exchange rate
Increase government investment	No invariant rule, in practice priority given to deficit reduction	*Yes*, at the expense of deficit reduction if necessary

demand compression. Thus, implicitly, the heterodox framework is tolerant of moderate inflation if interest rates are the only effective mechanism to restrict increases in the money supply.

Both approaches favour real devaluation; the difference lies in the mechanism to achieve it. In the orthodox framework, the exchange rate would be deregulated, while in the heterodox approach it would be administered (regulated) to ensure real devaluation. This intervention to devalue the exchange rate is especially important if trade has been liberalized. Trade deregulation tends to bring internal prices of tradables in line with 'border' prices (the so-called Law of One Price). If product markets are relatively efficient, this tendency will negate the devaluation; the purpose of the devaluation in the heterodox approach is to reduce the price of exportables below their world price, and lower the domestic price of importables below border prices. By repeated, moderate devaluations, the real exchange rate stays ahead of the internal price adjustment forced by the Law of One Price.

Finally, the key element in the growth strategy is an increase in government investment. While the orthodox approach is not opposed to this in principle, it places priority on reduction of the fiscal deficit; in contrast, the heterodox approach would sacrifice deficit reduction for the growth-generating effect of increased investment.

VI. Conclusion

In no region of the developing world have neoliberal policy reforms been so unsuccessful in stimulating recovery as in Africa south of the Sahara. There is an urgent need for policy formation to move from ideological generalizations to pragmatism. The structural characteristics of the region and empirical evidence indicate that policy should focus upon identifying effective forms of state interventions, rather restricting the role of governments. In the past, governments in the region engaged in many activities either ill-advised or beyond their capacity. But the time has come to move from the dismantling of the state to fostering and extending its positive role, a change recognized in rhetoric by the World Bank.[45] Further deregulation and restriction of government action would not produce a growth performance consistent with expanding employment and improving livelihoods. A less ideological and more growth-focused macroeconomic policy is essential to a new policy consensus. While this has been conceded in principle by the Chief Economist of the World Bank[46], it has yet to have its impact on the policies of the multilaterals in sub-Saharan Africa.

The first step towards an employment-generating and poverty-reducing strategy is faster growth. No matter how often it is asserted, deficit cutting, exchange rate liberalization and high real interest rates do not constitute a growth strategy. Were stimulating growth this simple, the sub-Saharan countries would have recovered long ago from their decades of stagnation and decline (Mosley 1995). Adjustment policies, as they are currently formulated for the countries of the region, constrain growth at the macro level. This might be justified were the region characterized by high inflation and other indicators of chronic instability. Except for a few countries, inflation is not rampant across the sub-Sahara; on the contrary, prior to the adjustment period the region-wide average rarely rose above 15 per cent. The problem in the sub-Saharan region has been slow growth and lack of export diversification, not macroeconomic instability.

Statistical Annex

This annex provides the details of the regression equations reported in Table 3.5. All equations are estimated using two World Bank data bases on CD-ROM: *World Development Indicators 1995* ('STARS') and *World Development Indicators 1997*. Degrees of freedom vary across equations because of missing observations.

Table 3A.1 OLS Estimated for Share of Investment in GDP across Sub-Saharan Countries, 1971–1995 [dependent variable: share of investment in GDP]

Variable	Coefficient	T-statistic	Significance
Constant	1.5116	8.813	0.000
$\Delta[GDP]$ $(t-1)$	1.2080	5.354	0.000
[*Imports/GDP*]t	0.3999	0.8.334	0.000
[*Inflation*]t	–0.2234	–1.959	0.051
[*Aid/GDP*]t	–0.0556	–2.278	0.023
[*Real Interest rate*] $(t-1)$	–0.0300	–0.244	0.8075
Adjusted R^2	0.6844		
F-statistic	25.98		
Degrees of freedom	491		
Countries with significant shift coefficients (0.10 or less): *twenty-two* (Omitted, Benin; no complete observations for Angola, Madagascar, Mozambique, Zaire)			

Note: All variables in logarithmic form.

Table 3A.2 OLS-Estimated Model for Saving in GDP across Sub-Saharan Countries, 1971–1995 [Dependent variable: (Saving)/GDP]

Variable	Coefficient	T-statistic	Significance
Constant	0.2071	21.394	0.000
ΔGDP *(t* – 1)	0.2605	3.174	0.002
[*real interest rate*]	0.0911	2.276	0.023
(*3 year average, t, t* – 2)			
[*Aid/GDP*] *(t* – 1)	–0.0537	–13.990	0.000
Adjusted R^2	0.3062		
F-statistic	68.56		
Degrees of freedom without country dummies	466		

Table 3A.3 OLS-Estimated Model for Imports as a Share of GDP, across Sub-Saharan Countries, 1971–1995 [Dependent variable: imports as a share of GDP]

Variable	Coefficient	T-statistic	Significance
Constant	3.5884	33.360	–0.000
Δ [*GDP*] *(t* – 1)	–0.4251	2.941	–0.003
[*Real exchange rate*](*t*)	–0.1012	–5.593	–0.000
Adjusted R^2	–0.7252		
F-statistic	75.29		
	(@.000)		
Degrees of freedom	1113		
Countries with significant shift coefficients (–0.10 or less): *twenty-nine* (Omitted, Benin; no complete observations for Angola)			

Note: All variables in logarithmic form.

Table 3A.4 OLS-Estimated Model for Exports as a Share of GDP, across Sub-Saharan Countries, 1971–1995
[Dependent variable: Exports as a share of GDP]

Variable	Coefficient	T-statistic	Significance
Constant	0.3217	1.359	0.175
[*Real exchange rate*] *(t* – 1)	0.0530	2.316	0.021
[*Terms of Trade*]*t*	0.3033	7.811	0.000
Adjusted R^2	0.7376		
F-statistic	74.00		

Table 3A.4 (continued)

Variable	Coefficient	T-statistic	Significance
Degrees of freedom	999		
Countries with significant shift coefficients (0.10 or less): *thirty-one* (Omitted, Benin; no complete observations for Angola)			

Note: All variables in logarithmic form.

Table 3A.5 OLS-Estimated Model for Inflation, across Sub-Saharan Countries, 1971–1995 [Dependent variable: change in the GDP deflator]

Variable	Coefficient	T-statistic	Significance
Constant	0.0238	4.475	0.000
$\Delta[GDP](t)$	−0.3994	−7.301	0.000
$\Delta[GDP](t-1)$	−0.2888	−5.38	0.000
[*sum*]	[−0.6882]		
$\Delta[Money](t)$	0.4034	21.971	0.000
$\Delta[Money](t-1)$	0.3315	17.655	0.000
[*sum*]	[0.3970]		
Adjusted R^2	0.5024		
F-statistic	254.63		
	0.000		
Degrees of freedom without country dummies	1001		

Note: All variables in logarithmic form.

Table 3A.6 OLS-Estimated Model for the Real Interest Rate, across Sub-Saharan Countries, 1971–1995 [Dependent variable: the real interest rate]

Variable	Coefficient	T-statistic	Significance
Constant	0.0431	4.681	0.000
Deficit/GDP $(t-1)$	0.2340	2.624	0.009
Money Growth (t)	−0.4723	−14.696	0.000
Adjusted R^2	0.3959		
F-statistic	110.79		
Degrees of freedom without country dummies	333		

Note: All variables in logarithmic form.

Table 3A.7 OLS-Estimated Model for Inflation (Quantity Theory), across Sub-Saharan Countries, 1971–1995 [Dependent variable: change in the GDP deflator]

Variable	Coefficient	T-statistic	Significance
Constant	–0.0349	–1.157	0.248
[ΔGDP](t)	–0.3189	–4.921	0.000
[ΔGDP](t − 1)	–0.2502	–4.047	0.000
[*sum*]	[–0.5691]		
[$\Delta Money$](t)	0.3336	14.761	0.000
[$\Delta money$](t − 1)	0.0011	11.102	0.000
[*sum*]	[0.3347]		
[*Aid/GDP*](t)	0.0243	3.002	0.003
Adjusted R^2	0.6148		
F-statistic	26.36		
Degrees of freedom	655		

Countries with significant
shift coefficients (0.10 or less):
fourteen
(Omitted, Benin; no complete
observations for Angola)

Note: All variables in logarithmic form.

Table 3A.8 OLS-Estimated Model for Inflation,* across Sub-Saharan Countries, 1971–1995 [Dependent variable: change in the GDP deflator]

Variable	Coefficient	T-statistic	Significance
Constant	0.1026	1.507	0.133
[ΔGDP](t)	–0.1650	–1.805	–0.019
[ΔGDP](t − 1)	–0.0750	–0.858	–0.858
[*Deficit/GDP*](t)	0.2358	2.122	0.0345
Adjusted R^2	0.4018		
F-statistic	8.47		
Degrees of freedom	405		

Countries with significant
shift coefficients (0.1 or less):
six
(Omitted, Benin; no complete
observations for Angola,
Mozambique & Zaire)

*Tests the hypothesis that the fiscal deficit is monetized.

Notes

1. See Mosley and Weeks 1993.
2. World Bank 1992, p. 21 and Chapter 12.
3. World Bank 1992, p. 278.
4. The ILO *Yearbook of Labour Statistics* includes 17 of the 46 sub-Saharan countries in its table giving the general level of employment (Table A3.3). Excluded are several of the large countries: Nigeria (most populous), Ethiopia (second most populous), Zaire (third), Sudan (fourth), Uganda (seventh), Mozambique (eighth), Cameroon (eleventh) and Tanzania (fifth). Of the ten most populous countries, only Ghana, Kenya and Côte d'Ivoire are found in the table.
5. Perhaps most of all in Nigeria, which is the most populous country in the region. It is uncontroversial to say that the country has never had a reliable census, and that population estimates (much less age and gender character-istics of the labour force) are no more than educated guesses. Closely related to this, Nigeria's statistics on non-traded agricultural products are among the most unreliable in the region (Mosley 1992).
6. Jamal provides estimates of the share of wage labour in the agricultural labour force for seven sub-Saharan countries. The average for the seven is just over 5 per cent, with Tanzania the highest at 11.8 (Jamal 1993). If one defines wage labour broadly to include those receiving wage payments but tied to employers by non-monetary obligations, the percentage would be higher.
7. A review of the literature on urban employment in Africa is found in van der Geest and Wignaraja (1996), which draws heavily on Lauchaud (1994).
8. Van der Geest 1994.
9. Jamal and Weeks 1993; and Mazumdar 1994.
10. The term is vague because it does not specify what is meant by the word 'led', and its usage is as loose as it is ubiquitous. Contraction arises when the term is applied within a treatment of the gains from trade using the standard assumption of full employment equilibrium. At full employment and free trade, resources are efficiently allocated, so no sector of the economy can be said to 'lead' (or 'follow'). If full employment is not assumed, then the case for trade liberalization loses its theoretical clarity. This point is pursued below. An excellent and balanced assessment of export-oriented strategies is found in Griffin (1989, Chapter 4).
11. The pressure from UNICEF via its 'adjustment with a human face' approach proved extremely influential in this regard.
12. The recommendation that targeted programmes for the poor might alleviate many if not all of the costs of transition from a liberalized regime can be found in numerous World Bank reports. Besley and Kanbur (in Balasubramanyam and Lall 1991) attempt to give analytical respectability to targeting.
13. Castaneda 1992.
14. World Bank 1994, Chapter 4.
15. Cramer and Weeks 1997.
16. The possibility of a substantial number of urban poor affected by adjustment is usually ignored or dismissed as unimportant: 'Within the urban population, there is no clear-cut evidence suggesting that the poor have suffered disproportionately more ... The poor have mostly suffered

from the indirect effect of contraction in the formal sectors' (World Bank 1992, p. 9).

17. This line of discourse can be found in virtually every World Bank report that focuses upon or refers in passing to the impact of structural adjustment on agriculture in the sub-Saharan region. See, for example, World Bank 1989 (pp. 3–4) and 1992 (Chapter 4). To give a typical quotation: 'The agricultural reforms that many governments have adopted ... increased the earnings of small farmers – who make up about 80 per cent of the population of Sub-Saharan Africa and include most of the poorest people' (World Bank 1989).

18. Two World Bank professionals offer evidence in support of this allegation (Demery and Squire 1996).

19. For example, a detailed analysis of the 1984/85 agricultural survey of Sierra Leone supports the above conclusion. Simulations of an increase in the price of food crops reduce the real income of the smallest landholders, who are net food buyers. A 10 per cent increase in the price of internationally tradable crops affected these landholders hardly at all (less than 1 per cent, Weeks 1993).

20. Jamal 1988.

21. The dynamics of this process are treated in Jamal and Weeks (1993) and Weeks (1993).

22. '... [I]mprovements in price or other incentives that lead the better-off rural households to increase their demand for labour or purchase more locally produced goods also help the incomes of the poor, though it may take output markets several years to adjust' (World Bank 1992, pp. 4–5).

23. This is also the conclusion of the World Bank:

> The rural population, most of whom are poor ... has benefited more when adjustment has led to increases in tradable crop incomes or agricultural incomes in general and relatively less when the gains were concentrated on exportable crops. (World Bank, 1992, p. 9)

24. A more nuanced approach is found in Khan (1987).

25. World Bank 1992, 1994.

26. See Mosley and Weeks 1993 and Mosley, Subasat and Weeks 1995, where the evidence is summarized.

27. Average deviations are calculated on the basis of a regression equation. A linear regression was estimated in which the independent variables were dummy variables for each year (with 1962 omitted). The predicted values were then generated for each year and the average calculated. The average value is subtracted from each predicted value to obtain the percentage point deviations. This method is an analysis of variance, which implicitly tests for the significance of the difference in means within cells (years) and among cells (across years).

28. This is defended as the pivotal date in Mosley and Weeks (1993).

29. World Bank and UNDP 1989.

30. Work for the World Bank by Elbadawi supports this conclusion (Elbadawi 1992 and Elbadawi, Ghura and Uwugaren 1992).

31. With 43 countries and 35 years (1961–1995) there are potentially 1500 observations. However, there are many incomplete observations, especially for equations involving the real interest rate.
32. World Bank 1994, pp. 222.
33. Ibid., pp. 260–261.
34. A variable is judged to be 'significantly different from zero' if it has a T-statistic that implies that its probability of being zero is 10 per cent or less.
35. Consider the basic quantity equation:

    $$PY = vM$$

    where P, Y, v and M are the price level, real output, the velocity of money and the nominal money supply.

    If one takes the total derivative, one obtains (all symbols rates of change):

    $$p = v + m - y$$

    If the velocity of money is constant, then seignorage $(m - y)$ is equal to the rate of inflation. Within the orthodox theoretical framework, the rate of inflation should be highly correlated with the real interest rate. If the fiscal deficit is financed through money creation, inflation and the deficit should be correlated. As shown below, both appear to be the case for the sub-Saharan region. Therefore, the equation is inappropriately specified.
36. In this specification, the interest rate does not impact directly on investment (modelled below) as a relative price, but through aggregate demand on expectation of future sales.
37. Note that the low coefficient does not imply a low elasticity. The coefficient is not the direct elasticity of GDP growth with respect to export growth, because of the intervention of the adjustment coefficient (and the specified mechanism of constrained demand (r_t, r_{t-1}).
38. For example, if the adjustment coefficient were 0.9, it is implied that a 10 per cent increase in the real interest rate would lower the growth rate by 1 per cent. While this may seem a small effect, it can prove quite substantial. The real Central Bank rate in Mozambique was approximately 11 per cent in 1995, and rose to 37 per cent in 1996, an increase of 236 per cent. The coefficient on the real interest rate in Table 3.6 implies that had the real interest rate remained at 11 per cent, GDP growth for 1996 would have been 8 per cent instead of 6.5 per cent (see Weeks 1998).
39. If the velocity of money is constant, then the constant term should be non-significant. If money is neutral and over the two periods adjustment is complete, the sum of the output coefficients should be minus unity and the sum of the money supply coefficients plus unity.
40. Most important, the implied elasticity of inflation with respect to the money supply drops below 0.5, and output becomes non-significant. Both contradict the quantity theory's prediction.
41. Other mechanisms by which a devaluation might be contractionary are discussed by Van Wijnbergen (1986).
42. These are the cross-country averages for 1970–1995 (for those countries and years with complete observations).
43. Bruno and Easterly 1995.

44. This is the case for Mozambique. See Weeks 1998.
45. World Bank 1997.
46. Stiglitz 1998.

References

Balasubramanyam, V.N. and Sanjaya Lall (1991) *Current Issues in Development Economics* (London: Macmillan).

Bruno, Michael, and William Easterly (1995) 'Inflation Crises and Long-run Growth', Policy Research Working Paper Number 1517, Policy Research Department, Macroeconomics and Growth Division (Washington: World Bank)

Castenada, Tarsicio (1992) *Combating Poverty: Innovative social reforms in Chile during the 1980s* (San Francisco: ICS Press).

Cramer, Chris, and John Weeks (1997) *Analytical Foundations of Employment and Training Programmes in Conflict-affected Countries*, ILO Action Programme on Skills and Entrepreneurship, Training for Countries Emerging from Armed Conflict (Geneva: ILO).

———— (1998) 'Adjusting Adjustment for Complex Human Emergencies', Paper prepared for a WIDER project on Complex Human Emergencies in SOAS, London.

Demery, Lionel and Lyn Squire (1996) 'Macroeconomic Adjustment and Poverty in Africa: An Emerging Picture'. *The World Bank Research Observer* 11, 1 (February).

Elbadawi, I. (1992) 'Have World Bank-Supported Adjustment Programs Improved Economic Performance in Sub-Saharan Africa?' *WPS 1001* (Washington: World Bank).

Elbadawi, I., D. Ghura and G. Uwugaren (1992) 'Why Structural Adjustment Has Not Succeeded in Sub-Saharan Africa'. *WPS 1000* (Washington: World Bank).

Griffin, Keith (1989) *Alternative Strategies for Economic Development* (London: Macmillan).

Jamal, Vali (1988) 'Getting the Crisis Right: Missing Perspectives on Africa.' *International Labour Review* 127, 6.

———— (1993) 'Changing Poverty and Employment Patterns Under Crisis in Africa'. Paper presented to the symposium on Poverty: New approaches to analysis and policy. 22–24 November at the International Institute for Labour Studies in Geneva.

Jamal, Vali and John Weeks (1993) *Africa Misunderstood* (London: Macmillan).

Khan, Mohsin S. (1987) 'Macroeconomic Adjustment in Developing Countries: A Policy Perspective.' *World Bank Research Observer* 2, 1 (January).

Krugman, Paul and Lance Taylor (1978) 'Contractionary Effects of Devaluation'. *Journal of Development Economics*, 8 (August).

Lauchaud, J.P. (1994) *The African Labour* Market (Geneva: ILO).

Mazumdar, D. (1994) *Wages in Africa* (Washington: World Bank).

Mosley, Paul (1991) 'Structural Adjustment: A general overview.' In *Current Issues in Development Economics*, ed., Balasubramanyam and Lall (London: Macmillan).

———— (1992) 'Policymaking Without Facts: A Note on the Assessment of Structural Adjustment in Nigeria'. *Africa Affairs* 91 (April).

———— (1994) 'Policy and Capital-Market Constraints to the African Green Revolution: A Study of Maize and Sorghum Yields in Kenya, Malawi and Zimbabwe 1960–91'. Occasional Papers 38 (Florence: UNICEF International Child Development Centre): 319–27.

———— (1995) 'Development Economics and the Underdevelopment of Africa' *Journal of International Development*, 7(7) (September–October).

Mosley, Paul and John Weeks (1993) 'Has Recovery Begun?' "Africa's Adjustment in the 1980s" Revisited'. *World Development* 21, 10: 1583–99.

———— (1994) 'Adjustment in Africa'. *Development Policy Review* 12.

Mosley, Paul, Turan Subasat and John Weeks (1995) 'Assessing Adjustment in Africa'. *World Development* 23, 9.

Serageldin, Ismail (1988) *Beyond Crisis Management: The World Bank's Comprehensive Program for Promoting Sustained Growth with Equity in Africa* (Washington: World Bank).

Stiglitz, Joseph (1998) 'More Instruments and Broader Goals: Moving Toward the Post-Washington Consensus' (Helsinki: WIDER).

United Nations Economic Commission for Africa (1989) 'Statistics and Policies: ECA Preliminary Observations on the World Bank Report: Africa's Adjustment and Growth in the 1980s' (Addis Ababa: ECA).

Van der Geest, W. (1994) 'A Review of Research Literature on the Impact of Structural Adjustment'. In *Beyond Structural adjustment and Beyond, Research and Policy Issues*, ed. Van der Hoeven and Van der Kraaij (London: James Currey).

Van der Geest, Willem, and Ganesh Wignaraja (1996) 'Adjustment, Employment and Labour Market Institutions' in 'Sub-Saharan Africa in the 1990s: A Survey' *Employment Papers 10* (Geneva: Employment Department, International Labour Office).

Van der Hoeven, Rolph (1993) 'The Design of Macroeconomic Policy to Reduce the Adverse Effects on Poverty of Structural Adjustment', paper presented to the Symposium on 'Poverty: New approaches to analysis and policy', 22–4 November at the International Institute for Labour Studies in Geneva.

Van Wijnbergen, Sweder (1986) 'Exchange Rate Management and Stabilization Policies in Developing Countries'. *Journal of Development Economics* 23.

Weeks, John (1993) *Development Strategy and the Economy of Sierra Leone* (London: Macmillan).

———— (1994) 'Macroeconomic Policies for Employment Generation: Africa South of the Sahara'. Paper prepared under the ILO/UNDP project 'Economic policy and employment' (Geneva: ILO).

———— (1998) *Macroeconomic Instability in Mozambique*. Centre for Development Policy and Research Weekly Paper: SOAS London.

World Bank (1989) *Sub-Saharan Africa, From Crisis to Sustainable Growth: A Long Term Perspective Study* (Washington: World Bank).

———— (1992) *World Bank Structural and Sectoral Adjustment Operations: The Second OED Overview* (Washington: World Bank).

———— (1994) *Adjustment in Africa: Reforms, Results, and the Road Ahead* (Oxford: Oxford University Press).

———— (1994) *International Development Indicators* (New York: World Bank).

———— (1995) *International Development Indicators* (New York: World Bank).

———— (1997) *International Development Indicators* (New York: World Bank).

———— (1997) *World Development Report 1997* (Washington: World Bank).

World Bank and United Nations Development Program (1989) *Africa's Adjustment and Growth in the 1980s* (Washington and New York: World Bank and UNDP).

4 Domestic Resource Mobilization and Enterprise Development in Sub-Saharan Africa

Keith Griffin and Mark D. Brenner

Since the early 1980s much of sub-Saharan Africa has been in the throes of economic crisis. Growth rates in real terms have remained stubbornly low or negative, real income per capita has fallen precipitously and despite repeated reassurances that prosperity was just around the corner, stabilization and structural adjustment policies have not delivered Africa from its misery. Humbled by this recent history, many are now seeking answers for why orthodox economic policy has failed to live up to its claims, and an active research effort is underway to find alternative solutions to the persistent problems of poverty and low levels of human development that afflict so much of Africa. This chapter should be seen as a contribution to the search for more effective policies. Specifically, we propose to analyse the questions of domestic resource mobilization and enterprise development in sub-Saharan Africa, within the context of an investment-led strategy for structural adjustment.[1]

I. Financing Investment-led Adjustment: External Sources

Foreign advisors and aid donors are not ignorant of the need to increase dramatically the rate of investment in sub-Saharan Africa. Indeed, they have sometimes seen themselves, and other external actors such as multinational corporations, as central to the process. There are problems with such a logic, which we explore in the following two subsections. We find, first, that foreign aid, even in relatively large amounts (whether expressed in per capita terms or as a percentage of GNP), has failed to spur overall investment, and, second, that foreign direct investment has not been forthcoming. Much of this can be attributed to problems internal to the countries of sub-Saharan Africa, but we also believe that to an important degree the problem resides in the inverted nature of the neo-classical logic.

African governments typically are offered specific assistance and unspecific hopes, namely, structural and sectoral adjustment loans by the international financial institutions to assist during the transition associated with resource reallocation, and the hope that foreign direct investment will follow, presumably attracted by profit opportunities associated with domestic restructuring and stabilization and structural adjustment policies. Indeed, the relationship between the two is critical to the logic of the neoclassical approach. It is implicitly assumed that 'getting prices right', along with other specific policies that accompany structural adjustment loans, will be sufficient to produce a structure of incentives that will attract foreign investment (often in export-oriented activities), which will then contribute to faster growth of the economy. Such an approach also assumes implicitly that adjustment follows the relatively frictionless path of resource reallocation, and thus structural and sectoral adjustment loans become part of the construction of a 'safety net' to alleviate the worst forms of hardship during the transition. These two assumptions, both incorrect in our view, reflect a misdiagnosis of the problem. In what follows we attempt to explain why that is the case, and to assess the ability of foreign aid and private foreign direct investment to finance the investment-led adjustment which we advocate. We begin with a consideration of foreign aid.

Official Development Assistance

Foreign aid, or Official Development Assistance (ODA), has been widely viewed as a critical element in the adjustment process. Indeed, structural adjustment loans have proliferated, and ODA has been abundant in many respects in sub-Saharan Africa. For the 38 countries where data are available, overall ODA per capita has risen from an average of $45.82 in the period 1980–85 to $71.71 in 1991–94, or by more than 56 per cent. In a region where many countries' per capita incomes fall well below $500 these numbers are not insignificant. Moreover, while not uniformly the case, this upward trend in ODA per person can be found in 25 of the 38 individual countries for which we have data.

An even more dramatic picture emerges from examining ODA as a percentage of GNP. For the 31 countries with available data, we record an average ODA as a percentage of GNP that rises from 13.75 per cent in the period 1980–85 to 15.80 per cent in the period 1986–90 and finally to 16.59 per cent in the period 1991–94.[2] That is, over the entire period the aid ratio increased by more than a fifth, from levels that already were high. Moreover, if all of the ODA had been productively invested, aid inflows alone would have been sufficient to finance a rapid rate of growth, even if domestic savings had been zero.

Unfortunately, however, these exceptionally high levels of ODA have not produced concomitant levels of growth or human development. In fact, for the 33 countries for which data are available, the simple average rate of growth of GDP was roughly 2.3 per cent per annum during the period 1980–94. Furthermore, the United Nations Development Programme classifies 79 per cent of sub-Saharan African countries as experiencing 'low human development'.[3] More importantly, the large aid inflows have yet to result in the levels of investment that are necessary to move the process of adjustment along any path other than that of contraction. This is in part due to inappropriate government policies that have directed foreign capital inflows to the financing of current public and private expenditures. It is remarkable, for instance, that between 1980 and 1994 government and private consumption increased as a proportion of GDP in sub- Saharan Africa while the weighted savings rate fell in the same period from 27 per cent to 16 per cent.[4] Low levels of investment are also in part due to the curious logic of adjustment embodied in the neo-classical orthodoxy.

By assuming a relatively frictionless reallocation of resources in the process of adjustment, economic hardship appears, at worst, to be a temporary by-product of the process. This necessitates, at most, the construction of a 'safety net' to alleviate the worst aspects of the transition. Such an outlook appears to have engendered a certain amount of complacency about current expenditure patterns, resting on the faith that restoring macroeconomic balance and 'getting prices right' will provide sufficient incentives for an increase in domestic savings and foreign direct investment. An implicit assumption of frictionless adjustment excludes the possibility of adjustment through contraction, as well as the severe, long-term human distress that accompanies it, and hence the approach ignores the fact that the resources required to construct an effective safety net in the face of such distress are immense, precisely at a time of dwindling available resources. Indeed, we find Africa in need of a different path of adjustment rather than merely a safety net.

Foreign Direct Investment

A second important element in the neo-classical adjustment strategy is Foreign Direct Investment (FDI). FDI, along with ODA, is often thought to help close the gap between domestic savings, both public and private, and the desired level of domestic investment. This logic, as alluded to above, holds that domestic adjustment, through 'getting prices right' and other specific policies, will create incentives sufficient to attract FDI. Moreover, foreign capital is frequently seen as a critical link to international technology and world markets, as well as a complement to, rather than competitor with, domestic capital formation. Consequently, it is regularly described, uncritically in our view, as beneficial to the receiving country. In this subsection we set aside questions of the desirability of or benefit from FDI and instead concern ourselves with the narrower question of whether FDI will be adequate to meet the needs of an investment-led adjustment process in sub-Saharan Africa.

The first measure of this adequacy that we will consider is an estimate of FDI per capita for three periods since 1980. It must first be noted that relatively few of the countries in sub-Saharan Africa have data available on FDI. This, along with the fact that measurement of FDI is often a more complicated and contentious issue than for ODA, for example, implies that these data should be interpreted with caution. For the 20 countries for which data are available, overall FDI per capita has risen steadily, from an average of $2.95 in the period 1980–85 to $4.43 in the period 1986–90 to $7.38 in the period 1991–94. Despite these minuscule absolute values of FDI per capita, the averages present a misleading picture of the importance of direct investment in a typical country in sub-Saharan Africa because of the concentration of direct investment. Indeed, 14 of the 20 countries for which we have data never achieved a level of FDI per capita as large as the average for 1980–85, the period when average inflows were smallest at $2.95. In addition, half the countries where data are available have at least one period where flows of direct investment were negative, representing a net outflow of productive resources. Finally, a word must be said about the upward trend of these three period averages. This too is misleading because in only 7 of the 20 countries under consideration did FDI per capita increase steadily over the three periods.

An exercise perhaps even more revealing is to put the levels of FDI in the context of the national economies of the region, using FDI as a percentage of GNP as one measure. For the 20 countries for which data are available, on average FDI was 0.1 per cent of GNP during the period 1980–85; it rose to 0.39 per cent of GNP during the period 1986–90 and reached a level of 0.49 per cent of GNP in the period 1991–94. As before, these numbers indicate the relatively minor role that direct investment has played in the adjustment process. Indeed, in over half the countries for which data are available FDI never rose above one half of 1 per cent of GNP. As with FDI per person, the apparent upward trend is representative only of a minority of the countries in question, with 8 out of 20 countries demonstrating an upward trend. Moreover, in three of these eight countries the initial period exhibited a negative trend, depicting a net capital outflow that improved over the two subsequent periods.

Thus, the above figures indicate that foreign direct investment has not contributed in any significant way to the adjustment process in sub-Saharan Africa, nor can we expect it to do so in future. On the contrary, we find much to support the argument that, rather than leading increased rates of growth in GDP, foreign investment tends to follow them. Thus, it is an economy which is already on a path of sustained high growth that is able to attract significant levels of direct investment. It is for these reasons that we believe that in sub-Saharan Africa, private foreign direct investment is more likely to be a consequence of a successful structural adjustment strategy than a cause of it.

II. Domestic Financing for Investment-led Adjustment: The Private Sector

It is likely that the financing of an investment-led strategy of adjustment will come primarily from domestic resources. In this section we explore some possibilities for increasing private sector savings, including possibilities for financing investment by mobilizing surplus household labour. In the following section we will consider the role of the public sector.

Gross domestic savings in sub-Saharan Africa are a lower percentage of gross domestic product than in any other developing region of the world. Such a situation clearly is incompatible with an investment-led strategy of structural adjustment and measures to mobilize resources for capital accumulation therefore deserve high priority. There is no simple formula for increasing savings, but there are a few cases where rapid progress might be possible. Too often, however, these opportunities are overlooked because they fall slightly outside conventional ways of thinking. Let us consider four examples.[5]

First, in some instances a judicious and discriminating rise in expenditures conventionally classified as consumption would result in a rise in output. For instance, increased food consumption among the very poor and those suffering from malnutrition, more extensive preventive health measures and expenditure on certain types of training and education (discussed below) can result in greater energy and morale, fewer days lost from work as a result of illness and higher productivity as a result of greater skills. These expenditures should be regarded as forms of human capital formation rather than current consumption.

Second, it sometimes is possible to increase investment not only by reducing unproductive consumption but also by reducing the amount of idle or unproductive labour time. Often labour is poorly utilized and in some areas seasonal unemployment is severe. Thus low-skilled labour power is not scarce but instead is waiting to be mobilized for development.[6] Experience shows that this surplus labour can be organized and that it can be used to 'finance' capital formation in rural areas. Indeed we discuss at some length below a guaranteed employment programme intended to accelerate investment. It is also important to recognize, however, that 'slack' labour at the household level can in principle be used to undertake small, labour-intensive investment projects. Whether on large public works schemes or on small household projects, additional investment and faster growth can be achieved by working longer and harder, and this need not imply a reduction in current consumption.

Third, in many instances 'savings' depend on the profitability of investment and will increase readily when investment opportunities arise. It often is incorrect to assume that in sub-Saharan Africa household savings and investment are two separate decisions taken by separate groups in the community. Most simple models are based on the assumption that it is households which save and firms which invest, and these two independent decisions are reconciled by the capital market through variations in the rate of interest and level of income.

In many African countries, however, savings and investment are interdependent and there is no capital market, or only a rather rudimentary one, to bring the two groups together. In these conditions savings and investment become indistinguishable; they are the same thing. A small farmer accumulates capital in the form of livestock by not slaughtering as many of his animals as are born. A small businessman increases the size of his firm by diverting part of his cash flow into the purchase of equipment rather than spending it on consumption goods. In other words, many of those who save do so in order to invest, and in the absence of a desire to invest no savings would be forthcoming. This suggests that until credit markets are fully developed, one way of increasing saving is to increase incentives and opportunities to invest.

Finally, one must be careful not to assume that low income households are unable to save because of their poverty and hence that policy makers should concentrate on medium and large enterprises and on the savings potential of upper income groups. There are a number of studies, mostly from Asia, which show that in rural areas the distinction between rich and poor households is less significant in explaining savings behaviour than the distinction between landless labourers and cultivating households. A study in Haryana, India indicates that there is no systematic relationship between the degree of inequality in rural areas and the savings ratio.[7]

Another study in the Indian Punjab and in Haryana shows that there is no tendency for large farmers to save proportionately more than medium and small farmers.[8] On the other hand, numerous studies have shown that non-cultivating rural households save a negligible proportion of their income whereas cultivating households, including secure tenants, save a significant amount. There is a suggestion that in Indonesia the marginal and average savings ratio varies positively with the proportion of total income originating from owned land,[9] but most studies indicate that the savings rate of tenants and small farmers are comparable with those of large farmers. Research in Taiwan, for instance, reveals that the marginal savings rates of large and small farmers are not significantly different.[10]

Experience in other parts of the world also demonstrates that small farmers are able to achieve high rates of savings and investment. In Colombia, for example, the coffee sector once dominated the economy (until it was superseded by cocaine), employing a quarter of the agricultural workers and producing a similar proportion of agricultural output.[11] Coffee is grown by over 300,000 farmers, the vast majority of whom are smallholders. Only 843 farms are larger than 50 hectares, while nearly 110,000 farms are less than one hectare in size. The coffee sector is efficiently organized. Producers can market their crop through their own Coffee Federation or through Federation-supported co-operatives or by selling directly to private merchants. The Federation maintains a support price for coffee, provides excellent extension services and runs a research station. Credit is available through the Banco Cafetero or the Caja Agrario. And the Federation even owns ocean-going ships to export the crop worldwide. Colombia's coffee commands a premium on the world market and the country's small coffee farmers have no difficulty competing with coffee grown on large plantations in Brazil, Guatemala, El Salvador, and so on.

Africa, too, has relevant experience. Until the very end of the colonial period, African farmers in Kenya were prohibited from entering cash crop export agriculture; their role under the colonial division of labour was to grow food for domestic consumption; the lucrative crops were reserved for large, European (mostly British) farmers. When the prohibition against coffee and tea cultivation was relaxed just before independence, small African farmers quickly responded to the newly created profit opportunities and almost overnight established a large, new sector of economic activity. Indeed between 1955 and 1964 the value of output from African smallholdings increased by 169 per cent.[12] Saving was not a constraint on development; when profitable investment opportunities were created, the production of coffee and tea increased dramatically. In Kenya, as elsewhere, the poor demonstrated that they are able to mobilize their own 'surplus' labour and to combine this with modest savings to undertake investment projects, provided of course that the structure of incentives is attractive.

III. Domestic Financing for Investment-led Adjustment: The Public Sector

Domestic private sector financing of investment-led adjustment, however, is only one part of the picture. Public sector financing of investment also has a large role to play in the adjustment process.[13] Indeed, public investment is essential for success because of the externalities and complementaries associated with it. There is much recent evidence that challenges the common assumption that public spending is competitive with or 'crowds out' private sector investment. Given the conditions that prevail in most of sub-Saharan Africa, the types of public expenditure we recommend are likely to be complementary to private sector investment, that is, public expenditure is more likely to 'crowd in' than 'crowd out.'[14] This will be true of many forms of human capital investment (primary and secondary education, applied agricultural research, certain types of vocational training and basic nutrition and health programmes) discussed in Section V as well as investment in rural and urban infrastructure (power, water and drainage and roads). These public expenditures are likely to enhance profitable opportunities for the private sector, and lead to higher rather than lower private sector 'savings'.

A separate issue from the size of the public sector investment programme is the debate about the appropriate size of the public sector as a whole. The conventional wisdom is that the public sector in Africa is too large and unwieldy, and should be reduced. This is not obvious from the basic facts on the size of the public sector, as can be seen from examining two indicators: total tax revenue as a percentage of GNP for 1980 and 1994 and total government expenditure as a percentage of GNP for 1980 and 1993. For those countries for which data are available, several patterns emerge. First, there is considerable variation within sub-Saharan Africa with regard to the size of the public sector. The range is from Uganda, where in 1980 tax revenue and central government expenditures represented 3 and 6.1 per cent of GNP, respectively, to the Congo, where in the same year the figures are 29.9 and 54.6 per cent, respectively. Second, in virtually every country, tax revenues are significantly smaller than total government expenditures, and in Africa the gap appears to be larger than in many other developing countries and is growing over time.

While on average the public sector in sub-Saharan Africa is larger than in most other developing regions, the difference is not very great. In neither 1980 nor 1994, the two years we are considering, did the average size of the public sector in sub-Saharan Africa exceed by more than 9 per cent the size of the public sector elsewhere.[15] This is true regardless of the indicator used, namely, the tax/GNP ratio or the ratio of total central government expenditure to GNP. Moreover, on average the size of the public sector in the OECD countries is larger than in Africa, again regardless of the criterion used.

The data for the various regions as a whole are summarized in Table 4.1. It is evident that sub-Saharan Africa's public sector, although above average in size, is not markedly out of line with other developing areas, and is not large by OECD standards. A more instructive comparison would be between Africa today and some of the Asian economies during the period when they were laying the foundations for their rapid growth, say Korea and Taiwan in the 1950s and 1960s.[16] In those economies a large, strong, development promoting state in the early stages of expansion encouraged the growth of the private sector which ultimately resulted in a relative decline in the size of the public sector. A small state, in other words, was a consequence of rapid development, not a cause of it.

We thus call into question the notion that the African state is too large and is an obstacle to development. Next let us consider a more pressing issue, namely, the composition of public spending. As we have noted, African nations are confronted by pervasive market failures that the

Table 4.1 Regional Averages for Tax Revenue and Total Central Government Expenditure (as a percentage of GNP)

Region or Group	Tax Revenue 1980	1994	Total Expenditures 1980	1993
Sub-Saharan Africa	17.3	16.9	26.8	28.7
	(27)	(15)	(25)	(15)
Asia	18.6	18.2	22.0	20.0
	(5)	(5)	(5)	(4)
OECD	28.1	31.0	34.7	41.4
	(19)	(20)	(19)	(17)
Central America	15.4	18.2	23.6	27.4
	(7)	(5)	(6)	(4)
South America	16.2	16.4	18.5	21.7
	(9)	(9)	(8)	(7)

Note: Values in parentheses represent the number of countries used in calculating the average.
Source: Authors' calculations based on World Bank, *World Development Report*, New York: Oxford University Press, 1995 and 1996.

private sector cannot overcome unaided. There is a need for the state to intervene to ensure that resources are allocated efficiently and in particular that investment in human and physical capital is directed towards areas that have the highest rates of return. In the context of education, for example, this implies that investment in primary education should be given priority over secondary and tertiary education, and rural education given higher priority than urban. Similarly for health, this implies a shift of investment in favour of preventive medicine and primary care, and away from curative medicine located in large urban hospitals. Similar considerations arise when considering allocations between categories, such as spending on the military as contrasted with social spending.

Finally, there is the question of the ability of the state in sub-Saharan Africa to design, implement and monitor an investment-led adjustment programme. Many assume that the state is incapable of managing such an investment programme for both narrow technical and broad political economy reasons. This view, however, may be too sweeping and too pessimistic. It is surely correct that a disintegrated state (Liberia, Somalia) or a rapidly decaying one (Sudan) cannot possibly implement the development strategy we recommend, but it is equally true that such a state cannot implement an alternative strategy either, including *laissez faire*. Cases of state disintegration or decay are the exception rather than the rule, however. Most states in sub-Saharan Africa are viable political entities with considerable development potential. Botswana, in fact, has achieved remarkable success by any standard. More generally, there is no *a priori* reason to assume that African states are fundamentally different from, say, the Korean or Taiwanese state and thus are incapable of adopting and successfully managing an investment-led development strategy.

IV. Role of the Informal Sector in the Broader Economic Context

There is much interest in the possibility of using the informal sector as a source of growth for developing countries in general, and particularly for sub-Saharan Africa. Indeed, this interest only deepens when one considers the dynamic, entrepreneurial segment of the informal sector engaged in formal sector subcontracting and supply relations. A central issue is the relationship between small and large businesses in the context of economic growth, and the very feasibility of a small-business-led growth strategy.

Those who are pessimistic about the potential of the informal sector to play a key role in an investment-led adjustment strategy emphasize the financial, material, managerial and legal constraints faced by 'informal' producers and their relative inability to expand beyond a certain (usually very small) size. The picture in Kenya, for example, is depicted in Table 4.2. In Kenya between 1983 and 1987 there was very slow growth in employment in small-scale manufacturing combined with a decrease in the number of firms employing between 20 and 49 persons. Moreover the mid-sized small-scale enterprises employing 20–49 persons accounted for less than 18 per cent of employment in small-scale enterprises as a whole. This 'missing middle' of small and medium-sized enterprises is a critical weakness in Kenya that limits the role of the 'informal' sector in the context of a growth strategy.

The situation in Kenya, however, need not be inevitable. While it is obvious that many firms in sub-Saharan Africa have not been able to grow beyond a very small size, there is no reason to believe that they cannot grow and survive because of something inherent in small firms. In fact the inability of firms to survive and grow is more likely to reflect the constraints they face than anything specific to their size. Indeed one of the purposes of the programmes discussed in Section V is to alleviate the constraints on the expansion of small businesses. Those programmes, when combined with a general reorientation of policy favouring investment and macroeconomic growth, should provide considerable indirect help to small enterprises by substantially reducing the risk of failure. Even so, failure rates among small enterprises are bound to remain high and expansion for most 'informal' producers will remain elusive, but some small enterprises *will* grow, and many *could* grow under the right conditions. The task of policy is to create the right conditions and not give up in despair.

Finally, there are potential linkages between small and large firms in industrial development and these linkages can help to foster growth in the informal sector. The experience of the Asian 'late-industrializers' is particularly informative.[17] In Japan and South Korea large corporate conglomerates (*zaibatsu*s and *chaebol*s, respectively) emerged as the leaders in industrialization, around whom smaller subcontractors and suppliers clustered. In Taiwan, in contrast, such large-scale conglomerates never emerged to lead the industrialization process and yet small enterprises flourished there too. In China, small and medium-sized enterprises, the so- called township and village enterprises, played a major role in transforming the countryside and industrializing the country as a whole. Thus there are several possible environments in which small and medium-sized enterprises can succeed.

Table 4.2 'Modern' Small-Scale Manufacturing Establishments, Kenya, 1983–87

Activity	No. of Establishments 10–19 persons		No. of Establishments 20–49 persons		Total Employees 10–49 persons		Employment Change
	1983	1987	1983	1987	1983	1987	1983–87
Wearing apparel, not footwear	21	28	51	38	1,914	1,793	-211
Wooden furniture	14	20	29	24	2,271	902	-139
Metal products	49	34	67	40	1,891	1,715	-176
Machinery	22	28	30	26	1,239	1,293	54
Railroad equipment	16	21	33	30	1,248	1,239	-9
Printing	37	46	36	38	1,575	1,785	210
Sawmills	15	29	26	25	1,004	1,172	168
Chemicals, paints, etc.	20	28	22	26	992	1,208	216
Bakeries	12	19	7	12	410	623	213
Grain Mill Products	2	2	5	2	198	95	-101
Dairy Products	8	0	4	1	200	46	-154
Other Food Preparation and processing	13	10	23	41	1,024	1,801	777
Other	41	64	59	73	2,532	3,560	1,028
Total	273	329	403	376	16,496	17,232	736

Source: Adapted from Ian Livingstone, 'A Reassessment of Kenya's Rural and Urban Informal Sector', World Development, Vol. 19, No. 6, 1991, Table 12.

Perhaps the Taiwanese case, however, is most instructive for sub-Saharan Africa. As Alice Amsden points out, Taiwan's decentralized and relatively small-scale production structure 'emerged more out of the throes of political economy than the play of free market forces.'[18] Indeed, she notes that small and medium enterprises developed in the shadow of an industrial base dominated by large public and private enterprises: 56.4 per cent of manufacturing value added in 1973 came from firms employing 500 or more workers. By 1984, however, almost 50 per cent of value added came from firms with fewer than 300 workers and smaller firms were clearly ascendant. None the less, the linkages between the large and small businesses were strong during the period of industrial development, and the small firms often depended on large ones for working capital, skill and technology transfers, and for subcontracting and supply relations.

Thus the East Asian experience demonstrates that there is more than one model of industrial development in which small and medium enterprises can play a central role. The challenge facing sub-Saharan Africa is to design an investment and growth strategy that builds on the latent potential of small enterprises and the energy and talents of the African people. It is to that challenge that we now turn.

V. Investment-led Structural Adjustment: Programmatic Elements

In this section we set forth several of the programmatic elements which should form part of an overall investment-led adjustment strategy. We recognize that some African governments will be unable to implement policies and programmes of the type we recommend, but it is equally unlikely that such governments would be able to implement more conventional structural adjustment programmes. Six issues will be treated in this section, each in the context of domestic resource mobilization and enterprise development. Specifically, we will discuss access to credit and the role of credit markets; targeted credit programmes; housing as a productive asset; education and technical training; guaranteed employment programmes; and finally, the commercialization of state enterprises.

Access to Credit and the Role of Credit Markets

The public sector has a major role to play in providing national infrastructure, both for human and physical capital. In addition, the public sector must ensure that actual and potential entrepreneurs have access to credit for investment purposes. This follows logically from our focus on an investment-led adjustment process, as access to credit is a critical condition for increased investment. Moreover, it is even more critical when small enterprises and informal producers are central actors in a future growth strategy, a perspective encouraged in our discussion of the informal sector. Many of our recommendations throughout this paper address non-financial constraints on enterprise development, such as low productivity and skill levels, as well as the absence of general profit-making opportunities. However, alleviating financial constraints also is crucial to enterprise development and therefore in this sub-section we will clarify some of the issues surrounding the functioning of credit markets in developing countries.

First, it is important to recognize that financial and non-financial constraints are intertwined. Lack of working capital or dependable access to it can be as severe a brake on growth, once constraints such as absence of profit-making opportunities have been alleviated, as were the original constraints themselves. Unfortunately, financial constraints are pervasive in developing countries, and obtaining credit from formal institutions such as commercial banks has not proved to be easy for many firms, even in the face of profitable economic activities. For example, Brian Levy, in his study of small and medium-sized enterprises in Tanzania, found that 97 per cent of the firms in his survey ranked access to finance as their most severe constraint.[19] Similarly, the ILO found that 95 per cent of microenterprises surveyed in Guinea were either self-financed or secured financing from family and friends during their initial start-up.[20] Results from Bangladesh further support the contention that credit is constrained, where the Bangladesh Institute of Development Studies found that a mere 14 per cent of rural households were benefiting from institutional credit.[21]

Next, we must address the many reasons that have been set forth to explain this poor penetration of formal credit institutions in developing countries, especially where services for the poor are concerned. Chief amongst these is the question of transactions costs. It is argued that, especially in rural areas and poor communities, the costs of organizing and operating formal financial services are prohibitive. For example, distances from banking centres in the urban areas are great and rural transportation and communication infrastructure is poor. In addition, where the average size of loans is small, the ratio of administrative overhead costs to the loan portfolio can be large. There are many complementarities between the programmatic elements discussed later and the constraints on financial deepening, such as the public provision of infrastructure. Moreover, there is much evidence from Africa and elsewhere that calls into question the notion that it is impossible to provide credit in the form of small loans to poor or rural borrowers at positive real interest rates, with positive bank profits. Indeed, what many cases indicate is the crucial roles that institution design and sensitivity to social context play in successful lending.

Furthermore there are two points worth noting with regard to administrative costs. First, while it is true that many of the lending programmes we will discuss shortly do have higher overhead and administrative costs compared to formal commercial banks on either a per loan or per loan officer basis, they are not so much higher as one might imagine. Design considerations and institutional arrangements have helped to prevent overhead costs from increasing proportionately with an increase in loan officers or transactions. Second, these administrative costs depend in part on the qualities of potential borrowers, including their literacy, numeracy and managerial expertise. Hence many of the educational and technical training programmes which we advocate will also help to reduce administrative overheads. Finally, where overhead and administrative costs are indeed higher, this should be reflected in the interest rate charged to borrowers.

Other often cited impediments to financial deepening are the direct and indirect barriers faced by potential borrowers. In Mali, for example, married women are legally prohibited from participating in commercial activities without the explicit consent of their husbands, and although they possess the legal right of access to banking services, many banks refuse to grant credit without the husband's authorization.[22] Such lending practices directly exclude half the population from expanding profitable economic activities in which they are engaged. Not only are such practices ethically questionable, they are economically unwise because such artificial barriers distort credit markets and seriously misallocate loanable funds. This impedes the efficiency of financial intermediation and also reduces economic growth.

Social norms of discrimination not codified into law are even more prevalent and equally distorting. Moreover, several other less transparent practices may also distort financial markets in developing countries. For example, collateral requirements, a standard instrument in commercial banking, serve to exclude many landless peasants and urban squatters from commercial borrowing, even when they have profitable projects. Similarly, many bureaucratic and administrative procedures required to secure loans necessitate literacy and numeracy in the official language, often marginalizing some indigenous people and the illiterate. Where formal, informal or bureaucratic barriers exclude sizeable portions of the population, there is potentially a positive role for the government to play. In fact there is much evidence that indicates that lending to women, the poor and other disenfranchised groups, at competitive interest rates, can be self-sustaining and even profitable.

Another argument that explains the prevalence of shallow and fragmented formal financial markets in developing countries is that these markets are credit rationed. Indeed, many authors in recent years have attributed the failure of domestic capital markets explicitly to policies and programmes adopted by governments, from subsidized interest rates for agricultural inputs to targeted sectoral credit.[23] Moreover, they argue that removing government interventions and liberalizing credit markets will promote a rational allocation of loanable funds and increased efficiency of financial intermediation.

While we agree that many, if not most, developing countries experience credit rationing in their capital markets, it is doubtful on both theoretical and empirical grounds that in the absence of 'clumsy' state intervention, credit markets would function efficiently and allocate loanable funds optimally. Empirically, recent evidence from both developed and developing countries has demonstrated that even in situations of relatively freely functioning capital markets, credit rationing is the norm rather than the exception. This is true even in countries which have introduced financial 'liberalization' programmes as part of structural adjustment.[24] These findings are not surprising, given the many recent theoretical insights on the functioning of credit markets. In particular, the work of Joseph Stiglitz and Andrew Weiss has focused attention on the role that information plays in the allocation of credit.[25] They have argued that where information concerning the creditworthiness of borrowers and the riskiness of their potential projects is incomplete or absent, serious deviations from both market clearing and efficient allocations may arise. Their explanation for credit rationing is divided into two effects induced by these informational asymmetries. First, interest rates may not rise in the face of excess demand for loanable funds if higher interest rates reduce the proportion of low risk borrowers in the applicant pool. Second, they may not rise because higher interest rates will induce borrowers to adopt riskier techniques or projects. Not surprisingly, informational asymmetries such as these are prevalent in developing country credit markets, and some authors even consider them to be the principal explanation behind the failure of formal financial sector institutions to broaden their lending base.[26] However, many institutions have emerged in developing countries that seem to have overcome the information, incentive and cost problems, and credit programmes directed to women and the poor have proven to be successful in a variety of situations. It is to a more detailed understanding of these institutions and their broader context that we turn in the next section.

Targeted Credit Programmes

A fundamental change in credit markets in developing countries has occurred in recent years, as the delivery of financial services has spread to some of the world's poorest inhabitants. Conventional wisdom that neither women nor the poor can utilize credit productively or repay loans on time has been abandoned, as numerous microcredit programmes operating in vastly different social and institutional contexts have demonstrated exactly the opposite.

One mechanism is the utilization of what is known as group (or solidarity) lending. Under such an arrangement, loans are disbursed to groups (or individuals in groups) and the group is required to play a role in securing the repayment of the loan.[27] Benefits to both the borrowers and lenders from this joint liability arrangement are numerous. For example, from the borrower's perspective joint liability often serves to reduce or eliminate collateral requirements, as group members represent multiple guarantors on each loan, spreading risk among themselves rather than assuming it individually. This spreading of risk among borrowers, in turn, reduces lender risk, and often eases credit rationing. Spreading risk through joint liability helps to reduce interest rates faced by borrowers and increase the proportion of funding for entrepreneurial projects coming from the loan.[28] Similarly, joint liability may serve to increase repayment rates on outstanding loans, as groups can and often do impose penalties on members who default, penalties which are generally not available to lenders.

Other non-financial considerations, which have influenced the success of group lending programmes, deserve mention. Avishay Braverman and J. Luis Guasch note that many successful group-lending programmes do much more than provide credit, as they support a wide range of institutional and human development initiatives, such as managerial training, general and technical education, and provision of health services. A recurring element in the experiences of the most successful group lending programmes is also the role played by mandatory savings. In addition to contributing substantially to the long-term viability of the lending programmes, compulsory savings provide additional credibility to sanctions imposed by group members on potential defaulters, as group members or the credit institutions often retain the right to disburse individual savings when members go into default.

Several of the points made above can perhaps best be illustrated through case studies. Here we shall consider only two, the Grameen Bank in Bangladesh and the Badan Kredit Kecamatan in Indonesia. Both institutions are examples of targeted credit programmes, but they operate in rather different ways.

Grameen Bank

Bangladesh's Grameen Bank, perhaps the most famous group lending programme, grew out of an action research project initiated by Dr Muhammad Yunus in 1976.[29] The goal of the bank is to provide financial resources at reasonable terms to the rural poor, primarily women. While there are many distinguishing features of the Grameen Bank, three are of particular note. The first is the Grameen Bank's group structure. Relatively homogeneous groups are formed consisting of five persons of the same sex, from the same village and of similar economic background.[30] This process of group formation screens members through self-selection, and the small size of the group and its homogeneity also increase the effectiveness of social sanctions. Second, group members participate in a multi-faceted mandatory savings programme, which mobilizes household savings. Moreover, group members are involved in the management of part of the savings, a process that reinforces the strength of social sanctions as well as the commitment of members to the group. Third, bank members also participate in the 'Sixteen Decisions' social programme, which strives to link education, discipline and unity to promote development. In practice this programme has led to investments in housing and education by group members, as well as to better health and standards of living.

Several other characteristics of the Grameen Bank are attractive. For example, by 1991, the Bank had spread its activities widely across the country, operating 880 branches covering 22,046 villages and serving 932,574 members.[31] Since its inception in 1976, the bank has enjoyed a very low default rate of only 4.09 per cent after the first year of a loan, and 1.48 per cent after the second year.[32] Despite this, the bank does not cover its full costs, but considerable progress has been made. In 1986 the cost of administration was 18.1 per cent of the total amount of loans, and the interest paid on external funds borrowed by the bank was 3.6 per cent; the interest rate charged by the bank was 16 per cent. The bank's operating deficit was covered by external funds. The administrative costs of mature branches, however, have fallen to roughly 9.3 per cent a year, and the interest rate charged to borrowers has been raised to 20 per cent. Provided the bank is able to continue to borrow at low interest rates, it should now be able to cover its full costs.[33] Finally, consider the bank's achievements in generating income and increasing equity. The Grameen Bank has generated new employment for roughly one third of its members and helped raise incomes for 98 per cent of its borrowers. By 1985 the increase in income per person was 696.01 taka on average.[34] As regards equity, by 1985 the bank was directing 59.9 per cent of its funds to its target group of households owning less than half an acre of cultivable land and total assets not exceeding the value of one acre. Moreover, the proportion of females among borrowers is higher than that of males, reinforcing the conclusion that the bank has been successful in reducing female poverty.

Badan Kredit Kecamatan (BKK)

Indonesia's Badan Kredit Kecamatan (BKK) was launched with a loan from the Central Java Regional Development Bank (BPD) in 1970 to promote small industry and the economic activities of the poor in Central Java.[35] The bank lends to individuals, not groups, and targets the rural poor. Since its establishment it has gone through many stages, but we will focus on the period from 1981 onwards. BKK is notable for having overcome many of the barriers to lending to the poor. Four features of its operations are of particular note. First, BKK recruits its staff from the areas in which it operates. This reduces the transactions costs associated with screening potential borrowers and strengthens the social sanction against defaulting. Second, the BKK has a mandatory savings programme, which is equivalent to 6.5 to 20 per cent of the total loan, depending on the repayment schedule.[36] An additional voluntary programme recently has supplemented the mandatory savings programme. These programmes help mobilize rural savings and ensure the financial viability of the BKK. The third important feature contributing to the BKK's success is its determination to charge interest rates that cover fully all operating costs. In 1988 the interest rate was 36 per cent a year. Finally, and perhaps most importantly, the BKK has been very successful in taking advantage of economies of scale. In 1989, there were 499 units of the BKK in operation and they provided almost complete coverage of Central Java's 492 subdistricts; in that year the BKK made 609,668 loans through its 3,440 subunits, the *pos desas* (village posts).

The BKK also has been successful in keeping default rates low and covering its full costs. As regards defaults, in 1989 the BKK's long-term loss ratio was only 2.1 per cent and arrears accounted for only 7.4 per cent of outstanding debt.[37] Moreover, the BKK made substantial profits throughout the late 1980s, 1.7 billion rupiah in 1989 alone, 90 per cent of which was retained by the bank to finance expansion. Turning to equity and income generation, the average size of a loan was less than rp. 75,000 (US $42), and approximately 90 per cent of the loans were for amounts less than rp. 100,000 (US $56). Sixty per cent of the borrowers were women, and more than 60 per cent of the rural borrowers had either no formal schooling or had not completed primary schooling. Evidently the bank was able to reach the poor and the disadvantaged, and to make a profit while doing so.

As the above case studies illustrate, targeted credit programmes directed to women and the poor have proven themselves to be not only sustainable but also in some cases profitable. They have succeeded in greater or lesser degrees in meeting all the goals of high repayment rates, long-term sustainability, enhanced income generation and increased equity. It is apparent, however, that no single model captures all the institutional and design criteria needed for success. Attention to the specific social and cultural context in which peer group and other sanctions operate, the degree of homogeneity amongst group members and the particular mix of information, incentive and cost mitigating structures are crucial.

Housing as a Productive Asset

It has long been recognized that housing in developing countries has multiple uses. In addition to shelter, dwellings provide space for workshops, retail outlets, restaurants, warehouse and storage, and a source of critical inputs such as electricity and water for many small and medium-sized home-based enterprises (HBEs). Yet many of the opportunities that derive from these home-based enterprises have not been fully exploited and their potential contribution to long-term development remains underdeveloped. In what follows we will briefly explore the empirical character of HBEs, discuss several reasons why HBEs should be better integrated into a development strategy and highlight the role that can be played by credit targeted at housing used as a productive asset.

The prevalence of HBEs, as well as their physical characteristics, qualities and economic activities, vary significantly across neighbourhoods, cities and regions. For example, in the periurban settlements of Lusaka, Zambia 25 per cent of the dwellings are utilized in home-based economic activity, while in the metropolitan area of Lima, Peru a mere 10.8 per cent of dwellings are HBEs.[38] Similarly, striking differences exist between two residential areas of Kumasi, Ghana, where 12.7 per cent of the dwellings in Asawase include space for HBEs, as contrasted with

40.2 per cent in Angola.[39] As with informal activities as a whole, those undertaken by HBEs display significant heterogeneity, as can be seen in Table 4.3 for Lima, Peru. Moreover, the evidence on market niches shows the substantial variation that occurs even *within* the particular activities in which HBEs are engaged. Finally, there is variation in the physical characteristics of HBEs as well. This is illustrated, for example, by the fact that 73 per cent of HBEs in Lima had indoor piped water, while in Kalutara, Sri Lanka this was true for a mere 16 per cent of HBEs.[40]

Despite this heterogeneity, it is evident that informal production based in the home is present to a significant extent in most, if not all, developing countries. Moreover, if the programmes we recommend are adopted – such as public works projects for infrastructure and targeted credit – the importance of home-based enterprises will increase. Consider for example, two types of irregular settlement – the *pirata* and invasion *barrios* – in Medellin, Colombia.[41] The invasion *barrios* are settlements where land possession is not recognized by a legal title, and conditions such as plot size and shape are unco-ordinated and irregular, a function of the dynamic of the land invasion itself. *Pirata* settlements, in contrast, refer to settlements where landowners promote subdivided plots and self-built houses, intentionally ignoring planning regulations concerning plot dimensions and infrastructural connections. In the case of Medellin, the *pirata* settlements are somewhat older than the invasion *barrios* and they exhibit a much more consolidated pattern of land use than in the invasion settlements. What is significant is that the *pirata* settlements

Table 4.3 Enterprise Types Amongst Home-Based Enterprises, Lima, Peru: 1983

Enterprise Type	Number in Survey	Percentage of Total
Manufacturing		
Food Products, Textiles and Clothing	332	19.46
Leather, Wood and Metal Products	92	5.39
Other Manufacturing	48	2.81
Services		
Retail Trade, Restaurants, Bars	898	52.64
Repairs	59	3.46
Medical Services	70	4.1
Laundries and Cleaning	23	1.35
Lodging	71	4.16
Miscellaneous	113	6.62
Total	1,706	100

Source: Adapted from W. Paul Strassman, 'Home-based Enterprises in Cities of Developing Countries', *Economic Development and Cultural Change*, Vol. 36, No. 1, 1987, Table 2.

utilize 36 per cent of their dwellings for economic purposes, as compared with 21 per cent for the invasion settlements. Consolidation appears to have played a role in that it permits further subdivision of plots for economic activities and indirectly facilitates access to infrastructure such as roads, power and water.

Another example comes from Manila, Philippines, where a 'sites and services' development project was undertaken in the slums of metropolitan Manila in the early 1980s.[42] The Zonal Improvement Programme (ZIP) was designed to resolve land tenure problems and introduce basic amenities and social services, primarily through a process of 'reblocking', which implied a realignment of road networks and land allocations in the selected neighbourhoods. Much of the reblocking was physical in nature, involving improvements of the existing infrastructure and land quality, as well as realigning existing structures into the block plans. Sample studies were conducted before and after implementing the programme in four of the thirteen ZIP sites, with results similar to those in Medellin. In 1981, before the ZIP was implemented, 19 per cent of the dwellings contained HBEs, whereas in 1984 after the ZIP improvements were introduced, 36 per cent reported HBE activity. Moreover, the monthly household median income rose from US$ 71.29 to US$ 114.10, a 60.2 per cent increase. These findings are not at all surprising. W. Paul Strassman, for instance, noted in his study of Lusaka and Colombo that in those households where HBEs were present, reported incomes were significantly higher than those without, namely, 10.7 per cent and 10.3 per cent higher, respectively.[43]

These experiences indicate that if well-conceived investment programmes are undertaken, there is likely to be an increase in HBEs. The provision of infrastructure and other services increases the profitability of home-based enterprises and economic activity consequently responds. Moreover, as the data from Manila, Lusaka and Colombo demonstrate, such activities are likely to increase household incomes as compared to those households which do not engage in home-based economic activity. Hence for these reasons housing as a productive asset should be incorporated into a long-term development strategy. Indeed, low-income housing is an attractive candidate for a targeted credit programme.

Additional reasons strengthen this conviction. First, home-based work is associated with low transport costs and a high degree of flexibility. This flexibility is one of the great virtues of HBEs, as domestic physical and human capital can be readily shifted into and out of a variety of uses. Moreover, the ability to reduce travel to and from work, as well as transporting goods to and from external storage, substantially reduces the real costs of operating microenterprises. No doubt this helps to explain why, judging from the responses from HBEs in Lima, home-based work is popular for so many people. Indeed, 71 per cent of those employed in HBEs in W. Paul Strassman's survey responded that in order to induce them to switch to formal sector work, wages would have to be 'much more' than they were earning at present, and only 5.7 per cent were considering moving their business from their dwelling.[44]

A second major reason why housing as a productive asset can play a central role in long-term development is that investment in housing provides substantial direct employment and income benefits and also generates large forward and backward linkages to the local economy. For instance, the direct employment and income benefits from housing come not just from the construction and improvement of homes, but also from the necessary investments in roads, sewers and other public infrastructural improvements. Indeed, there are many opportunities to provide 'sites and services' under the guaranteed employment programmes discussed below. Furthermore, housing and related investments will generate backward and forward linkages to construction materials, capital equipment and home furnishings. While this does not guarantee large employment effects, if small-scale, local, labour-intensive techniques are favoured both backwards and forwards, the probability is high that much employment will be created.

Finally, an emphasis on housing as a productive asset confers an obvious direct benefit in the form of improved shelter for low-income families. There continues to be great interest, nationally and internationally, in affordable and adequate shelter, as witnessed, for example, by the United Nations Global Strategy for Shelter (GSS).[45] Investing in housing has the dual advantage of enhancing productive capacity while strengthening the provision of basic needs. Moreover, if a housing programme is carefully designed and implemented, it is likely to have a favourable impact on equity as well.

Thus there is much to be said in favour of housing as a productive asset. The potential benefits for developing countries are many, as are the complementarities between this and other programmatic elements discussed in this paper. None the less, it must be recognized that a higher level of investment in housing and an improved composition in favour of low-income housing will not happen automatically under conventional structural adjustment programmes. As indicated above, credit markets in sub-Saharan Africa will continue to misallocate funds even after 'liberalization' and hence a targeted credit programme for housing merits careful consideration.

The informational asymmetries between borrowers and lenders are very great in the case of home-based enterprises and access to credit is further complicated by the fact that the income stream generated by HBEs often is ignored when decisions are taken about lending for housing. This occurs despite the fact that income generated by HBEs significantly increases the ability of borrowers to service a housing loan. W. Paul Strassman confirms this conclusion in his discussion of Lima, where he notes that of the 1,706 HBEs surveyed, only 37 had received credit from the Banco Industrial del Peru (BIP), the official institution charged with such lending, and those who did receive credit tended to be one third larger in terms of housing floorspace than those who did not. This suggests that providing collateral was a severe constraint.[46] As with all special financial programmes, a targeted credit programme for housing should be conceptualized as an entrepreneurial development programme: interest rates should be set to cover all costs fully and attention should be devoted to efficient targeting and screening. Where these elements of success are ignored, results will be disappointing.[47]

Education and Technical Training

It has long been known that investment in human capital – and particularly expenditures on education and technical training – enjoys high rates of return,[48] indeed rates of return that are comparable to the returns on investment in physical capital.[49] The 'market' for human capital, however, does not operate efficiently, primarily because the benefits from investing in education and technical training are widely dispersed: they accrue partly to the individual receiving the education, partly to those who employ educated and well-trained workers and partly to the society at large. In other words, investment in human capital is characterized by widespread positive externalities and this results in 'market failure' and underinvestment in education. The consequence of underinvestment, in turn, is a slower rate of growth than would otherwise be possible.

The problem of underinvestment in education and training is exacerbated by market failure in the credit markets. Low income people wishing to invest in their education, or in the education of their children, are unable to finance educational expenditures out of their own resources because of their poverty, and they are unable to finance the expenditures with borrowed resources because investment in education, from the perspective of a bank, is very risky: collateral usually is not available; the income stream from investment in human capital, out of which the loan would be serviced, is uncertain; and the possibility of default is high. Thus investment in education usually can be neither self-financed nor bank-financed.

Employers evidently have no incentive to finance the general education of present and future workers. The ability of employees to read, write and calculate clearly is of benefit to employers, but they are unable to appropriate those benefits because, short of 'bonding' labour, there is no means to ensure that those whose education is financed by a particular enterprise will end up working for that enterprise or, if they do work for the enterprise, they will remain long enough for the employer to recover his outlay.

A similar problem arises in the case of employer-financed training programmes. Some apprenticeship schemes, in effect, are jointly financed by the employer and the apprentice, the latter by agreeing to accept a low wage and to spend many years working as an apprentice. Some training programmes are fully funded by the enterprise, but these programmes usually train workers in skills which are specific to the enterprise and hence are of little value to other potential employers. These training programmes, in other words, do not significantly increase the job mobility of workers outside the enterprise. Training programmes that do increase the mobility of workers – by providing skills that are in general demand in the marketplace – tend to be underfunded because of the difficulty of employers in recovering their costs.

Thus for a variety of reasons investment in human capital requires substantial financial support by the state, and in fact governments in sub-Saharan Africa have responded to the challenge by allocating a significant proportion of public expenditure to education. This relatively generous allocation, however, has yielded lower returns than anticipated because of a series of biases in the expenditures, namely, biases in favour of tertiary education, biases in favour of urban residents, biases in favour of the formal sector and biases in favour of males.

The 'expenditure pyramid' in education typically concentrates resources on university and other tertiary education, where expenditure per student often is extraordinarily high; expenditure per student in secondary education is much lower while expenditure per student in primary education is lower still.[50] Yet the empirical evidence indicates that the returns to expenditure on education are highest at the primary level, declining at the secondary level and further still at the tertiary level. That is, the composition of expenditure is the opposite of what it should be if the objective is to achieve a rapid rate of growth. There is thus a strong case for reallocating expenditure away from tertiary education in favour of primary education.

There is a similar bias in favour of urban areas: most schools are located in the cities and large towns while the rural areas are neglected.[51] Yet most people live in the countryside and the agricultural sector usually is the largest source of employment and a major source of output. Moreover, there is considerable evidence that expenditure on rural education, extension services and agricultural research can generate high returns.[52] Equally, we now have evidence that there are substantial returns to education for informal sector workers and for women.[53] Hence there are significant gains to be reaped by eliminating the biases in educational expenditure and increasing allocations in favour of primary and secondary education, vocational training, the rural and informal sectors, and women. Such a reallocation of investment in human capital is especially important for the type of strategy recommended in this chapter, since our emphasis is on creating investment opportunities for the largest possible number of people by concentrating on the development of small enterprises, particularly in the informal sector.

If entrepreneurship is to flourish in sub-Saharan Africa, public expenditure on human capital must be substantial and efficiently allocated. Efficiency implies not only the elimination of the biases we have highlighted but also a concern with the quality of education that young people receive. Students must have access to books, classrooms should be properly equipped, teachers should be well trained and the pay structure should reward good teaching. In some cases expenditure on raising the quality of education can yield as much as expenditure on increasing the quantity of education.[54]

Finally, expenditure on education and technical training should be seen within the context of a broad development strategy. The point has already been made that if domestic entrepreneurship and small business development are to be sources of growth, then special attention must be paid to primary and secondary education. The expansion of small enterprises and the expansion of human capital are complementary: the returns to both activities taken together are much greater than the return to each taken separately.

Consider, for example, the credit market. Small entrepreneurs need access to credit and hence there is a strong case to be made for special credit schemes aimed at those currently excluded from the market: workers in the informal sector, small farmers, fishermen, artisans and women in general. Credit institutions, however, encounter high costs of lending to such people, in part because they are illiterate (and cannot, for example, read and complete loan application forms) and cannot make simple calculations or maintain accurate accounts. A universal programme of basic education, by increasing literacy and numeracy, would lower the costs of lending, increase the number of potential borrowers and raise the likelihood of success of credit programmes aimed at low-income people. Thus small enterprise development depends in part on the availability of credit and the availability of credit to small entrepreneurs depends in part on a minimum level of human capital. If either credit or education is provided in isolation, the returns may be disappointing, but if both are provided simultaneously, the strong complementarities between the two may ensure that the overall returns are high.

Guaranteed Employment Programmes

Sub-Saharan Africa has long suffered from underutilization of labour in the form of seasonal unemployment in the countryside and open unemployment in the cities. The stabilization and structural adjustment policies adopted in recent years, however, have greatly aggravated the problem and the region now finds that its greatest asset, its labour power, is massively underemployed. At the same time there are very great needs for physical capital accumulation and there are many socially profitable investment projects which can be undertaken with labour intensive methods of production. An acute social and economic problem can be transformed into a development opportunity by mobilizing underemployed labour on capital construction projects.

The best way to do this is by organizing a guaranteed employment programme.[55] The purposes of the programme would be, first, to increase the overall rate of investment by launching nation-wide public works projects and, second, to provide employment opportunities for all able-bodied workers willing to perform unskilled manual labour for a minimum wage. There have, of course, been public works projects in many countries, including sub-Saharan Africa,[56] but these have been largely emergency relief schemes introduced during periods of famine or severe distress rather than a component of a development strategy designed to accelerate investment and growth.

Several Asian countries, however, have viewed public works projects as an integral part of their long-term development policy and their experience is relevant to sub-Saharan Africa. In Bangladesh, for example, there has been a large food-for-work programme for about three decades and by the second half of the 1980s it provided approximately 15 days of work per year (or three weeks) for all those households which owned less than 0.5 acres of land (that is, for the landless and near-landless).[57] The experience in China during the Maoist period was much more extensive and the mobilization of surplus labour within the commune system was a key mechanism for rural capital construction, which succeeded, in large part, in transforming the countryside.[58] Indeed in 1960 (when de-colonization began in Africa), per capita incomes in China were well below those in sub-Saharan Africa; today, China has caught up and in many cases exceeded the per capita income of countries in the region. One reason for this success was massive investment in labour intensive public works projects. Perhaps the most relevant example for sub-Saharan Africa, however, comes from India. The state of Maharashtra has implemented a successful employment guarantee scheme in the rural areas since 1975 and this has made a major contribution to reducing poverty.[59] The key to success of such schemes is wage policy.[60]

Any able-bodied person seeking employment and willing to do manual work should be guaranteed a job at a subsistence wage. The daily wage rate or piece rate should be set at a level which does not attract workers from other jobs, notably from the private sector, since the purpose of the scheme is to provide work to those who have no other source of gainful employment. In the rural areas this means that the wage should be set marginally below, say 5–10 per cent below, the wages received by hired workers in the lowest-income regions of the country. A similar principle could be applied in urban areas, that is, the wage should be set fractionally below the going wage for unskilled workers. Such wages probably would reflect fairly closely the opportunity cost of labour and would ensure that the guaranteed employment scheme does not raise labour costs and damage employment prospects in other sectors of the economy.

Projects should be designed in such a way that labour costs account for a high proportion of the total. As a guideline, one might aim for projects in which the costs of employment represent about two-thirds or more of total project costs. The experience of Maharashtra indicates that this is realistic. If, for any reason, work cannot be provided to those who seek it, and the government is in fact unable to guarantee employment, unemployment compensation should be paid at a rate equivalent to the daily wage rate on works projects. This will provide an incentive to government to design and implement useful projects since, if they do not, the workers will be entitled to a wage payment in any case.

Whenever feasible, the assets created by a guaranteed employment programme should become the property of the labourers who construct them.[61] If instead the assets are owned by the state and the services produced by the assets are provided free of charge, as is often the case, 'externalities' are generated and usually these are captured by property owners. For example, the benefits of a public highway or of soil conservation works or of drainage and irrigation facilities are reflected in part in a higher price of land and in part in higher returns to farmers and in higher rents received by landowners. Except where land is equally distributed among all rural households, public works programmes are likely to increase inequalities in the distribution of income and wealth. On the other hand, in principle it would be possible in many cases to combine capital formation with progressive income redistribution by ensuring that the assets are constructed by the poor, such as the landless and near-landless, and that upon completion, ownership of the assets is transferred to a co-operative consisting solely of those who supplied their labour. The purpose of the co-operative would be to manage the assets and charge for their use, distributing part of the income to the members and retaining part to finance future capital accumulation. In this manner the productive base of the poorest households could be strengthened on a continuing basis. In addition, an institutional basis for small-scale entrepreneurship would be created and a mechanism for generating a steady flow of savings for financing new projects would be in place.

A great many projects could be undertaken which could yield a permanent flow of income to organized groups of the rural poor. Examples include the reclamation of waterlogged or salinated land, the construction or rehabilitation of fish ponds and fish farms, the construction of irrigation facilities of various sorts, construction of bridges and roads, and the planting of timber forests, plantations and fruit orchards. Income from projects such as these would be derived from the sale of products (fish, fruit, timber), fees for services provided (irrigation water and drainage facilities) and tolls for the use of social infrastructure (roads, bridges). Reclaimed land could either become commercial property and cultivated under the authority of the co-operative (for example, by renting it out) or sold and the proceeds reinvested in other activities. Similarly, the products produced by the co-operative could be sold on the market, distributed among the members for direct consumption or used to provide the major input into commercially run processing enterprises such as canneries, timber mills and fish processing plants.

Linking asset creation by the poor with asset ownership by institutions organized for the poor provides both a mechanism and an incentive for the works constructed under an employment guarantee programme to be maintained and improved. In this way the chronic problem of inadequate or non-existent maintenance could be overcome. Moreover, some of the net income generated by the co-operatives of the poor could be set aside as savings for investment in other productive activities, thereby initiating a sustained if modest process of cumulative expansion. Public land could be leased by the co-operative and private land could either be bought by the co-operative from the landowner at the unimproved site value or rented, or the landowner could be offered a share of the output. Members would participate in the distribution of income generated by the co-operative in proportion to the number of days of work contributed. In these ways a guaranteed employment scheme could simultaneously increase investment, generate jobs, contribute to a steady flow of savings and raise incomes among the very poor.

Commercialization of State Enterprises

The conventional view is that the disposal of state-owned enterprises should be an integral part of any structural adjustment programme. This is said to be a universal principle, applicable alike in the United Kingdom, the ex-socialist countries and sub-Saharan Africa. Advocates of the 'privatization' of state enterprises usually cite three reasons. First, it is claimed that public ownership is incompatible with the operation of a market economy. Second, in practice state enterprises are said to be inefficient in their use of resources. Third, many state enterprises operate at a loss that has to be covered by the government; these losses, in effect, are negative savings that reduce the overall rate of investment and growth.

The first claim clearly is false and the last two must be carefully qualified. Economic theory provides no justification for the claim that a market economy requires a particular ownership regime. Owner-operators, partnerships, co-operatives, limited liability corporations and state ownership are all compatible with a market system and indeed most market economies contain examples of all of these forms of ownership. Mainstream theory provides no case for privatisation of state enterprises.[62]

It is true that many state enterprises in sub-Saharan Africa, and elsewhere, are inefficient. This inefficiency, however, is not inherent in public ownership, but arises from macroeconomic and microeconomic policies. At the macroeconomic level, the strategy of development often has resulted in a structure of incentives that is highly distorted. Relative factor prices do not reflect opportunity costs (for example, because of overvalued exchange rates and artificially low real rates of interest) and product prices (for example, because of tariffs or other trade restrictions) do not reflect the country's comparative advantage. The solution to the problem in this case is not privatization but a change in the development strategy.

At the microeconomic level a problem may arise from the inability of the owners of the enterprise (the state) to ensure that management (the state's agent) operates the enterprise in the interests of the state (or of society as a whole). In sub Saharan Africa this principal agent problem takes several forms: plunder of the enterprise by its managers (corruption), interference in the day-to-day operation of the enterprise by politicians (political interference) and poor service to customers (exploitation of monopolistic advantages). In this case the solution is not privatisation but rather the commercialization of state enterprises.

It is also true that many state enterprises fail to earn a profit. Rather than generating savings out of retained profits, they require heavy subsidies from the exchequer and these subsidies reduce national savings. This behaviour evidently is incompatible with an investment-led strategy of structural adjustment. What, then, should be done?

The first thing to do is to reform the state enterprises. Where they enjoy monopoly protection, their protection should be removed and they should be subjected to competition from other enterprises, domestic and foreign. Barriers to entry into industries dominated by state enterprises should be dismantled. Where state enterprises enjoy subsidies, these subsidies should be gradually reduced over a fixed time period and the firm's budget constraint continuously tightened. Decision making should be decentralized, management given greater autonomy in day-to-day decision making and ministerial and political interference terminated. Management should report to an independent Board of Directors (on which there may be ministerial representation) and be responsible to it. In other words, state enterprises should be commercialized and managed much like a large private corporation.

If despite organizational and economic reforms some state enterprises continue to operate at a loss, they should be declared bankrupt and closed down and their remaining assets sold. Subsidies should not be continued indefinitely except in those few cases where market prices do not reflect social benefits produced by the firm, that is, except in cases where positive externalities exist. Normally, state enterprises should be expected to pay their way and produce a profit, part of which can be retained by the firm to finance its expansion and the rest paid to the state as owner. Government revenues from state enterprises can then be used to help finance the government's contribution to an investment-led structural adjustment strategy.

An alternative to the commercialization of state enterprises is privatisation. Experience has shown, however, that privatization is neither necessary nor sufficient for a successful reform programme. In China, for example, privatization played almost no role in the reform process, yet structural adjustment and the transition from central planning to a market-guided economy have been highly successful.[63] In Russia, in contrast, privatization has occurred on a massive scale, yet the economy remains depressed, inefficiency is very widespread and savings rates are low. Similarly in Mongolia, where privatization was put at the centre of the reform programme, the disposal of state enterprises (by giving vouchers to the entire population) has proved to be irrelevant to the reform process and the economy continues to be severely depressed.[64] Even in Eastern Europe, where the transition proceeded much more smoothly than in the former Soviet Union, privatization of large-scale state enterprises encountered serious difficulties.[65]

Sub-Saharan Africa can learn from these experiences. First, many state enterprises are monopolies. Hence successful privatization would have to be accompanied by a well conceived and implemented competition policy, including a liberal import policy, in order to prevent the newly privatized enterprises from exercising market power and engaging in uncompetitive behaviour. Implementation of an effective competition policy takes time and, in any case, should be done whether or not state enterprises are privatised. In the absence of anti-monopoly measures, however, privatisation actually could result in greater inefficiency in the allocation of resources.

Second, short of giving the enterprises away, it is not obvious how the government can efficiently transfer state enterprises to the private sector when relative prices are subject to very large change, as they are during a structural adjustment programme. If state enterprises are given away or sold at bargain basement prices, the government will lose an opportunity to obtain revenue from the sale of assets, revenue that could be used to finance other public sector investments. Moreover, depending on how the privatised assets are given away, inequalities in the distribution of income and wealth probably will increase. This certainly will occur if the enterprises are transferred to the former state managers, as has often happened, for example, in Russia.

If the government wants to avoid these consequences, state enterprises should be sold at their full market value. The problem then becomes how to determine full market value. Given the distorted prices that are present during structural adjustment, it is virtually impossible to know which state enterprises ultimately will be profitable and which are likely to operate at a loss, and hence should be allowed to become bankrupt.

Third, if state enterprises are sold during a period of falling per capita incomes, the market values of the enterprises are likely to be depressed, even if they reflect the current full market value. That is, the timing of privatization is important. Market values of state enterprises will be much higher at the end of the period of structural adjustment than at the beginning. Finally, if foreigners are allowed to bid for state enterprises, this could result in a welcome inflow of foreign capital, but the larger is the inflow of foreign capital, the larger will be the proportion of the stock of physical capital under the control of non-citizens. A market economy in which the large capitalists are mostly foreigners and the workers are local people may not be socially or politically attractive.

Thus for all these reasons privatization is more likely to be a distraction during the reform process rather than a source of recovery. Efforts should instead be concentrated on commercializing the state enterprises and creating an attractive environment in which new private enterprises can emerge and entrepreneurship flourish.

VI. Conclusions

Structural adjustment should be seen not as a resource reallocation strategy but as part of a long-term growth strategy. The key to successful structural adjustment in sub-Saharan Africa is an increase in investment in human, physical and natural capital and an improvement in the allocation of investment. This is also the key to an acceleration in the rate of growth.

Sub-Saharan Africa's dependence on foreign aid has not been helpful and its hopes of receiving substantial inflows of private foreign capital have not materialized. Official development assistance has indeed been exceptionally large, but foreign aid has not resulted in an acceleration of investment or an improvement in the effectiveness of investment. Foreign direct investment, despite economic liberalization, has not been forthcoming, providing support for the view that foreign investment is a consequence of growth rather than a cause of it.

The conventional approach to structural adjustment implicitly posits a sequence that begins with a change in the structure of incentives ('getting prices right') which then leads to an inflow of foreign direct investment (supplemented by foreign aid) which, in turn, results in an increase in the pace of economic expansion. We argue in this chapter, however, that the correct sequence should begin with an increase in the level of investment and an improvement in its composition; this would lead to structural change and to an acceleration of growth, which in turn would attract private foreign capital and further accelerate growth.

The financing of an investment-led strategy consequently will have to come from domestic resources. It does not follow from this, however, that the solution to Africa's problem is further belt tightening and a squeeze on consumption in an attempt to raise domestic savings. In many instances it should be possible to finance human capital accumulation merely by changing the composition of expenditures conventionally classified as current consumption, for example, by reducing military expenditure while increasing expenditures on basic health programmes. It is also possible to undertake investment by mobilizing labour both at the household level (digging an irrigation ditch) and at the local or regional level (constructing a farm-to-market road). That is, small, labour-intensive investment projects can be 'financed' not just by consuming less (saving) but by working longer (reducing unemployment).

In the absence of comprehensive and well functioning capital markets, saving largely depends upon the existence of profitable investment opportunities. That is, people save in order to invest and where there is no desire to invest, there will be no savings. Public policy should therefore concentrate on creating a favourable climate for private investment rather than attempt to raise savings directly. Moreover, the possession of wealth or assets (say, in the form of land or a house) often provides investment opportunities and a profitable outlet for savings. That is, the linkages run from asset ownership to investment opportunities and thence to savings behaviour. The policy implication is that government should encourage a wide ownership of productive resources and ready access to land, housing and credit because this will lead to greater investment and savings, and of course to a more equitable society.

There is no compelling evidence that the size of government in sub-Saharan Africa is too large and ought to be reduced. There is evidence, however, that the composition of government expenditure could be improved in order to contribute more to human development and capital accumulation. For example, a reallocation of expenditure from tertiary to primary education, from urban hospitals to rural health clinics, and from airports to expanded and improved road networks would greatly increase the contribution of government to development. Moreover, a reallocation of expenditure within functional categories should be accompanied by a reallocation between categories. A switch of expenditure from armaments to public health, mentioned above,[66] is an obvious example.

It is commonly argued that public investment 'squeezes out' private investment, that is, that public and private investment are competitive. We believe this view is mistaken. Indeed it is much more likely that a well-designed public investment programme in sub-Saharan Africa would be complementary to private investment rather than competitive with it. The reason for this is that public investment in physical infrastructure (transport, communications, power), in human capital (basic health services, nutrition, primary and secondary education, family planning services) and in many other areas (applied research, irrigation systems) creates investment opportunities for the private sector and strong incentives to save. A reduction in investment in the public sector could well lead to a reduction in savings in the private sector.

The private sector includes, of course, the informal sector. The informal sector, in turn, is very heterogeneous, but it does contain a dynamic, entrepreneurial segment that can make an important contribution to an investment-led strategy of adjustment. Indeed, microenterprises and small businesses have considerable potential for growth in their own right and, in addition, they can establish mutually advantageous linkages with medium and large businesses.

The development potential of small business, however, will be frustrated if entrepreneurs from small enterprises and informal producers generally do not have access to credit to help finance investment. Unfortunately, credit markets in sub-Saharan Africa, as elsewhere, do not function efficiently – they are prone to 'market failure' – and consequently government has an important role in improving the performance of capital markets.

There is now considerable evidence that targeted credit programmes – which facilitate group lending, or which are aimed specifically at women, small farmers or small business persons – can succeed in reaching the poor. Moreover, it is now clear that it is possible to design such programmes to cover their full costs while charging positive real rates of interest. That is, targeted credit programmes can be profitable and sustainable over the long term. Here again, however, there are complementarities that should be taken into account when constructing an overall strategy. For instance, the cost of lending depends in part on the literacy and numeracy of borrowers as well as upon the transportation and communication network. Hence investments in human capital and in physical infrastructure will affect the viability of the credit market and the access of poor people to finance capital.

The potential dynamism of the housing sector in sub-Saharan Africa has long been overlooked and investment in housing is widely regarded as unproductive. This is a serious mistake. Housing not only provides shelter (and thereby contributes directly to the well being of people), it also represents a productive asset which can create profitable investment opportunities. Home-based enterprises have been neglected, yet micro-enterprises centred on private housing are common throughout sub-Saharan Africa and they can contribute to long-term development. Government can encourage the growth of home-based enterprises by, for example, providing secure titles to homesteads and by providing 'sites and services' for low-income housing developments. In addition, investment in low-income housing is a good candidate for a specially designed targeted credit programme. Just as there are specialized mortgage lending institutions in most developed economies, so too there should be specialized institutions in Africa that finance investment in housing. The added dimension in sub-Saharan Africa, however, is that lending for house construction should be regarded, at least in part, as a microenterprise development programme.

The market for human capital, like the credit market, is prone to market failure. There are high rates of return on investment in education and training and other forms of human capital, but because of pervasive externalities these returns are hard to capture. As a result, there is underinvestment in human capital. Government thus has an important role to play in encouraging or directly financing investment in human capital, and particularly in education. Unfortunately, however, government expenditure on education has been biased in a number of ways, namely, in favour of tertiary education, urban residents, the formal sector and males. Removal of these biases would greatly increase the contribution of educational expenditures to development while reducing inequality. Moreover, because of complementaries, greater and more efficient investment in human capital would promote a more rapid expansion of physical capital, and particularly more rapid growth of small enterprises.

A guaranteed employment programme represents yet another opportunity to mobilize domestic resources in support of an investment-led growth and adjustment strategy. Labour power is sub-Saharan Africa's greatest asset and unemployed labour power can be used to 'finance' physical capital accumulation in a wide range of activities, yet these opportunities sometimes are obscured by lumping them together under the label of public works projects. There is enormous scope for labour intensive investment in Africa: in the cities as well as in the countryside, in directly productive activities as well as in infrastructure and on small projects as well as large.

One suggestion we make is that asset creation by the poor should be linked with asset ownership by institutions organized for the poor. That is, the physical capital assets created under a guaranteed employment programme should, whenever possible, become the property of those who constructed them, namely, the poor. Cooperatives could be formed which would own and manage the assets, and the income generated would partly be distributed to the members of the cooperative and partly be retained by the cooperative to finance future investment projects. In this way, underemployed, low-skilled, poor people gradually would be transformed into people who construct, maintain, manage and accumulate assets from which they obtain a modest but welcome addition to their income.

Finally, there is the vexed question whether state-owned enterprises should be reformed or privatised, that is, their ownership transferred to the private sector. We recommend reform. The reforms we advocate would include the following: exposing state enterprises to competition from the private sector, gradually reducing the subsidies they receive from government, terminating political influence in the conduct of day-to-day affairs, decentralizing management while holding management accountable to an independent Board of Directors, and generally 'commercializing' state enterprises so that they behave much like private enterprises. The purpose of the reforms would be to increase the efficiency of state enterprises and ensure that they produce a profit, and thereby contribute to financing investment.

The mere transfer of ownership of large enterprises from the public to the private sector is unlikely to increase efficiency in the allocation of resources or to accelerate the rate of accumulation of capital. Privatisation, in other words, is largely a distraction; with few exceptions, it is not relevant to the serious problems faced in sub-Saharan Africa. Rather than enlarging the private sector artificially by privatising state-owned enterprises, efforts should be concentrated on creating opportunities for new, small-scale and medium-sized private enterprises to develop and prosper. If profitable investment opportunities are created, savings will be forthcoming to take advantage of those opportunities, and the foundations for an investment-led strategy of adjustment and growth would then be in place.

Notes

1. See Keith Griffin, *Macroeconomic Reform and Employment: An Investment-Led Strategy of Structural Adjustment in Sub-Saharan Africa* (International Labour Office, Development Policies Department, Issues in Development Discussion Paper 16, 1996) included in this volume.
2. It must be noted that while these numbers would surely be much smaller were the average weighted by population, we reiterate our commitment to treating each country as a separate experiment in adjustment.
3. See Griffin, *Macroeconomic Reform and Employment.* Note that this estimate for GDP growth has been calculated in much the same way as the previous figures, taking country averages for the 14 years in question and then taking a simple average of the 33 countries where data are available. Also note that while low compared to the rest of the world, this figure should be considered

an upper bound on the growth rate for the entire region, as many of the countries for which data are unavailable were racked by political violence, a fact likely to lower their growth rates below the average of the rest of sub-Saharan Africa.

4. World Bank, *World Development Report 1996* (New York: Oxford University Press, 1996). It is worth noting that even if ODA were promoting capital formation at a rapid pace, given the political climate in many donor countries, present prospects for its continued availability let alone increased levels are slim.

5. Keith Griffin and Azizur Rahman Khan (eds), *Poverty and Landlessness in Rural Asia* (Geneva: ILO, 1977) pp. 29–37.

6. The classic statement for mobilizing surplus labour for investment is Ragnar Nurkse, *Problems of Capital Formation in Underdeveloped Countries* (New York: Oxford University Press, 1953).

7. K.N. Ray, D.K. Grover and D.S. Nandlal, 'Investment and Saving Pattern in Irrigated and Unirrigated Zones of Haryana State', *Indian Journal of Agricultural Economics* (October–December 1969).

8. A.S. Kahlon and Harbhajan Singh Bal, *Factors Associated With Farm and Farm Family Investment Pattern in Ludhiana (Punjab) and Hissar (Haryana) Districts: (1966–67 through 1969–70)* (Department of Economics and Sociology, Punjab Agricultural University, Ludhiana, n.d.).

9. Allan C. Kelly and Jeffrey G. Williamson, 'Household Saving Behaviour in the Developing Economies: The Indonesian Case', *Economic Development and Cultural Change* (April 1968).

10. Marcia L. Ong, Dale W. Adams and I.J. Singh, 'Voluntary Rural Savings Capacities in Taiwan, 1960 to 1970', *Economics and Sociology Occasional Paper* 175 (Ohio State University, n.d.).

11. Keith Griffin, *Land Concentration and Rural Poverty* (London: Macmillan, 2nd ed, 1981), Ch. 3.

12. Colin Leys, *Underdevelopment in Kenya: The Political Economy of Neo-Colonialism* (London: Heinemann, 1975), p. 53.

13. For example, see Helen Shapiro and Lance Taylor, 'The State and Industrial Strategy', *World Development* 18, 6 (1990) and Lance Taylor, 'Stabilisation and Adjustment', in United Nations Development Programme Structural Adjustment Advisory Teams for Africa (UNDP/SAATA), *Stabilisation and Adjustment* (New York: United Nations Publications, 1991).

14. For evidence of 'crowding in' and the complementarity between public investment in infrastructure and private investment in directly productive activities, see, for example, David A. Aschauer, 'Is Public Expenditure Productive?', *Journal of Monetary Economics* 23, 2 (March 1989); Ernst R. Berndt and Bengt Hausson, 'Measuring the Contribution of Public Infrastructure Capital in Sweden', *Scandinavian Journal of Economics* 94 (Supplement 1992); M. Ishaq Nadiri and Theofanis P. Mamuneas, 'The Effects of Public Infrastructure and R&D on the Cost Structure and Performance of U.S. Manufacturing Industries', *Review of Economics and Statistics* 76, 1 (February 1994); and Catherine J. Morrison and Amy Ellen Schwartz, 'State Infrastructure and Productive Performance', *American Economic Review* 86, 5 (December 1996). These studies use data from the United States and Sweden. Given the paucity of infrastructure in sub-

Saharan Africa, the complementarity between public and private investment should be stronger there than in developed countries. See World Bank, 'Infrastructure for Development', *World Development Report 1994* (New York: Oxford University Press, 1994).

15. As with the calculations in Section II, averages are calculated unweighted for each region. See endnote 6 above.

16. For example, Alice Amsden reports that in 1952 as much as 56 per cent of total industrial production in Taiwan was accounted for by the public sector. Alice H. Amsden, 'Big Business and Urban Congestion in Taiwan: The Origins of Small Enterprise and Regionally Decentralized Industry (Respectively)', *World Development* 19, 9 (1991).

17. This term has been coined by Alice Amsden to distinguish between the industrialisation experience of East Asia, Mexico, Brazil and others, as compared to that of Europe and the United States. She argues that the success of the late industrializers crucially depended on their ability to borrow existing technologies and adapt them to local conditions. This often included designing methods of production to conform more closely to domestically available inputs, reverse-engineering and down-scaling, as well as other process innovations. In the discussion that follows, we will draw from Alice H. Amsden, 'Big Business and Urban Congestion' Amsden, 'Third World Industrialisation: "Global Fordism" a New Model?', *New Left Review*, no. 182 (July–August, 1990); Amsden, 'Taiwan in International Perspective', in N.T. Wang (ed.), *Taiwan's Enterprise in Global Perspective* (New York: M.E. Sharpe, Inc. 1992); and Amsden, *Asia's Next Giant: South Korea and Late Industrialization* (New York: Oxford University Press, 1989).

18. Amsden, 'Big Business and Urban Congestion'.

19. Brian Levy, 'Obstacles to Developing Indigenous Small and Medium Enterprises: An Empirical Assessment', *World Bank Economic Review* 7, (1993). It must be noted that due to small sample size, 19 observations, care should be taken when drawing conclusions from these results. However, many other surveys support the contention that access to credit is a major constraint to enterprise development.

20. ILO, 'L'economie informelle en Guinee: Analyse et strategie de developpement.' Geneva, 1990, as cited in Leila Webster and Peter Fidler (eds), *The Informal Sector and Microfinance Institutions in West Africa* (Washington, DC: The World Bank, 1996).

21. See the Bangladesh Institute of Development Studies and International Food Policy Research Institute, *Development Impact of the Food for Works Program in Bangladesh*, a report prepared for the World Food Programme, Washington, DC, 1985, as cited in Atiur Rahman and M. Mahabub-ul Islam, 'The General Performance of the Grameen Bank', in Abu N.M. Wahid (ed.), *The Grameen Bank: Poverty Relief in Bangladesh* (Boulder: Westview Press, 1993).

22. See Pierre-Olivier Colleye, 'Mali', as cited in Webster and Fidler (eds), *The Informal Sector*.

23. See for example J.D. Von Pischke, Dale W. Adams and Gordon Donald eds, *Rural Financial Markets in Developing Countries* (Washington, DC: The World Bank, 1983) and World Bank, *World Development Report 1989: Financial Systems and Development* (New York: Oxford University Press, 1989).

24. For evidence of credit rationing in the UK, US, Italy and Japan, respectively, see M. Devereux and F. Schiantarelli, 'Investment, Financial Factors, and Cash Flow: Evidence from U.K. Panel Model', in R.G. Hubbard (ed.), *Information, Capital Markets and Investment* (University of Chicago Press, 1990); S. Fazzari, G. Hubbard, and B. Peterson, 'Financing Constraints and Corporate Investment', *Brookings Papers on Economic Activity* no 1, (1988); M. Galeotti, F. Jaramillo, and F. Schiantarelli, 'Investment Decisions and the Role of Debt, Liquid Assets and Cash Flow: Evidence from Italian Panel Data', Boston University Working Paper, March 1990; and T. Hoshi, A. Kashyap, and D. Scharfstein, 'Corporate Structure and Investment: Evidence from Japanese Panel Data', MIT Sloan School of Management Working Paper, 1988, as cited in Joseph E. Stiglitz and Andrew Weiss, 'Asymmetric Information in Credit Markets and its Implications for Macro-Economics', *Oxford Economic Papers* 44 (1992). For China see, for example, Gershon Feder, Lawrence J. Lau, Justin Y. Lin, and Xiaopeng Luo, 'The Nascent Rural Credit Market in China', in Karla Hoff, Avishay Braverman, and Joseph E. Stiglitz (eds), *The Economics of Rural Organization* (New York, Oxford University Press, 1993).

25. See Joseph Stiglitz and Andrew Weiss, 'Credit Rationing in Markets with Imperfect Information', *American Economic Review* 71, 3 (1981); Joseph Stiglitz and Andrew Weiss, 'Incentive Effects of Terminations: Applications to the Credit and Labor Markets', *American Economic Review* 73 (1983); and Joseph Stiglitz and Andrew Weiss, 'Credit Rationing: A Comment', *American Economic Review* 77, 3 (1987).

26. See, for example, Irfan Aleem, 'Imperfect Information, Screening, and the Costs of Informal Lending: A Study of a Rural Credit Market In Pakistan', in Hoff, Braverman and Stiglitz (eds), *Economics of Rural Organization*, and Siamwalla Ammar, Chirmsak Pinthong, Nipon Poapongsakorn, Ploenpit Sasanguan, Prayong Nettayarak, Wanrak Mingmaneenakin, and Yuavares Tubpun, 'The Thai Rural Credit System and Elements of a Theory: Public Subsidies, Private Information, and Segmented Markets', in Hoff, Braverman, and Stiglitz (eds), *Economics of Rural Organization*.

27. For a more detailed discussion of the design of various group lending programmes, and the variations on liability that are observed, see Monika Huppi and Gershon Feder, 'The Role of Groups and Credit Cooperatives in Rural Lending', *The World Bank Research Observer* 5, 2 (1990).

28. See Joseph E. Stiglitz, 'Peer Monitoring and Credit Markets', *World Bank Economic Review* 4 (1990).

29. See Wahid, *Grameen Bank*, Chs 2, 5, 10 and 15, from which our account is drawn.

30. An important element of the group structure is that only one member of a household is allowed to join any one group, and relatives are not allowed to form groups with each other.

31. Wahid, *Grameen Bank*, Ch. 4.

32. These repayment rates are reported as of August 1992, as cited in *ibid.*, Chapter 10.

33. A small subsidy to targeted credit programmes is not necessarily undesirable. First, since formal credit markets do not clear because of imperfect information, a subsidy in the informal credit market may actually increase overall efficiency. Second, targeted credit programmes may generate positive

externalities, for example, by providing rudimentary management training, by encouraging basic education or by promoting family planning.

34. *Ibid.*, Ch. 5.
35. The following material is drawn from Richard H. Pattern and Jay K. Rosengard, *Progress with Profits: The Development of Rural Banking in Indonesia* (San Francisco: ICS Press, 1991), Ch. 4.
36. Forced savings linked to targeted credit programmes are common. The lender retains, say, 5–10 per cent of the group's (or an individual's) loan as an interest bearing deposit, which is returned to the group (or individual) when the loan is repaid.
37. The long-term loss ratio is defined as the ratio of the total amount overdue to the total amount due.
38. W. Paul Strassman, 'Home-based Enterprises in Cities of Developing Countries', *Economic Development and Cultural Change* 36, 1 (1987).
39. Samuel Kofi Afrane, 'Job Creation in Residential Areas: A Comparative Study of Public and Private Residential Communities in Kumasi, Ghana', in Mulkh Raj and Peter Nientied (eds), *Housing and Income in Third World Urban Development* (London: Aspect Publishing, 1990).
40. Strassman, 'Home-based Enterprises'.
41. This case study of Medellin is drawn from Nora Elena S Mesa, 'Economic Use of Housing "Pirata" and Invasion "Barrios Medellin"', in Raj and Nientied, (eds), *Housing and Income.*
42. See Angelo F. Leynes, 'Impact of the Slum Upgrading Programme in Metropolitan Manila on the Housing-based Income Generation Activities', in Raj and Nientied (eds), *Housing and Income.*
43. Strassman, 'Home-based Enterprises'.
44. *Ibid.*
45. UNCHS (Habitat), *The Global Strategy for Shelter to the Year 2000* (Nairobi: UNCHS, 1990).
46. Strassman, 'Home-based Enterprises'.
47. Neelima Risbud, 'Housing and Income Generation Policies for the Urban Poor – Linkages and Limitations (A Case Study of Madhya Pradesh)', in Raj and Nientied (eds), *Housing and Income.*
48. T.W. Schultz, 'Investment in Human Capital', *American Economic Review* (March 1961).
49. George Psacharopoulos, 'Education and Development: A Review', *World Bank Research Observer* 3, 1 (January 1988).
50. Keith Griffin and Terry McKinley, *Implementing a Human Development Strategy* (London: Macmillan, 1994): Ch. 3.
51 For a study of the impact of education on the urban areas of East Africa, see John Knight and Richard Sabot, 'Educational Policy and Labour Productivity: An Output Accounting Exercise', *Economic Journal* 97, 385 (March 1987).
52. For a study of the rural areas in Latin America, see Daniel Cotlear, 'The Effects of Education on Farm Productivity', in Keith Griffin and John Knight (eds), *Human Development and the International Development Strategy for the 1990s* (London: Macmillan, 1990). Also see Marlaine Lockheed, Dean Jamison and Lawrence Lau, 'Farmer Education and Farm Efficiency: A Survey', *Economic Development and Cultural Change '*(October 1980). For a survey of research on the returns to expenditure on extension services, see Dean Birkhaeuser,

Robert Evenson and Gershon Feder, 'The Economic Impact of Agricultural Extension: A Review', *Economic Development and Cultural Change* 39, 3 (April 1991).

53. Douglas Marcouiller, Veronica Ruiz de Castilla and Christopher Woodruff, 'Formal Measures of the Informal- Sector Wage Gap in Mexico, El Salvador and Peru', *Economic Development and Cultural Change* 45, 2 (January 1997).

54. See J. Behrman and N. Birdsall, 'The Quality of Schooling: Quantity Alone May Be Misleading', *American Economic Review* (1983) and John Oxenham with Jocelyn DeJong and Steven Treagust, 'Improving the Quality of Education in Developing Countries', in Griffin and Knight (eds), *Human Development*.

55. For details see Griffin and McKinley, *Human Development Strategy*, Ch. 5.

56. See Jacques Gaude and Steve Miller, 'Rural Development and Local Resource Intensity: A Case-Study Approach', in Griffin and Knight (eds), *Human Development*.

57. UNDP, *Human Development in Bangladesh* (Dhaka: UNDP, 1992): 25. On the public works programme in Bangladesh see Ahmed Raisuddin and Mahabub Hossain, *Developmental Impact of Rural Infrastructure in Bangladesh* (Washington, DC: International Food Policy Research Institute, 1990); and 'Food for Work Program', Special Issue of *Bangladesh Development Studies* 11 (1983).

58. Thomas Rawski, *Economic Growth and Employment in China* (New York: Oxford University Press, 1979).

59. Sarthi Acharya, *The Maharashtra Employment Guarantee Scheme: A Study of Labour Market Intervention* (New Delhi: ILO, ARTEP, Working Paper, May 1990).

60. The next two paragraphs are taken from Griffin and McKinley, 1994, p. 75. Slight alterations have been made to the original text.

61. This proposal is taken from Keith Griffin, 'Rural Poverty in Asia: Analysis and Policy Alternatives', in Rizwanul Islam (ed), *Strategies for Alleviating Poverty in Rural Asia* (Dhaka: Bangladesh Institute of Development Studies and Bangkok: ILO, ARTEP, 1985), pp. 63–65.

62. Keith Cowling, 'Reflections on the Privatisation Issue', in Ha-Joon Chang and Peter Nolan (eds), *The Transformation of the Communist Economies* (London: Macmillan, 1995).

63. See Keith Griffin, *Studies in Globalization and Economic Transitions* (London: Macmillan, 1996), Ch. 7.

64. Keith Griffin (ed), *Poverty and the Transition to a Market Economy in Mongolia* (London: Macmillan, 1995), Ch. 1.

65. For analysis of the experience in Poland, Hungary, Slovakia and the Czech Republic see Yilmaz Akyüz, Detlef Kotte, Andràs Köves and László Szamuely (eds), *Privatisation in the Transition Process: Recent Experiences in Eastern Europe* (Geneva: UNCTAD, 1994).

References

Acharya, Sarthi (1990) *The Maharashtra Employment Guarantee Scheme: A Study of Labour Market Intervention*. New Delhi: ILO, ARTEP, Working Paper (May).

Afrane, Samuel Kofi (1990) 'Job Creation in Residential Areas: A Comparative Study of Public and Private Residential Communities in Kumasi, Ghana.' In *Housing and Income in Third World Urban Development*, ed. Mulkh Raj and Peter Nientied (London: Aspect Publishing).

Akyüz, Yilmaz, Detlef Kotte, Andràs Köves and László Szamuely (eds) (1994) *Privatisation in the Transition Process: Recent Experiences in Eastern Europe* (Geneva: UNCTAD).

Aleem, Irfan (1993) 'Imperfect Information, Screening, and the Costs of Informal Lending: A Study of a Rural Credit Market In Pakistan'. In *The Economics of Rural Organization*, ed. Karla Hoff, Avishay Braverman, and Joseph E. Stiglitz (New York: Oxford University Press).

Ammar Siamwalla, Chirmsak Pinthong, Nipon Poapongsakorn, Ploenpit Sasan-guan, Prayong Nettayarak, Wanrak Mingmaneenakin, and Yuavares Tubpun (1993) 'The Thai Rural Credit System and Elements of a Theory: Public Subsidies, Private Information, and Segmented Markets'. In *The Economics of Rural Organization*, ed. Karla Hoff, Avishay Braverman, and Joseph E. Stiglitz (New York: Oxford University Press).

Amsden, Alice H. (1989) *Asia's Next Giant: South Korea and Late Industrialisation.* (New York: Oxford University Press).

Amsden, Alice H. (1990) 'Third World Industrialisation: "Global Fordism" or a New Model?' *New Left Review* no. 182 (July-August).

Amsden, Alice (1991) 'Big Business and Urban Congestion in Taiwan: The Origins of Small Enterprise and Regionally Decentralised Industry (Respectively)'. *World Development* 19, 9.

Amsden, Alice H. (1992) 'Taiwan in International Perspective'. In *Taiwan's Enterprise in Global Perspective*. ed. N.T. Wang (New York: M.E. Sharpe, Inc. 1992).

Aschaur, David A. (1989) 'Is Public Expenditure Productive?' *Journal of Monetary Economics* 23, 2 (March).

Bangladesh Institute of Development Studies and International Food Policy Research Institute. (1985) *Development Impact of the Food for Works Program in Bangladesh.* A report prepared for the World Food Programme, Washington, DC.

Behrman, J. and N. Birdsall (1983) 'The Quality of Schooling: Quantity Alone May Be Misleading'. *American Economic Review*, 73, 5.

Berndt, Ernst R. and Bengt Hausson (1992) 'Measuring the Contribution of Public Infrastructure Capital in Sweden'. *Scandinavian Journal of Economics* 94, Supplement.

Birkhaeuser, Dean, Robert Evenson and Gershon Feder (1991) 'The Economic Impact of Agricultural Extension: A Review'. *Economic Development and Cultural Change* 39, 3 (April).

Colleye, Pierre-Olivier 'Mali' (1996) As cited in *The Informal Sector and Microfinance Institutions in West Africa*. ed. Leila Webster and Peter Fidler (Washington, DC: The World Bank).

Cotlear, Daniel (1990) 'The Effects of Education on Farm Productivity'. In *Human Development and the International Development Strategy for the 1990s*, ed. Keith Griffin and John Knight (London: Macmillan).

Cowling, Keith (1995) 'Reflections on the Privatisation Issue'. In *The Transformation of the Communist Economies*, ed. Ha-Joon Chang and Peter Nolan (London: Macmillan).

Devereux, M. and F. Schiantarelli (1990) 'Investment, Financial Factors, and Cash Flow: Evidence from U.K. Panel Model'. In *Information, Capital Markets and Investment*. ed. R.G. Hubbard (University of Chicago Press).

Fazzari, S., G. Hubbard, and B. Peterson (1988) 'Financing Constraints and Corporate Investment' *Brookings Papers on Economic Activity* no. 1.

Feder, Gershon, Lawrence J. Lau, Justin Y. Lin, and Xiaopeng Luo (1993) 'The Nascent Rural Credit Market in China'. In *The Economics of Rural Organization*, ed.

Karla Hoff, Avishay Braverman, and Joseph E. Stiglitz (New York: Oxford University Press).

Galeotti, M., F. Jaramillo, and F. Schiantarelli (1990) 'Investment Decisions and the Role of Debt, Liquid Assets and Cash Flow: Evidence from Italian Panel Data'. Boston University Working Paper (March).

Gaude, Jacques and Steve Miller (1990) 'Rural Development and Local Resource Intensity: A Case-Study Approach'. In *Human Development and the International Development Strategy for the 1990s*, ed. Keith Griffin and John Knight (London: Macmillan).

Griffin, Keith (1981) *Land Concentration and Rural Poverty*, 2nd edn (London: Macmillan).

Griffin, Keith (1985) 'Rural Poverty in Asia: Analysis and Policy Alternatives'. In *Strategies for Alleviating Poverty in Rural Asia*, ed. Rizwanul Islam (Dhaka: Bangladesh Institute of Development Studies and Bangkok: ILO, ARTEP).

Griffin, Keith (ed.) (1995) *Poverty and the Transition to a Market Economy in Mongolia* (London: Macmillan).

Griffin, Keith (1996) *Macroeconomic Reform and Employment: An Investment-Led Strategy of Structural Adjustment in Sub-Saharan Africa*, International Labour Office, Development Policies Department, Issues in Development Discussion Paper 16.

Griffin, Keith (1996) *Studies in Globalization and Economic Transitions* (London: Macmillan, 1996).

Griffin, Keith and Azizur Rahman Khan (eds) (1977) *Poverty and Landlessness in Rural Asia* (Geneva: ILO).

Griffin, Keith and Terry McKinley (1994) *Implementing a Human Development Strategy* (London: Macmillan).

Hoshi, T.A. Kashyap and D. Scharfstein (1988) 'Corporate Structure and Investment: Evidence from Japanese Panel Data'. MIT Sloan School of Management Working Paper. As cited in Stiglitz, Joseph, E. and Andrew Weiss (1992) 'Asymmetric Information in Credit Markets and its Implications for Macro-Economics.' *Oxford Economic Papers* 44.

Huppi, Monika and Gershon Feder (1990) 'The Role of Groups and Credit Cooperatives in Rural Lending'. *The World Bank Research Observer* 5, no. 2.

ILO (1990) 'L'economie informelle en Guinee: Analyse et strategie de developpement'. Geneva. As cited in *The Informal Sector and Microfinance Institutions in West Africa*. ed. Leila Webster and Peter Fidler (Washington, DC: The World Bank).

Kahlon, A.S., Harbhajan Singh Bal. *Factors Associated With Farm and Farm Family Investment Pattern in Ludhiana (Punjab) and Hissar (Haryana) Districts: (1966–67 through 1969–70)*. Department of Economics and Sociology, Punjab Agricultural University, Ludhiana, n.d.

Kelly, Allan C. and Jeffrey G. Williamson (1968) 'Household Saving Behaviour in the Developing Economies: The Indonesian Case'. *Economic Development and Cultural Change* (April).

Knight, John and Richard Sabot (1997) 'Educational Policy and Labour Productivity: An Output Accounting Exercise'. *Economic Journal* 97, 385 (March).

Levy, Brian (1993) 'Obstacles to Developing Indigenous Small and Medium Enterprises: An Empirical Assessment'. *World Bank Economic Review* 7, 1.

Leynes, Angelo F. (1990) 'Impact of the Slum Upgrading Programme in Metropolitan Manila on the Housing-based Income Generation Activities'. In

Housing and Income in Third World Urban Development, ed. Mulkh Raj and Peter Nientied (London: Aspect Publishing).

Leys, Colin (1975) *Underdevelopment in Kenya: The Political Economy of Neo-Colonialism* (London: Heinemann).

Lockheed, Marlaine, Dean Jamison and Lawrence Lau (1980) 'Farmer Education and Farm Efficiency: A Survey'. *Economic Development and Cultural Change* (October).

Marcouiller, Douglas, Veronica Ruiz de Castilla and Christopher Woodruff (1997) 'Formal Measures of the Informal-Sector Wage Gap in Mexico, El Salvador and Peru'. *Economic Development and Cultural Change* 45, 2 (January).

Mesa S., Nora Elena (1990) 'Economic Use of Housing "Pirata" and Invasion "Barrios" Medellin'. In *Housing and Income in Third World Urban Development*, ed. Mulkh Raj and Peter Nientied. (London: Aspect Publishing).

Morrison, Catherine J. and Amy Ellen Schwartz (1996) 'State Infrastructure and Productive Performance'. *American Economic Review* 86, 5 (December).

Nadiri, Ishaq, M. and Theofanis P. Mamuneas (1994) 'The Effects of Public Infrastructure and R&D on the Cost Structure and Performance of U.S. Manufacturing Industries'. *Review of Economics and Statistics* 76, 1 (February).

Nurkse, Ragnar (1953) *Problems of Capital Formation in Underdeveloped Countries* (New York: Oxford University Press).

Ong, Marcia L., Dale W. Adams and I.J. Singh. 'Voluntary Rural Savings Capacities in Taiwan, 1960 to 1970'. *Economics and Sociology Occasional Paper* No. 175, Ohio State University, n.d.

Oxenham, John, Jocelyn DeJong and Steven Treagust (1990) 'Improving the Quality of Education in Developing Countries'. In *Human Development and the International Development Strategy for the 1990s*. ed. Keith Griffin and John Knight (London: Macmillan).

Pattern, Richard H. and Jay K. Rosengard (1991) *Progress with Profits: The Development of Rural Banking in Indonesia* (San Francisco: ICS Press).

Psacharopoulos, George (1988) 'Education and Development: A Review'. *World Bank Research Observer* 3, 1 (January).

Rahman, Atiur and M. Mahabub-ul Islam (1993) 'The General Performance of the Grameen Bank'. In *The Grameen Bank: Poverty Relief in Bangladesh*. ed. Abu N.M. Wahid (Boulder: Westview Press).

Raisuddin, Ahmed and Mahabub Hossain (1983) 'Food for Work Program'. Special Issue of *Bangladesh Development Studies* 11.

Raisuddin, Ahmed and Mahabub Hossain (1990) *Developmental Impact of Rural Infrastructure in Bangladesh* (Washington, DC: International Food Policy Research Institute).

Rawski, Thomas (1979) *Economic Growth and Employment in China* (New York: Oxford University Press).

Ray, K.N., D.K. Grover and D.S. Nandlal (1969) 'Investment and Saving Pattern in Irrigated and Unirrigated Zones of Haryana State'. *Indian Journal of Agricultural Economics* (October-December).

Risbud, Neelima (1990) 'Housing and Income Generation Policies for the Urban Poor – Linkages and Limitations (A Case Study of Madhya Pradesh)'. In *Housing and Income in Third World Urban Development*, ed. Mulkh Raj and Peter Nientied (London: Aspect Publishing).

Schultz, T.W. (1961) 'Investment in Human Capital'. *American Economic Review* (March).

Shapiro, Helen and Lance Taylor (1990) 'The State and Industrial Strategy'. *World Development* 18, 6.

Stiglitz, Joseph E. (1990) 'Peer Monitoring and Credit Markets'. *World Bank Economic Review* 4.

Stiglitz, Joseph and Andrew Weiss (1981) 'Credit Rationing in Markets with Imperfect Information'. *American Economic Review* 71, 3.

Stiglitz, Joseph and Andrew Weiss (1983) 'Incentive Effects of Terminations: Applications to the Credit and Labor Markets'. *American Economic Review* 73.

Stiglitz, Joseph and Andrew Weiss. (1987) 'Credit Rationing: A Comment'. *American Economic Review* 77, 3.

Strassman, Paul W. (1987) 'Home-based Enterprises in Cities of Developing Countries'. *Economic Development and Cultural Change* 36, 1.

Taylor, Lance (1991) 'Stabilisation and Adjustment'. In *Stabilisation and Adjustment*. United Nations Development Programme Structural Adjustment Advisory Teams for Africa (UNDP/SAATA), (New York: United Nations Publications).

UNCHS (Habitat) (1990) *The Global Strategy for Shelter to the Year 2000* (Nairobi: UNCHS).

UNDP (1992) *Human Development in Bangladesh* (Dhaka: UNDP).

Von Pischke, J.D., Dale W. Adams and Gordon Donald (eds) (1983) *Rural Financial Markets in Developing Countries* (Washington, DC: The World Bank).

Wahid, Abu N.M. (ed) (1993) *The Grameen Bank: Poverty Relief in Bangladesh* (Boulder: Westview Press).

World Bank (1989) *World Development Report 1989: Financial Systems and Development* (New York: Oxford University Press).

World Bank (1994) 'Infrastructure for Development'. *World Development Report 1994* (New York: Oxford University Press).

World Bank (1996) *World Development Report 1996* (New York: Oxford University Press).

5 Macroeconomic Policies and Poverty: An Analysis of the Experience in Ten Asian Countries

Azizur Rahman Khan

This chapter draws upon the experience of Bangladesh, China, India, Indonesia, Malaysia, Mongolia, Nepal, Pakistan, the Philippines and Thailand in discussing the relationship between macroeconomic policies and poverty.[1] This is not a chapter on how to design policies for the alleviation of poverty. Changes in the incidence of poverty are due to a wide variety of policies and circumstances, encompassing institutions, resources, politics, environment, culture and different kinds of economic policies. In designing a credible programme for the alleviation of poverty, one must consider many other factors in addition to macroeconomic policies. It is even possible that often macroeconomic policies would not rank very high in the league of factors that affect the incidence of poverty. It is nevertheless clear that macroeconomic policies can have a powerful effect on the welfare of the poor. In recent years this has become a subject of much discussion in the context of the dramatic change of course that macroeconomic policies in less developed countries (LDCs) came to adopt as part of structural adjustment and adjustment to a globalizing world economy.[2]

Section I of this chapter discusses the linkage between macroeconomic policies and the determinants of poverty. Section II summarizes the main features of the linkage as documented in the ten country studies. Section III makes a comparative analysis of the country experience in determining the effect of some of the major instruments of macroeconomic policy on the change in the incidence of poverty. The concluding section provides a brief summary.

I. The Relationship between Macroeconomic Policies and Poverty

It is useful to start with the definition of macroeconomic policy instruments. We shall include all those policies that affect economic activity at the aggregate or broad sectoral level: fiscal policy, taxation, monetary and credit policies and public expenditure policies; price policy and policies concerning sectoral terms of trade; trade and exchange rate policies and policies towards foreign investment; and employment policies.

The ten country studies under review follow the nearly universal practice of measuring the incidence of poverty by identifying the threshold level of income or consumption below which a person is considered poor and finding some summary measure to aggregate the characteristics of all persons below that level. A change in such an index of poverty is completely determined by (i) the average rate of growth of the indicator chosen and (ii) the change in the Lorenz distribution of the indicator. Macroeconomic policies can affect both: they affect both the rate of growth and the distribution of income, consumption and other indicators of welfare.

The relationship between a particular instrument of macroeconomic policy on the one hand and growth and distribution on the other is, however, not unique. It depends on the specific circumstances of a country in which the policy is being applied. Thus a rise in the rate of public investment may either 'crowd out' private investment – by competing for investment funds – or 'crowd in' private investment – by improving the infrastructure and increasing the profitability of private investment. How conducive a rise in public investment is to growth depends on which of the two possible effects dominates in a given situation. Consider again an adjustment in the exchange rate to a value closer to the equilibrium value. In an LDC with a large agricultural sector producing tradable goods, this will increase the price of agricultural products. Whether this will improve or worsen the distribution of income will depend on the distribution of the benefits of higher agricultural prices. In an egalitarian peasant agriculture, with a limited incidence of net buyers of food among the low-income groups, this will improve the distribution of income. In an economy with a high concentration of landownership and a high incidence of landless labourers, this may easily worsen the distribution of income.

The composition of macroeconomic policies that reduces poverty would therefore depend on the actual circumstances of a country and would vary from one country to another. A comparison of the ten case studies – relating to countries differing in institutions, resource endowments, levels of development and structures of the economy – should inform us on how a given instrument of macroeconomic policy can produce different outcomes with respect to growth and distribution under different country circumstances.

It should, however, be noted that few countries have the choice of selecting a package of macroeconomic policies that maximize the alleviation of poverty. The choice of macroeconomic policies is often driven by considerations of macroeconomic balance and adjustment. The urgency of attaining macroeconomic targets often limits the range of choice of instruments of macroeconomic policy. It is quite possible that the package that is dictated by macroeconomic priorities aggravates, rather than alleviates, poverty. An example is an economy in which low-income groups are net buyers of food who are adversely affected by a rise in food prices that results from an adjustment of the exchange rate. A devaluation may still be forced by an unsustainable external imbalance. In this case it is essential for the policy makers to know what effect devaluation has on the poor so that they may pursue the goal of offsetting this adverse effect on the poor by other policies, including other kinds of macroeconomic policies.

In discussing the effects of growth and distribution on poverty, frequently growth is measured by the rate of growth of per capita GDP or GNP and distribution is measured by some summary index, for example, the Gini ratio of personal income distribution. These measurements may be quite inappropriate in identifying the factors affecting changes in the incidence of poverty. Consider a poverty threshold in terms of a level of per capita personal income that is anchored to a certain minimum level of nutrition. Consider also that poverty estimates are measured separately for rural and urban areas and that most of the poor live in rural areas. A change in the head count or any other standard index of rural (urban) poverty is then uniquely determined by (a) the average increase in per capita rural (urban) personal income and (b) the change in the Lorenz distribution of per capita rural (urban) personal income. Clearly, the reduction in poverty is greater the greater the increase in per capita rural personal income, given that the Lorenz distribution is unchanged. The rate of change in per capita GDP may be a very bad predictor of the rate of change in per capita rural personal income. This may be because:

(a)   the growth in GDP is concentrated in non-rural economic activities so that rural GDP does not increase at the same rate;

(b) there has been a change in the sectoral terms of trade for agriculture, the dominant rural economic activity; or
(c) the increase in GDP has not been passed on in the form of an increase in personal income due, for example, to a rising share of the public sector in incremental GDP.

All these are subject to influence by macroeconomic policies.

Similarly a summary index of distribution – for example the Gini ratio – may fail to be affected by a change in the Lorenz distribution that affects the welfare of the poor. Thus a redistribution of income between the decile just below the poverty threshold and the decile just above the poverty threshold may be offset by a redistribution of income between the ninth and tenth deciles in such a way that the Gini ratio remains unchanged. In this case the Gini ratio will fail to detect a relevant change in distribution affecting the poor (assuming of course that the ninth decile is above the poverty threshold). The nature of the change in distribution may also be influenced by macroeconomic policies.

The indices of poverty that are typically used in quantifying the incidence of poverty focus on a single dimension of poverty (for example, inadequacy of consumption or income). The welfare of the poor, however, has many dimensions. Thus, for example, apart from assuring a threshold level of consumption, the welfare of the poor can be enhanced by endowing them with improved human capital. This is particularly important from the standpoint of creating the capability for overcoming poverty in the future. Macroeconomic policy instruments that achieve this – namely a rise in public expenditure on the appropriate kind of education and health facilities – are often quite different from the ones that contribute to the growth and distribution of current income. Thus we shall often go beyond the direct effect of macroeconomic instruments on growth and distribution of the particular variable that features in the poverty threshold and consider their effects on other dimensions of welfare of the poor.

II. Main Features of Country Experience

This section summarizes only the main findings about the effects of macroeconomic policies on the poor although most of these studies go well beyond this issue.[3] We also limit ourselves to the actual document-ation provided in these studies. Occasionally we point out the omission of some important issue but rarely insert any evidence from outside these studies.

Bangladesh

The country study provides estimates of poverty at six points over the period 1973/4–1991/2. The poverty threshold refers to a level of income that satisfied basic nutritional and other needs in a benchmark year and was updated by the consumer price index (CPI) for the poor for other years. Head count, poverty gap and 'weighted poverty gap' indices of poverty are shown.[4] All indices show a decline in the incidence of poverty until 1985/6 and a rise in the incidence of poverty thereafter.

Per capita income grew more or less steadily, albeit modestly, over the entire period. Indeed the rate of growth in per capita income was higher in the post 1985/6 period than before. There was some rise in the Gini ratio of income distribution, modest in rural areas and more significant in urban areas. That poverty increased after 1985/6, in spite of a significant rise in per capita income, was perhaps due more to the change in the sectoral composition of growth than the increase in inequality. After 1985/6, especially since the late 1980s, the growth of the agricultural sector declined sharply. This must have adversely affected the growth of personal income in rural areas, where the poor are concentrated.

The aggregate investment rate has been stagnant throughout the period after 1985/6 and indeed lower than in the early 1980s. Growth in public investment has been insignificant and this appears to have adversely affected the rate of growth of aggregate investment. Empirical evidence suggests that public investment has a 'crowding in' effect on private investment in Bangladesh.

Public development expenditure in agriculture drastically fell after the mid-1980s. This was not offset by a rise in the proportion of public expenditure in the non-agricultural sector in the rural economy. Reform of prices resulted in the drastic reduction or complete withdrawal of subsidies on agricultural inputs and this was not replaced by alternative incentives for agriculture.

Financial sector reforms were focused on raising the real rate of interest. This was not matched by institutional reform to improve the flow of credit to small producers. On balance this may have been detrimental to the interests of the small producers. Also empirical evidence suggests that the elasticity of savings with respect to GDP and bank branches is much higher than it is with respect to the real interest rate.

China

Estimates of poverty consist of nine sets of observations for rural China and six sets of observations for urban China over the period of reform, ranging over 1980–94. Per capita personal income, anchored to an acceptable level of nutrition given consumer preferences in the benchmark year, and adjusted in other years by the CPI for the poor, is used as the poverty threshold. Head count, poverty gap and weighted poverty gap indices are estimated. In rural China there was a rapid decline in poverty until the mid-1980s. After 1985 there was a dramatic reduction in the rate of decline in the incidence of rural poverty. In the early 1990s there was a complete halt in the reduction in the headcount index in rural China with the consequent rise in the number of poor. Performance in reducing more abysmal kinds of rural poverty was worse in this period. In urban China there was a steady fall in the incidence of poverty until the end of the 1980s. In the 1990s there was a rise in the head count index for more extreme kinds of poverty.

The asymmetrical performance in poverty reduction in the pre-1985 and post-1985 period in rural China is largely explained by a fall in the growth rate in personal income (the variable featuring in the poverty threshold). In the earlier period personal income grew rapidly aided by the high rate of growth of agricultural output and a sharp improvement in agriculture's terms of trade. This was strong enough to outweigh the effect of moderately rising inequality in the distribution of personal income. In the later period the growth in personal income was drastically reduced, due to a decline in the growth of agricultural output and a decline and/or stagnation in agriculture's terms of trade. The growth in personal income was no longer high enough to offset the effect of inequality, which continued to rise. The shift in the composition of rural income in favour of non-farm activities was a source of increased inequality of rural income distribution because non-farm income is more unequally distributed than farm income. Since most of China's poor are located in rural areas, the decline in the growth of rural income was detrimental to overall poverty reduction in China.

In urban China the rate of growth in personal income was high, easily outweighing the effect of the moderate rise in inequality until the late 1980s. Since then growth in personal income accelerated but was still not able to outweigh the effect of the sharp increase in the inequality of income distribution.

An important point emerging in the case of China is that the overall growth rate of GDP is a poor predictor of the growth rate in personal income, the variable that features in the estimation of poverty. This is partly due to macroeconomic policies concerning the rate of accumulation. Partly this is due to the change in sectoral terms of trade, which features prominently in the transmission of aggregate growth to sectoral growth.

The unprecedented rate of industrialization in the era of globalization (1984–94) contributed to income concentration in two very important ways. First, the output elasticity of employment in manufacturing fell drastically. Secondly, there was a high concentration of growth in the richer coastal and eastern provinces. These were closely related to reforms aimed at facilitating the integration of China with the globalizing world economy, not complemented by offsetting policies to protect the unemployed and the poorer regions.

Institutional changes in liberalizing the provision of education and health services were not complemented by offsetting changes in the allocation of public funds for protecting the access of the poor to these services.

Some of the specific macroeconomic policies deserve to be highlighted. The push for an ever higher rate of accumulation was an obstacle to the transmission of the growth of GDP to growth of personal income. Brinkmanship in the quest for as high a rate of growth as possible led to periodic spurts of high inflation; years of high inflation have also been years of reduced poverty alleviation. The change in the composition of public expenditure and credit, away from the rural sector and in favour of the urban sectors of the richer provinces, was detrimental to overall poverty alleviation. The policy of allowing the state and collective enterprises to shed underemployed labour – to enable them to integrate with the globalizing world economy – was not matched by an adequate policy to protect the unemployed. While the *de facto* tolerance of migration has been beneficial to the poor, the remaining discrimination against the migrants is an impediment to the welfare of the poor.

India

The Indian case study covers the longest time period of any study; it estimates the incidence of poverty at 18 points over the period 1966/7–1993/4. The poverty threshold relates to a constant per capita real *expenditure*, anchored to an acceptable level of nutrition given consumer preference in the benchmark year and adjusted by the CPI for the poor in other years.[5] The head count ratio is the principal index although a number of other distributional measures have been presented. The main finding is that there has been a trend decline in poverty over the entire period. The rate of decline in poverty was higher in rural India (0.9 percentage point of head count ratio per year) than in urban India (0.7 percentage point). Another fact, not highlighted by the authors, is that the rate of decline in the head count index of poverty appears to have slowed down in the period after 1983 compared to the period before.[6]

The country study identifies two determinants of the index of poverty: per capita value added (in agriculture for rural India and in the non-agricultural economy for urban India), which varies negatively with the index of poverty; and the ratio of food price to overall consumer price, which varies positively with the index of poverty. In rural India the effect of a per cent change in the income variable on poverty is greater than in urban India. The relative magnitudes of the effect of a per cent change in the price variable in rural and urban India are exact opposites.

The country study takes the view that per capita value added is exogenous in the short run so that the short-run macroeconomic instruments for poverty alleviation should focus on the stabilization of the relative food price. The non-quantifiable time trend is found to be the single most important determining factor behind the rise in the relative food price. The volume of public food stock has a negative impact on food prices while the government fiscal deficit and exchange rate devaluation have positive impacts on the relative food price.

State level poverty estimates, combining observations for 5 time periods for 15 states, confirm the above analysis. In addition they show that in rural India the level of poverty varies positively with inequality although the elasticity of rural head count index with respect to inequality (measured by the inter quartile range) is rather low. For rural India inequality does not have a significant effect on the head count ratio.[7]

The study concludes by suggesting different kinds of safety net for rural and urban India. To cope with weather-induced supply shocks in rural India, public works for employment and income generation should have high priority because of the high elasticity of head count ratio with respect to income. In urban areas, with lower elasticity of poverty index with respect to income and a much higher elasticity with respect to relative food price, it is far more important to stabilize food prices. Stabilizing food prices in rural India is also of high priority though not as high as in urban India. The authors also conclude that the absence of a relationship between inequality and poverty in urban India and the low elasticity of poverty with respect to inequality in rural India suggest that the pursuit of equality at the cost of growth is not a sound strategy for poverty reduction.

A reduced fiscal deficit helps stabilize food prices; but its effect on the growth of output and employment may be negative, which may offset the positive effect due to lower food prices. Greater export orientation of the Indian economy would mean higher food prices, which should be compensated by offsetting policies such as high public food stock and higher food imports. On the whole the study strongly argues for higher growth of agriculture both to raise rural income and to stabilize food prices.

Indonesia

The country study reports official poverty estimates at nine points over the 23-year period from 1970 to 1993. Poverty thresholds refer to two alternative bundles of minimum consumption for the benchmark year, updated by the CPI for other years. Head count index is the principal measurement reported although occasional estimates of poverty gap are also shown. These estimates show steady decline in poverty in both rural and urban Indonesia especially since the mid-1970s. The rate of poverty reduction was higher in urban areas than in rural areas.

The country study has only a limited discussion of the linkage between macroeconomic policies and poverty. Reduction in poverty has been achieved through a combination of rapid growth and stable inequality in distribution. The relationship between growth and poverty alleviation has varied over time. Between 1981 and 1987 – the period of stabilization – the GDP growth rate slowed down appreciably. But this did not result in a slow down in the rate of poverty reduction mainly because a rise in inequality was avoided. Reduction in public expenditure was concentrated in capital-intensive sectors (for example grants to public enterprises were reduced), which did not much impact on employment. Budgetary retrenchment was not so drastic as to induce stagnation and worsen the distribution of income.

During 1970–76 rural poverty increased due mainly to a rapid increase in food (principally rice) prices. The government thereafter followed a policy of stablizing rice prices. To stem the transmission of instability in international prices, self-sufficiency in rice was identified as a key policy and virtually achieved by the mid-1980s.

Malaysia

The country study reports six official observations spaced over 25 years (1970–95), using a constant per capita real income that was only 17 per cent of per capita GNP in 1989. The head count ratio is the index of poverty that is used. In spite of the questionable nature of the estimates,[8] it is beyond doubt that the incidence of poverty has steadily declined over time in both rural and urban Malaysia. For urban areas the head count ratio had become negligible by the late 1980s while for rural areas it still remains significant. Hardcore poverty, showing the population below a poverty threshold which is half as high as the standard poverty threshold, declined faster than absolute poverty. Poverty declined for all ethnic, locational and economic groups.

The main source of poverty reduction was the rapid growth of the economy. Inequality declined somewhat between 1973 and 1987 and increased moderately in the 1990s. The discussion of the linkage between macroeconomic policies and poverty is generally weak. Directed credit, quotas on employment and asset redistribution were used to bring about a shift in the distribution of income among ethnic groups, with an uncertain outcome for overall equity. Public expenditure was directed to promote research and development in high yielding rice and improved varieties of seed for cocoa and tobacco, with a favourable effect on growth. Major changes in taxation policy consisted of a sharp reduction in the progressivity of taxes, which could not have helped either equality or poverty alleviation. Significant reduction in export and import duties may have helped make food cheaper for low income groups. Nothing is known about the redistributive effects of public expenditure. The same is true about the effects of privatization, which was promoted after the late 1970s and reversed the previous emphasis on public enterprises. Monetary policy was strongly focused on price stability, resulting in a low rate of inflation (averaging 4.5 per cent per year between 1973 and 1990).

Mongolia

Official poverty estimates are available only for 1992–94. These use a poverty threshold that is based on the cost of a largely arbitrarily chosen minimum consumption basket. There are many questions concerning the appropriateness of the methodology of estimating the poverty threshold and adjusting it over time. The head count index of poverty rose sharply from 17 per cent in 1992 to 26.5 per cent in 1994. Although no comparable estimates are available for the past, it is pretty certain that poverty in the sense of income inadequacy to satisfy the specified consumption basket did not exist until about 1989.

The increase in poverty was due almost entirely to the large fall in output precipitated by the external shock due to the loss of foreign assistance and the disruption of external trade as a result of the decline and the ultimate breakdown of the Soviet Union. A small economy such as Mongolia could simply not avoid contraction in the face of such massive external shocks. This was aggravated by the failure to bring about an orderly change in the rural institutions that replaced the state and collective institutions of the past. Public resources for education and health fell sharply, leading to a reduced access of the poor to these services. Unemployment rose and real earnings fell.

Nepal

Only four observations of poverty head count ratio are reported for the period 1977–92. Even these estimates are seriously flawed in so far as the poverty threshold does not represent a constant level of real living standard over time. The study claims, presumably on the grounds that the variations in the real living standard between poverty thresholds used by different studies were small, that there was steady and significant increase in the incidence of poverty over the period under review in both rural and urban areas.

Real GDP grew steadily at about 4.7 per cent per year, resulting in a rise in per capita income of about 2 per cent per year. For poverty to increase in spite of this, there should have been significant worsening of distribution for the poor. The distributional data are very messy although it seems unlikely that intra-rural inequality increased much.[9] The Gini ratio of landholding fell significantly between 1981/2 and 1991/2.

While the growth rate in GDP was sustained at a reasonable level, the growth rate of agricultural GDP fell steadily to only 1.3 per cent per year in the early 1990s. This could have led to too slow a growth in rural income to prevent a rise in the incidence of rural poverty.

There is uncertainty about the effects of recent macroeconomic reforms. The interest rate has been reformed to make the lending rate highly positive in real terms. The study argues that due to capital market imperfections the deposit rate remains very low, with a very large spread between the deposit rate and the lending rate. As a result both the incentive to save and the incentive to invest are adversely affected. The saving rate has been nearly stagnant at 12 per cent of GDP in recent years while the rate of investment, at 22 per cent of GDP, has been quite respectable.

The exchange rate was devalued substantially *vis-à-vis* the US$. Since Nepal is a net importer of food, this, along with the reform of the trade regime, resulted in a faster rate of increase in food prices than in other prices. This has adversely affected those large numbers among the poor who are net buyers of food. This problem has been further exacerbated by the rapid rate of inflation (11.5 per cent per year since the late 1970s) that macroeconomic policies permitted.

While Nepal's currency has depreciated in real terms *vis-à-vis* the US$, it has appreciated substantially relative to the currency of India, by as much as 22 per cent between 1977 and 1993. This has rendered many Nepalese industries uncompetitive relative to Indian industries, creating a serious problem of incentive to invest in industries.

Pakistan

The country study reports eight observations of head count indices of poverty over the period 1963/4 to 1992/3 spaced at unequal intervals. Three observations each of poverty gap and weighted poverty gap indices are also reported over the period 1984/5 to 1990/91. The poverty income threshold for the benchmark year refers to per capita expenditure that is adequate for a specified level of basic nutrition with allowance for non-food expenditure that is based on the proportion of such expenditure for the poor households.

Poverty trends are shown for four broad periods:

(1) the period of high growth in GDP during the 1960s when the incidence of rural and overall poverty increased;
(2) the period of slower growth in GDP between 1969/70 and 1977 when the incidence of poverty declined sharply;
(3) the subsequent decade of high growth when the declining trend of poverty continued; and
(4) the period of structural adjustment since 1987/8 when the incidence of rural and overall poverty increased again.

Increased poverty in spite of high growth during the decade of the 1960s was due to structural changes – for example increased inequality in the distribution of landholdings – leading to greater inequality in living standards. During the 1970s the adverse effect of the reduction in the rate of growth of GDP was more than offset by the dramatic rise in the rate of income remittance which augmented the earnings of the poor, both directly and indirectly, through the employment effect of the increased investment that a part of the remittance flow financed. The declining trend in the incidence of poverty continued into the 1980s, when remittances peaked (in 1982/3) before beginning a decline and the growth in GDP accelerated again. After 1987/8 the incidence of rural and overall poverty increased again once structural adjustment policies were implemented on a broad front.

The country study focuses especially on the effect of structural adjustment on poverty by comparing poverty trends in the immediate pre-structural adjustment period (1984/5 to 1987/8) with poverty trends in the early structural adjustment period (1987/8 to 1990/91). In the pre-adjustment period the incidence of rural, urban and overall poverty fell according to all available estimates. In the structural adjustment period the incidence of rural, urban and overall poverty increased according to most available estimates. The country study identifies the following causes of these asymmetrical trends in the incidence of poverty:

- the overall growth rate was lower in the second period than in the first;
- growth in employment was far lower in the second period than in the first both because of lower growth in GDP and because of the reduced output elasticity of employment. As a result, the growth rate in real wages for unskilled workers changed from a significantly positive value in the first period to a significantly negative value in the second period, thereby contributing to increased inequality in income distribution;
- the poverty-reducing effect of high growth in the first period was accentuated by the poverty-reducing effect of mild reduction in inequality, while the weakened poverty-reducing effect of slower growth in the second period was accentuated by the poverty-inducing effect of increased inequality;
- the income remittance in real terms was far lower in the second period than in the first;
- the rate of inflation accelerated from 4.7 per cent in the first period to 9.5 per cent in the second period, which made the gap between the change in prices and the change in money wages and earnings of the poor greater in the second period than in the first;
- the system of taxation became more regressive in the structural adjustment period; and
- the decline in subsidies and the reduction in the growth of public expenditure on primary education and basic health care in the second period, as compared to the first period, adversely affected the welfare of the poor.

Limited econometric analysis further supports the view that the head count rate of poverty is a decreasing function of income growth, increases in real wages (a proxy for greater equality in the distribution of income), income remittances by migrants and the per capita availability of food grains; and an increasing function of labour supply.

The Philippines

Using a constant real consumption that buys a minimum bundle of goods as the poverty threshold, estimates of head count index are available for the period 1985–94. Estimates of poverty gap and weighted poverty gap are also available between 1985 and 1991. There was some decline in the head count index between 1985 and 1988 in both rural and urban areas. Between 1988 and 1994 the head count index rose in rural areas and fell in urban areas. All other indices of poverty showed an increase between 1988 and 1991.

The relationship among growth, inequality and poverty has been different in different periods. During 1985–88 real GDP per capita increased by a total of 12 per cent. According to the Family Income and Expenditure Survey the real consumption per capita was unchanged, representing a failure of transmission of aggregate GDP growth to a growth in the household living standard. The incidence of poverty, however, declined due to an improvement in the distribution of expenditure in rural areas. During 1988–91 there was almost no growth in GDP per capita while the inequality in distribution increased. The incidence of poverty increased.

Simulation with a macro model shows that a 5 per cent devaluation will increase the rural head count ratio of poverty by 1.9 percentage points and the urban head count ratio by 2.5 percentage points. Since agriculture is more tradable than industries in the Philippines, devaluation substantially raises rural prices. The resulting terms of trade improvement does not benefit the rural poor, who are largely landless workers and small farmers – namely, net buyers of food. Urban poor also face a higher rise in food prices than in nominal incomes.

Another controversial policy change concerns the rise in the price of utilities and public services due to the removal of subsidies. Simulation with a macro model shows that this too will increase the incidence of poverty though only slightly. A 20 per cent increase in utilities prices would increase rural and urban head count ratios respectively by 1.44 percentage points and 1.17 percentage points. Similar simulation is also made to demonstrate that increased public investment in infrastructure, increased education and tenancy reform in agriculture are highly poverty alleviating, especially if such measures are concentrated in poor areas.

Thailand

There are eight observations over the 30-year period stretching from 1962/3 to 1992 although the estimates for the years before 1968/9 are not comparable with the later ones. Even within the period between 1968/9 and 1992 there were breaks in methodology raising questions about comparability. The poverty threshold is based on the cost of a minimum nutritional basket and other basic consumption goods in the base year, adjusted by the CPI in later years. The head count ratio is the principal index while estimates of poverty gap are available for a shorter period. There was steady reduction in the head count ratio over the entire period with the exception of the year 1986, in which there was a rise. Also the average intensity of poverty of the poor rose between 1988 and 1990 although the number of poor declined.

There was little by way of targeted action for poverty reduction in Thailand until recently due to the absence of a fiscal surplus for this purpose. The focus of the poverty alleviation strategy was on the generation of rapid growth trickling down to the poor. Over time growth has been accompanied by increasing inequality. The poverty-alleviating effect of growth was only partly offset by the poverty-inducing effect of increased inequality. The study reports that during 1988–90 about 36 per cent of the reduction in the head count ratio that would have resulted from income growth with unchanged distribution was offset by the adverse change in distribution. Over time the offsetting effect of increasing inequality has been becoming weaker.

Until the 1980s effective protection was highly positive for industries and highly negative for agriculture (due to an export tax and high tariffs on agricultural inputs). This began to change radically in the late 1980s resulting in a sharp reduction in protection. Using a computable general equilibrium (CGE) model showed that a reduction in protection significantly reduces all indices of poverty. Curiously, an earlier CGE model had shown that an increase in manufactured exports would increase inequality, though not poverty, due to a lower rate of increase in wages than in profits.

Monetary policy in Thailand successfully stabilized prices to an average inflation rate of 5.8 per cent per year during 1987–95, the period of ultra rapid growth. Widespread reform of the financial system improved the efficiency of the sector. It is, however, not very clear how these outcomes benefited the poor.

The overall effect of the tax system on income distribution in Thailand is disequalizing. Since the mid-1980s this began to change. The direct effect of these changes on poverty can not be ascertained. The effect of public expenditure on income distribution is equalizing. Since the mid-1980s the share of economic and social services in total public expenditure has been increasing rapidly. Some of this is due to increasing amounts of resources for rural projects that are directly poverty alleviating.

III. Macroeconomic Policy Instruments and Poverty: an Analysis of the Evidence

This section analyses the evidence from the ten country studies to determine the effect of specific macroeconomic policy instruments on poverty.

Growth, Distribution and Poverty

We begin with an analysis of the evidence on the effects of the broad goals and/or outcomes of macroeconomic policies, namely growth and distribution. Often the design of a macroeconomic policy package is confronted with the dilemma of whether to pursue the goal of efficiency leading to high growth or to sacrifice efficiency in order to avoid a worsening of the distribution of income. What does the evidence from the case studies tell us about the effect on poverty of a particular way of blending the two goals?

Table 5.1 summarizes the experience of ten countries. Countries experiencing a reduction in the incidence of poverty all achieved moderate to high growth.[10] It should, however, be noted that a rapid rate of increase in per capita GDP is not a guarantee of poverty reduction. As discussed in Section I, for poverty to decline, growth in GDP must get translated into growth in income/consumption of the poor. In the case studies reported above, there are numerous cases in which this transmission did not happen.

Thus in Bangladesh after the mid-1980s, poverty increased in spite of a moderately high rate of growth in per capita GDP – higher than the rate of growth in per capita GDP in the preceding period when poverty declined – because: (a) the growth of agricultural GDP, the largest source of income in rural areas, in which the poor are concentrated, declined sharply; and (b) the inequality of distribution increased. Macroeconomic policies were largely responsible for at least the first of these two factors. Public expenditure in agriculture declined sharply and taxation and subsidy policies reduced incentives in agriculture.

In China since the mid-1980s, the rate of growth in rural personal income was low in spite of an extraordinarily high growth in GDP. This was due to a decline in the growth of the agricultural sector and a decline/ stagnation in agriculture's terms of trade. Once again, macroeconomic policies appear to be responsible for much of this. Public sector accumulation policies drove a wedge between growth in GDP and growth in personal income. Agriculture's share of public resources declined. Agricultural prices were depressed because of public policies which overly emphasized a very high rate of accumulation. In addition inequality in distribution increased. In urban China the rate of increase in personal income was higher, but the increase in inequality was also much higher, resulting in a dismal performance in poverty alleviation in the 1990s.

In Nepal the overall growth in GDP was high enough to prevent a rise in the incidence of poverty if not to bring about a fall in it. But the growth in GDP was largely concentrated in the growth of income in non-agricultural

Table 5.1 Evidence on Poverty, Growth and Distribution

Country	Poverty Trend	Growth Performance	Distribution
Bangladesh	Fall until the mid-1980s; rise thereafter	Moderate growth in GDP per capita which was higher after 1985; growth in agricultural GDP slowed after 1985	Moderate rise in inequality within rural and urban areas
China	Rural: Fall until the mid-1980s; stagnant or rise thereafter. Urban: Fall until the end of the 1980s; stagnant or rise thereafter.	GDP growth very high; until the mid-1980s this was transmitted to rural personal income growth; thereafter very low personal income growth in rural areas; urban personal income grew rapidly throughout the period.	Inequality rose moderately in rural China. In urban China rise in inequality accelerated in the 1990s.
India	Steady decline	Moderate growth	Trend in inequality not documented; probably a modest rise in inequality
Indonesia	Steady decline	Rapid growth; growth slowed during the stabilization period 1981–87	No evidence of increasing inequality; during the stabilization period inequality declined.
Malaysia	Steady decline	Rapid growth	Declining inequality until 1987; rise thereafter
Mongolia	Sharp rise	Negative growth; sharp fall in per capita GDP	No evidence
Nepal	Steady increase	Moderate growth in GDP; sharp fall in the growth in agricultural GDP	Evidence unclear; probably moderate rise in inequality in rural areas and sharper rise in urban areas
Pakistan	Rise in the 1960s; fall between 1970 and 1987/8 and rise thereafter	Rapid growth in the 1960s; slower growth in the 1970s; return to rapid growth in the 1980s until the slowdown after 1987/8	Rising inequality in the 1960s and after 1987/8. In between, trend in inequality not well documented, perhaps not rising much if at all
The Philippines	Fall during 1985–88; rise during 1988–91	Moderate growth in GDP during 1985–88 not transmitted to growth in personal income; insignificant growth in per capita GDP during 1988–91	Improved distribution during 1985–88; increasing inequality during 1988–91
Thailand	Fall in poverty	Rapid growth in per capita income	Rise in inequality

and non-rural activities. The growth of agricultural GDP declined sharply. This, along with a moderate rise in inequality in the rural economy and a sharp rise in inequality in the urban economy, resulted in a rise in the incidence of poverty.

In Pakistan growth in GDP was by and large high enough to permit a steady reduction in the incidence of poverty. Paradoxically poverty increased in the 1960s, the period of most rapid growth in GDP, due to increased inequality, mainly caused by structural factors. After 1987/8 poverty increased again. This time it was due to a combination of slower growth of GDP and greater inequality in income distribution, due substantially to macroeconomic policies under the structural adjustment programme.

Failure of GDP growth to be transmitted to the growth of personal expenditure – the variable in the poverty threshold – is also observed in the Philippines during 1985–88. An increase in poverty was avoided because of an absence of an adverse change in income distribution.

Clearly a high rate of GDP growth is not enough. Two kinds of distributional outcomes must be combined with it: it must be translated into a growth in personal income/consumption of the sectors of the economy where the poor are concentrated; and it must not be accompanied by a large increase in inequality. There are many examples in the case studies of high growth successfully overcoming the effects of moderate increase in inequality in bringing about a decline in the incidence of poverty. But even a very high rate of growth may be offset by a dramatic rise in inequality. This appears to have happened in urban China in the 1990s.

Food Prices

The effect of a rise in food prices appears to be detrimental to poverty alleviation in India and the Philippines. The Nepal study also surmises that a rise in food prices may have adversely affected the poor. The same was the experience of Indonesia in the 1970s.

The effect of a rise in food prices is quite different in other cases. In Thailand, an improvement in agriculture's terms of trade, due to a reduction in the rate of negative effective protection, seems to have reduced the incidence of poverty. In rural China too an improvement in producers' prices would have reduced the incidence of poverty. There is some evidence that an improvement in agriculture's terms of trade in Bangladesh might have helped reduce the incidence of poverty.[11]

The issue is extremely complex. First, it should be recognized that the effect of a rise in the price of food would depend on the structure of the economy. In an economy dominated by agriculture with an egalitarian peasant ownership there is a small incidence of net buyers of food among the poor. In this case a rise in agricultural prices, including the price of food, helps alleviate poverty by raising the income of the poor peasants. The effect is particularly strong if this comes about by abolishing discrimination against peasant exports. The poor in urban areas are adversely affected; but usually they are a numerical minority, often very small. Furthermore, a thriving rural economy should facilitate an acceleration of urban growth by providing both increased resources and additional demand for urban products. In an economy characterized by an inegalitarian agriculture, with a high concentration of net buyers of food among the poor, a rise in food price may easily aggravate the incidence of poverty. This may explain the asymmetrical effect of a rise in prices in China and India.

A second question is, what to do when food prices are suppressed by distortionary policies even though it is known that a rise would adversely affect the poor. Macroeconomic reform may want to dismantle distortions – for example, negative effective protection of agricultural exports and low procurement prices for food and agricultural goods in a regulated market – which reduce the efficiency of economic performance and adversely affect growth. It is quite possible that in the long run the adverse indirect effect on the poor, due to a reduction in economic growth, would outweigh the favourable direct effect of lower food prices. Furthermore, it should be possible to design some programme of compensating the net buyers of food among the poor for the adverse effect of a rise in food price by an expansion of employment through public works or targeted income subsidy or targeted public distribution of subsidized food.

Reform of the Trade Regime and Poverty

The above discussion directly leads to the issue of reforming the trade regime, as a part of the macroeconomic reform programme, for greater efficiency and growth of the economy. Often the objection to trade reforms is that they are harmful to the standard of living of the poor. An example of the process through which this takes place is the rise in food prices and/or the prices of basic consumer goods. The case studies of India and the Philippines argue that the reforms of the trade regime are likely to be harmful to the poor. The Philippines study reports the result of a simulation exercise that finds the adverse effect of a devaluation on the head count index of poverty to be rather large.

Reform of the trade regime is so central to economic efficiency that it is hard to justify its postponement because of its adverse direct effect on the poor. One must hope that in the long run the indirect effect of higher efficiency and growth would offset the adverse direct effect. During the transition, policy makers might find it possible to protect the poor by alternative methods.

Public Expenditure

Public expenditure and public investment are powerful macroeconomic instruments to affect aggregate economic activity and poverty. One of the principal orthodoxies of structural adjustment sponsored by some multilateral development agencies is that a rise in public expenditure is detrimental to economic efficiency because it crowds out the more efficient and productive private investment. The evidence in the case studies hardly supports this view. Both in Bangladesh and in the Philippines there is strong evidence of the crowding in effect of public expenditure and investment.

The composition of public expenditure can be a powerful tool in influencing the distribution of income. The Philippines simulation exercise demonstrates that by influencing the location of infrastructural public investment in areas and activities with a concentration of the poor, public expenditure can dramatically alleviate poverty. Reduction in public expenditure on subsidies and the reduction in growth in public expenditure on primary education and health care appear to have hurt the poor in Pakistan.

Public investment and expenditure need not compete with private investment. Indeed, there is little advantage to be had in expanding public ownership of industries and directly productive enterprises. Even in infrastructure, there is no need for the public sector to shut out private participation. What is needed is intervention when a lack of infrastructure and an inadequate access to human capital prevent an enhancement of the productivity of the poor.

Price Stability

The case studies have a limited involvement with the effect of price stability, or its absence, on the poor. The China study notes that the years of high inflation have been relatively difficult years for poverty alleviation. Some of the other studies (for example, Pakistan and Nepal) suggest that price stability is good for the poor. Yet other studies (for example, Thailand) argue that the relationship between price stability and poverty is tenuous. By and large, the conclusion that emerges is that extreme price instability is harmful for poverty alleviation; it makes the task of adjusting nominal incomes of the poor to the rate of inflation very difficult. This calls for the avoidance of large public sector fiscal deficits and too permissive a monetary policy. On the other hand some studies (for example, India) warn against the policy of restricting the fiscal deficit to such an extent as to negatively impact output and employment growth.

Globalization, Employment and Poverty

A good deal of macroeconomic reform and structural adjustment since the early 1980s – especially the reform of the trade and exchange rate regime, including the policy towards capital flows – was intended to facilitate the integration of the LDCs with the globalizing world economy. The hope was that greater integration with the world economy would lead to higher and more poverty-alleviating growth. This expectation was based on the reasoning that increased integration with the world economy would mean an end of the notoriously employment-hostile regime of import-substituting industrialization and change the structure of industries in favour of exports which, given the relative abundance of labour in the LDCs, are likely to consist of labour-intensive goods. The reform of the trade regime and other related incentives should facilitate this process by promoting specialization in goods intensive in the use of the abundant factors. An inflow of foreign capital, especially foreign direct investment (FDI) pursuing low real costs of labour, should provide an additional impetus to employment expansion.

The experience of even the most successful cases of adjustment to globalization is very mixed on the expansion of industrial employment. Contrary to the expectation outlined above, the output elasticity of employment in manufacturing industries fell in China, India and several other countries.[12] This is in spite of the fact that empirical studies show that at least in China's case the growth of manufactured exports was concentrated in labour-intensive products. The explanation of the paradox seems to lie in the initial conditions of manufacturing industries in many of these countries. The pre-globalization system of incentives permitted an absorption of labour far in excess of requirement in the manufacturing industries of these countries. In the case of China this mainly happened in state and collective enterprises and in India in public sector industries. The phenomenon was very much a part of the social policies that these countries were committed to at the time. Economic reform to promote integration with the globalizing world economy made it increasingly difficult to continue with this system of concealed social protection. Thus a process of shedding the concealed surplus labour began. The observed low output elasticity of employment hides the fact that it represents the sum of two effects:

(1)   a fairly high output elasticity of employment measured at constant intensity of employment per worker; and

(2)   a rise in the intensity of employment per worker due to a reduction of concealed unemployment in industries.

It is possible to argue that reforms leading to globalization should not be blamed for the slow growth of employment in industries. Industrial employment, measured at constant intensity of employment per worker, has increased quite rapidly but is hidden due to the effect of the reduction in concealed surplus labour in public sector industries. Once the process of shedding surplus labour is completed, industries will become more efficient. A proper method of protecting surplus industrial workers is to institute either a formal system of unemployment insurance or transitional public works programmes if the objective is to avoid the social cost of the employment consequence of globalization. Both these alternatives were hard to pursue in an environment of macroeconomic policies emphasizing fiscal retrenchment.

Globalization has aggravated the problem of poverty in China in another important way. In its nearly single-minded pursuit of FDI, China went for a concentration of public expenditure and investment in infrastructure in the richest provinces, which are the most attractive locations for investment projects. This has exacerbated the regional imbalance in growth and the neglect of the regions which have a concentration of poverty.

IV. Conclusions

This concluding section can now highlight some of the main findings of the comparative country experience on the relationship between macroeconomic policies and poverty. One very clear conclusion that emerges from the case studies is that economic growth is a necessary precondition of poverty reduction. Macroeconomic policies should therefore focus on ensuring an adequate rate of growth of the economy.

The accumulated country experience, however, makes the powerful point that growth by itself does not ensure poverty reduction. There are numerous reasons why a high rate of growth of per capita GDP/GNP may fail to improve the living standard of the poor. These factors can be lumped together as 'adverse distributional changes'. But they consist of distinct elements that are worth identifying in view of the different ways that macroeconomic policies affect them. First, the composition of growth is important. The economies of most LDCs with high incidence of poverty are characterized by very large rural sectors which have far greater than average incidence of poverty. It is therefore important for poverty alleviation that the overall growth in per capita GDP is consistent with a high growth of rural GDP. This in turn calls for a high growth of agricultural output, an avoidance of adverse terms of trade for agriculture and a growth in rural non-agricultural activities. Macroeconomic policies can powerfully affect all these outcomes.

Secondly, growth in per capita GDP, or its sectoral components, does not automatically mean an equivalent growth in per capita personal income or expenditure, variables that feature in poverty thresholds. Macroeconomic policies can bring about a redistribution between public and personal income and/or a redistribution between accumulation and consumption. There is a distinct conflict between the objectives of immediate poverty reduction and economic growth (future poverty reduction) that macroeconomic policies must arbitrate.

Thirdly, given the growth in per capita personal income/consumption, the reduction in poverty is a matter of the distribution of personal income/ consumption. While rapid growth in personal income can offset the adverse effect of a modest rise in inequality, a sharp increase in inequality can easily offset the positive effect of a high growth in personal income. Macro-economic policies – those relating to the composition of public expenditure and taxation, credit policy and trade regime – can have important effects on the distribution of personal income. But this is a matter that is also subject to strong influences from social institutions and incentive structures. Macro-economic policies by themselves are an inadequate instrument to direct the evolution of income distribution along a desirable path.

The extent to which macroeconomic policies can pursue the objective of growth, without aggravating inequality, is essentially an empirical question. Higher growth requires a higher rate of accumulation. Other things being equal, the pursuit of higher growth thus reduces the proportion of the increase in current output that can be allocated to immediate poverty reduction. To reduce the conflict between growth and the reduction of current poverty, macroeconomic policy must avoid a strategy of accumulation that subjects the poorer sectors and population groups to an involuntary generation of surplus, for example, a policy-induced adverse terms of trade on peasant agriculture.

Other conflicts between growth and the reduction of current poverty may be due to the fact that macroeconomic policies for greater efficiency can hurt the poor. An example is the reform of a foreign trade regime that keeps the price of food artificially low, thereby benefiting the poor – who in the given case are the net buyers of food – while reducing the efficiency of resource allocation in agriculture. In this case the reform of the trade regime should be combined with additional policies for the protection of the poor, for example, public works programmes for the augmentation of the income of the poor and/or targeted income subsidies to offset the reduction in real income due to the adjustment of food prices.

The case studies show that the effect on the poor of a given policy can be very dissimilar under different circumstances. Macroeconomic policies that lead to a rise in the price of food can hurt the poor in an agrarian society characterized by large inequalities in land and asset holding (the poor being the net buyers of food in this case). The same policies can have a favourable effect on the incomes of the poor in an agrarian society in which land and assets are equitably distributed by improving the terms of trade for the poor producers of food and agricultural goods in general. The design of macroeconomic policies should therefore take into account the specific context.

Macroeconomic policies for price stability are generally conducive to poverty alleviation. In a period of rapid inflation it is very hard to protect the real living standards of the poor. It should, however, be noted that the pursuit of price stability should not be taken to such extreme limits that economic growth and targeted expenditure for the poor are adversely affected.

It is generally believed that macroeconomic stabilization is inconsistent with the protection of the poor. This is probably true for stabilization of the extreme kind that leads to a collapse of economic growth. It is, however, clear – as amply demonstrated by the Indonesian experience – that reasonably effective stabilization can be consistent with the protection of the poor. There are components of public expenditure that can be eliminated with little adverse effect on the poor. It should, however, be noted that the incidence of such components is usually limited. An extreme programme of stabilization goes beyond these options and adopts policies that hurt the poor. The success of Indonesian stabilization in avoiding an adverse effect on the poor was due to the avoidance of extreme stabilization. This was possible because the donors made it feasible for Indonesia to avoid a more extreme programme.

Integration with the globalizing world economy, pursued within a carefully planned framework of orderly transition to a structure of production that is consistent with resource endowment, should be of advantage to the poor in the long run. Policy makers should, however, be alert to the possibility of a short-run adverse impact of globalization on certain poverty groups. This is usually due to the inefficient initial structure of the economy which becomes unsustainable under the new 'rules of the game' in a globalizing world economy. An example is the observed low output elasticity of employment in manufacturing industries in the initial phase of otherwise successful integration with the world economy in countries which allowed a large concealed underemployment in (public) enterprises in the past. Careful compensatory action needs to be adopted in order to protect the incrementally unemployed work force in this case.

Notes

1. The experience in these ten countries have been documented in the country studies listed in the references. These country studies were prepared under the United Nations Development Programme/ILO project 'Regional Poverty Alleviation Programme for Asia and the Pacific (RAS/95/001)'. Individual country studies are referred to simply by naming the country (for example, 'the Bangladesh country study').

2. Nor is this chapter concerned with an analysis of the entire experience considered by the ten country studies. The terms of reference of these studies went beyond macroeconomic policies and included 'sectoral and targeted policies to benefit the poor and women'. More importantly, the country studies often went beyond the terms of reference and considered the entire range of poverty reduction policies. Indeed the ten studies differ considerably in scope. Some (for example, India) limit themselves exclusively to macroeconomic policies strictly and, in the opinion of the present author, narrowly defined. In several cases (for example, Bangladesh, the Philippines and Thailand) the studies discuss a broad range of policies for the alleviation of poverty. In some cases (for example, Malaysia, Indonesia and Nepal) the link between macroeconomic policies and poverty appears to have received inadequate focus.

3. See endnote 2 above.

4. For the definition and interpretation of these indices see the Annex to the China country study (Khan 1996).

5. The use of expenditure, instead of income, appears to provide a lower estimate of head count of poverty because household surveys show that at the threshold level expenditure typically exceeds income.

6. Statistical testing of the hypothesis of a slowdown in the rate of reduction of head count poverty is ambiguous. This is seen from the following fitted regressions:

$$RHCR = 64.19 - 8.53Z - 0.96T + 0.44ZT \qquad \text{Adjusted } R^2 = 0.83$$
$$\qquad\qquad\quad (-2.45) \qquad\quad (0.81)$$

$$UCHR = 53.59 - 8.57Z - 0.89T + 0.47ZT \qquad \text{Adjusted } R^2 = 0.90$$
$$\qquad\qquad\quad (-3.51) \qquad\quad (1.30)$$

based on the data shown in the paper, where

$RHCR$ = Rural head count ratio

$UCHR$ = Urban head count ratio

T = Time

Z = Dummy (=0 for years before 1983 and =1 since 1983).

and figures in parentheses are t values.

The positive coefficient for *ZT* shows that the point estimate of the rate of reduction in *HCR* since 1983 is lower than it is for years before 1983. Note, however, that the coefficient of *ZT* is not significant at any reasonable level for rural India and is significant only at a relatively low level for urban India.

7. As we have argued before, given the value of per capita expenditure, a rise in inequality due to an adverse shift of the Lorenz distribution must increase the head count ratio. This particular result is therefore not convincing. It is either an econometric quirk or due to the use of an inappropriate index of inequality.

8. Some of the questionable features of poverty measurements reported in the country study are as follows. In Samudram (1996), Table 6, overall head count ratios for 1989 and 1995 are higher than either the rural or the urban head count ratio which does not seem possible. The head count ratio is higher for population in some years and for households in other years with the range of the ratio of the two crossing the boundary of plausibility. Unfortunately, the country study does not explain these problems.

9. The study reports a fall in the Gini ratio for rural *household* income distribution and a sharp rise in inequality in urban *household* income distribution between 1977 and 1989. It then says that the Gini ratios for *per capita* income distribution in 1989 were as low as 0.23 and 0.26 for rural and urban areas respectively. If these latter estimates are right then Nepal's income distribution was so egalitarian by 1989 that there could not have been a significant rise over time. The author of the country study (Guru-Gharana, 1996) casts doubt on these estimates but does not provide any convincing alternative estimate.

10. One possible exception is the Philippines during 1985–88 when there was no rise in per capita real expenditure. Per capita real GDP, however, increased at a moderately high rate.

11. This is not analysed in the Bangladesh country study. The subject is controversial. See Khan 1990 for a statement of the case in favour of this argument.

12. The decline in the case of China is documented in the country study (Khan, 1996). The India country study (Tendulkar *et al.*, 1996) does not discuss this issue. Employment in Indian manufacturing industries increased at an annual rate of 3.9 per cent during the 1970s. During 1980–91, despite a significant acceleration in the rate of growth of the economy, the trend rate of growth in employment in manufacturing was not significantly different from zero (based on the data shown in World Bank 1995). In the Philippines the share of manufacturing industries in total employment declined a little during the period of globalization (1980–93).

References

Amjad, Rashid and A.R. Kemal (n.d.) 'Macroeconomic Policies and their Impact on Poverty Alleviation in Pakistan' (Manila: ILO/South-East Asia and the Pacific Multidisciplinary Advisory Team (SEAPAT)).

Balisacan, Arsenio (1996) 'Philippines: Policy Reforms and Poverty Alleviation.' ILO/SEAPAT, Manila.

Booth, Anne (1996) 'Poverty in Indonesia'. ILO/SEAPAT, Manila.

Guru-Gharana, Kishore Kumar (1996) 'Macroeconomic Policies and Poverty in Nepal.' ILO/South Asia Multidisciplinary Advisory Team (SAAT), New Delhi.

Khan, A.R. (1990) 'Poverty in Bangladesh: A Consequence of and a Constraint on Growth.' *The Bangladesh Development Studies* 18, 3 (September).

Khan, A.R. (1996) 'The Impact of Recent Macroeconomic and Sectoral Changes on the Poor and Women in China.' ILO/The East Asia Multidisciplinary Advisory Team (EASMAT), Bangkok.

Krongkaew, Medhi (1996) 'Macroeconomic Policies and Poverty: The Thai Experience'. ILO/EASMAT, Bangkok.

Mujeri, Mustafa *et al.* (1996) 'Poverty, Macroeconomic Policies and Gender Issues in Bangladesh'. ILO/(SAAT), New Delhi.

Raychaudhury, Bijoy (1996) 'Adapting Macro-economic, Sectoral and Targeted Policies to Benefit the Poor and Women: Study on Mongolia.' ILO/EASMAT, Bangkok.

Samudram, Muthi (1996) 'Macroeconomic Policies and Poverty: The Malaysian Experience.' ILO/EASMAT, Bangkok.

Tendulkar, Suresh *et al.* (1996) 'Macroeconomic Policies and Poverty in India, 1966–67 to 1993–94.' ILO/SAAT, New Delhi.

World Bank (1995) *World Tables 1995.* Baltimore and London: The Johns Hopkins University Press.

6 The Macroeconomic Context to Promote Social Development and Combat Poverty in Latin America and the Caribbean

Albert Berry[1]

I. Introduction

This chapter summarizes the evidence on income distribution trends and the factors behind them, including the market reforms put in place since 1975 in nearly all the countries of the region, and then attempts to identify the policy areas and instruments that would be most important in reducing poverty in light of these trends. An important relationship that is examined is that between macroeconomic policies and direct anti-poverty programmes.

The macroeconomic context must be taken into account in the design and implementation of poverty policies for several reasons. To begin with, poverty alleviation is one outcome of healthy growth, so the rate and pattern of growth are a major determinant of the size of the poverty challenge and the task left to be carried out by direct anti-poverty programmes. Up to a point, therefore, healthy growth and direct anti-poverty programmes are substitutes for each other. Second, however, the macro context and performance also determine where direct anti-poverty efforts need to be focused; even healthy growth creates strains and hurts some people at least in the short run, so policy should respond to such threats. Finally, there are certain dimensions of poverty in most Latin American countries which will not in the foreseeable future be resolved by economic growth, so these problems must be approached in a different and more direct way.

Though economic growth is in most cases essential to long-run poverty alleviation, the increase in productive, stable and increasingly well remunerated employment – the direct source of most poverty alleviation

– may or may not be closely correlated with growth. When labour displacing technological change is an important source of economic growth, the expansion of productive employment may be significantly less than that of output.[2] Links between growth and poverty reduction may occur primarily either through creation of productive employment or through wage increases at the lower end of the earnings spectrum. In 'labour surplus' economies whose large populations tend to 'flood' the labour market, the benefits of growth will mainly take the form of increased employment but may have little impact on the basic wage rate; after this 'surplus labour' condition has disappeared (that is, when the labour market tightens up) growth will pull the basic wage up while simultaneously expanding the level of employment.[3]

In this analysis of Latin America's post-1970 economic performance, we focus extensively on the distribution of income[4] and the rate of growth, since these two variables essentially determine the effects of economic performance on the rate of poverty alleviation, when poverty is defined by income level.[5] A highly unequal distribution of income means that the number of jobs paying somewhere close to the average income in the economy is low relative to the size of the labour force. Other indicators, such as the rate of open unemployment, the level of underemployment and job stability, are also relevant to social welfare, as are the various direct and indirect poverty redressal programmes.

The Latin American style or 'model' of development has involved a set of special characteristics which distinguish the region in varying degree both from the 'average' LDC and from the historical experience of North America, Japan and most of the countries of Europe. It is useful to have these in mind when considering policy options to relieve poverty:

1. The distribution of land as the process of structural change began was atypically unequal. That original inequality of land led to extreme income inequality both because it implied that the land/capital income was concentrated in a few families rather than distributed widely, but also because it limited the demand for labour and hence the level of productive employment. The initial inequality with roots in the distribution of land was then passed on from one stage of development to the next.

2. As growth shifted the fulcrum of the Latin American and the Caribbean (LAC) economies toward urban and non-agricultural activities, the creation of adequate employment opportunities came to depend less on how agriculture functioned and more on the non-agricultural sector. Though the modern or formal sector did create increasing levels

of productive employment over time, the path of development during the growth phase (prior to the crisis of the 1980s) was less labour intensive than in the economies of Southeast Asia and less labour intensive than it could have been.

3. Over time the urban informal sector became substantial, though its size may not be out of line with the level of development of these economies. The claim that over-urbanization was related to an undue expansion of this sector has frequently been made but is difficult to demonstrate, beyond the obvious point that with more labour-intensive agrarian systems the rural areas would have retained more workers; given the absence of such systems the distribution of labour between rural and urban areas may have been reasonably efficient.

4. Through a combination of lack of fiscal conservatism, high inflation and currency overvaluation, LAC countries frequently discouraged exports, encouraged overuse of imported inputs and suffered from stop-go cycles associated with periodic balance of payments crises. Still, most countries of the region have evolved away from their previously high dependence on primary exports to a greater focus on manufactures and some degree of service exports. On balance these exports have been less labour intensive than in the East Asian experience. In most countries, policy biases worked against such labour-intensive goods as garments, leather products and furniture.

II. Growth, Distribution and Poverty Effects of the Market-friendly Economic Reforms

The post-1970 economic evolution of Latin America breaks naturally into three phases, both for the region as a whole and, with some differences in dates, for most of the individual countries as well. The period of growth under the import substituting industrialization (ISI) strategy, which in some cases evolved substantially toward a 'mixed' strategy of fostering exports as well as import substitutes, continued into or through the 1970s;[6] it was followed by macroeconomic crisis, in most cases associated with the international debt crisis; and the third phase was the post-crisis one that brought a return of modest growth to the region as a whole.

The debt crisis provided the push to induce and/or oblige the region to jettison its import-substitution strategy for a more liberalized trading system and to adopt other elements of what is now a standard package of reforms to labour markets, financial markets and the public sector. Some countries (especially Colombia and Brazil) had already taken significant steps away from the traditional combination of protectionism and overvalued exchange rates and the resulting bias against trade. These approaches were qualitatively similar to the East Asian practice of encouraging exports while continuing to protect against imports. Chile went much further as the Pinochet regime introduced the most free-trade, free-market system in the region, including a real import liberalization bringing tariff rates down to 10 per cent by 1980; though they were raised somewhat in the mid-1980s, the average was back down to 15 per cent as the decade came to a close. Argentina had an important liberalization episode between 1976 and 1982, in which the average effective rate of protection fell from 158 per cent to 54 per cent.[7] In the second half of the 1980s most of the countries of the region initiated significant reforms, varying in detail and in timing, and having few if any close precedents in the developing (or the developed) world. The remaining countries followed suit in the early 1990s.

Labour and capital market reforms have also been widely undertaken as has public sector downsizing. Many aspects of the traditional set of labour practices and institutions have been weakened. In the area of financial markets the reforms have focused on increasing the share of the private sector at the expense of state institutions, and diminishing the extent of credit subsidization in favour of market-determined interest rates. Downsizing of the state has involved both the privatisation of parastatals and an attempt to cut back on employment and the wage bill in the more narrowly defined or 'core' part of the public sector.

By now, in short, the LAC countries are launched in the direction of a different, more outward-oriented and less interventionist economic model. This model shows signs of working well in some countries, but has been slower than hoped in bringing the region as a whole back to its former growth and has also either caused or coincided with a marked deterioration of income distribution. Unless growth accelerates quickly in the next few years (and in some countries even if it does), it will not provide an adequate antidote to poverty.

The Employment and Distribution Impacts of the Reforms

The employment and distributional impacts of the market-friendly economic reforms are especially important to the evolution of poverty incidence and the design of poverty policy in the LAC countries. Expectations have varied widely, especially with respect to the most-discussed component of the reforms, the liberalization of trade. Several bodies of research bear, in different ways, on this issue. Simple two (or perhaps three) factor trade models tend to suggest that trade liberalization should have a positive effect on labour demand and on income distribution, as long as labour is considered to be an abundant factor. But it is not obvious that the countries of Latin America are relatively labour abundant within the global context; in a world involving only them and the industrialized countries this would clearly be the case, but in the presence of huge low income countries which are mounting trade offensives, the picture becomes murky.

A set of country studies directed by Krueger[8] addressed one aspect of this issue; manufactured exports were found to be more labour intensive than domestically produced import substitutes in all cases except the Republic of Korea. For the nine countries excluding Korea (Brazil, Chile and Colombia were the LAC countries included) the average employment per dollar of value added was 49 per cent higher for the exports. The measurements were based on industry-wide average factor proportions and did not take account of the fact that in any given industry (at least at that time in the LAC countries) exports tended to come from the larger more capital-intensive firms; this created some degree of bias in favour of the conclusion reached. Note also the extensive evidence that import-substitute and export production is often carried out by the same firms.[9] The main implication of this research, however, is that the static effect of even a fairly large shift from import substituting to exporting sectors would produce only a quite modest total increase in the demand for labour. The main employment benefits from experiences such as those of the East Asian NICs came from the rapid growth of exports and of the economy as a whole.

The employment implications of mineral exports are, as is well known, very limited. Those from agriculture are less so but it is probable that the average labour content of agricultural exports is in many cases low and will get lower in future.

A number of observers have, however, expressed optimism with regard to impacts of outward orientation through an expanding agricultural sector, on the grounds that this sector has tended to be disfavoured by ISI policies. But here, as in manufacturing, liberalization has recently coincided with difficult times for important agricultural groups (for example in Colombia and Mexico); models which treated agriculture as homogenous in relation to trade policy were seriously over-simplified. Many of the newer agricultural exports appear to be produced in relatively capital-intensive ways (one factor in this is the inegalitarian agrarian structure), though some (for example flowers in Colombia) are strong exceptions to this. For crops such as oil palm, coffee and cocoa, export pessimism seems largely justified as demand is inelastic, so even when their production is labour intensive this feature may not show up in expanding demand for labour. All this said, in fairness to the export-employment optimism view, it may be that the longer-run effects of outward orientation on employment will be substantially more favourable than the short-run ones. More detailed analysis of trends in the rural and overall labour markets of the region could help to identify such trends without waiting for the full history to unfold.

Based on factor proportions arguments it would seem unlikely that trade policy has had a major direct impact on income distribution (that is, an impact independent of that occurring through its impact on growth), judging from the modest size of the trading sectors in relation to the economy and the fact that many exports are not very labour intensive. It is nevertheless important to encourage labour-intensive exports and import substitutes through the selection of policy instruments, but it appears unrealistic to expect this to be the normal outcome. For most LAC countries comparative advantage is likely to be more in middle- and upper-skill areas.

The ultimate test of the employment/distribution impact of a more open system must of course come from the empirical record; though, as discussed below, it is hard to sort out which causal factors have been dominant, the record of widespread deterioration of income distribution around the time of the policy reforms is very worrisome. Exports have for the most part not been particularly labour intensive[10] and import liberalization seems usually to have been accompanied by worsening income distribution. The Chilean experience, plus less complete evidence from Argentina and Colombia, hints that export-fuelled growth may widen the earnings differentials between highly educated people and others. Rama's[11] analysis for Uruguay suggests a negative employment effect.

Accordingly, any optimism to the effect that policy reforms in this area would have positive distributional effects as well as accelerating growth should be shelved until there is some empirical evidence to support it. In place of that optimism should be a realistic recognition that the reforms may have a generalized negative effect on distribution in both the short and the medium run, and that carefully planned policy, especially in the areas of education/training, may be needed to counteract those effects. In particular, the hope that opening up of trade would fairly directly raise the relative incomes of the poorer agricultural workers on the grounds that the old protectionist system disfavoured them should be abandoned. It is increasingly clear that in such countries there is a major part of the agricultural sector which cannot compete easily with an onslaught of imports, and whose labour resources are unlikely to be quickly mobile to other sectors.[12]

Distribution Impacts: The Empirical Record[13]

Although considerable uncertainty still surrounds the precise evolution of income distribution during the crisis and adjustment periods in many of the countries of Latin America, and it is difficult to sort out the effects of policy changes from those of the crisis itself and of longer-run structural trends dating back to the pre-crisis years, analysis of the record is nevertheless quite revealing, as summarized in Table 6.1. There has been a clear preponderance of negative shifts in distribution around the time of the introduction of policy reforms, an impact not readily explicable by other obvious candidates such as stage of the cycle, rate of inflation and so on. Such shifts have occurred in Argentina, Chile, Colombia, the Dominican Republic, Ecuador, Mexico and Uruguay. In no case with data of satisfactory quality is there clear evidence of the opposite pattern. Costa Rica is a special and important case since distribution appears to have remained roughly constant during the relevant period.[14]

The three Southern Cone countries, Chile, Argentina and Uruguay, differ from the rest of the LAC nations in that all introduced significant liberalising economic reforms in the early or mid-1970s, before such efforts were undertaken elsewhere.[15] These cases thus offer a longer period during which possible impacts of the reforms might have been felt. Argentina and Chile suffered unusual worsening of income distribution, with high unemployment an aspect of the period in question in Chile, and falling labour incomes for the lower deciles the dominant feature in Argentina. Uruguay also appears to have suffered a major deterioration of distribution.

Chile

Chile's experience is the most important in terms of the lessons it may provide, since the policy experiments date well back in time and, despite some vacillation, their basic direction has been maintained subsequently. Since 1973, during which period there have been two severe recessions, the economy has undergone the most radical policy 'reforms' of any nation in the region. As of the late 1960s inequality was a little less severe than in most Latin American countries. What happened over the next couple of decades has been widely debated in the Chilean literature. Data on the distribution of consumption among Greater Santiago households imply one of the largest deteriorations ever recorded statistically in a developing country, occurring primarily between 1969 and 1978 but also over the decade which followed (Table 6.2). Since distribution at the end of the Allende years was almost certainly better than that of 1969 (to which the first data point refers), it would appear that the worsening was

Table 6.1 Summary of the Relationships Between Economic Reforms and Distribution (Countries for which data are available)

Country	Main Period of Worsening	Degree of Worsening, Main Period	Degree of Worsening to Present	Characteristics of Main Period of Worsening
Argentina (Greater Buenos Aires)	1976–1978	8 points followed by some easing	8 points	Liberalization, labour repression, no net growth
Chile (Greater Santiago)	1974–1976	7–9 points	7–9 points	Liberalization, labour repression, sharp recession
Uruguay (Montevideo)	1976–1979 or 1982–1984	9 points to 7 points	not available	Liberalization, labour repression, growth or recession, increased exports, transition towards democracy
Mexico	late 1980s	3–5 points	3–5 points	Liberalization, some labour reform, slow growth
Dominican Republic	In period 1984–1989	8 points	not available	May have coincided with adjustment
Colombia (Three major cities)	1990–1992	4–7 points	4–7 points	Liberalization, labour market reforms, moderate growth
Ecuador (Urban)	1989–1991	5 points	5 points	Liberalization, labour reform, slow growth
Costa Rica	1985–1987 (?)	0–4 points (?)	–1 to +3 points	Liberalization, mild labour reforms (?), moderate growth

Note: (i) Distribution worsening measured in percentage point increases of the Gini coefficient; (ii) depending on data availability, the Gini coefficient may refer to income earners, households ranked by household income, households ranked by per capita income or other distributions available. Completeness of income coverage varies with the case, as discussed in the text.

Table 6.2 The Quintile Distribution of Consumption Among Households in Greater Santiago, 1969, 1978 and 1988 (percent of total consumption)

Quintile	1969	1978	1988
1	7.6	5.2	4.4
2	11.8	9.3	8.2
3	15.6	13.6	12.6
4	20.6	21.0	20.0
5	44.5	51.0	54.9
Total	100.0	100.0	100.0

Source: Encuesta de Presupuestos Familiares, Instituto Nacional de Estatisticas.

dramatic over the first five post-Allende years. Poverty would have increased sharply since together with the worsening of inequality came a sharp drop in average income associated with the post-Allende economic recession. The figures of Table 6.2 have been criticized on the grounds that the implicit average consumption levels show virtually no change among the three points of time, suggesting a high degree of underreporting in 1988. Meanwhile, the other estimates of trends in distribution (of income rather than consumption) show less marked increases in inequality, but also enough inconsistency among themselves to imply that the true story remains something of a mystery, even if it is likely that some degree of deterioration occurred. Whatever the precise time path of poverty, a combination of make-work policies for low-income groups and targeted poverty redressal seems to have helped to limit the most serious poverty impacts of the negative income trends.

A number of the policy steps taken by the Pinochet regime would be expected to contribute to rising inequality. The extensive privatization, mainly carried out during the severe recession of 1972–74, led to acute concentration of ownership and the formation of large conglomerates.[18] Curtailment of agricultural credit to small farmers led to land concentration as well. Preferential financing to small entrepreneurs was cut back. Perhaps most important was the reform of the labour legislation, which relaxed worker dismissal regulations, suspended unions (until 1979, when they were again authorized to operate, but with many restrictions), greatly reduced the social security tax paid by the employers and reduced other non-wage costs as well. After the second crisis (1981–1983), wage indexation was abolished, replaced by a real wage 'floor', specified to be the real wage prevailing in 1979. Wealth and capital gains taxes were eliminated, profit tax rates substantially reduced, and public employment greatly cut back. Unemployment rates (for greater Santiago) rose to unprecedented levels, in the neighbourhood of 20–25 per cent (depending on the definition used). Only in 1989 did this rate fall below 10 per cent but after that the fall was continuous, to just 5 per cent in 1992.[19] The coverage of the minimum wage was restricted considerably and its level fell in the 1980s. Fringe benefits had been greatly reduced from their 1970 level and public expenditure per capita in health care, education and housing had also decreased.

One feature of the post-1975 period which probably contributed to increasing income inequality is an increase in the relative income of persons with university *vis-à-vis* those with less education. Robbins'[20] analysis indicates that the increase was not primarily the result of shifts in the composition of employment among industries, but rather a 'within sector' phenomenon. It may reflect a greater relative payoff to higher education under a more open economy or the dismantling of union power and changes in labour legislation in Chile.

Argentina

Until the early 1980s, Argentina had a long period of very slow growth – only a total of 4 per cent for the whole period between 1974 and 1988. Accompanying this macroeconomic failure was an unusually sudden and large increase in inequality: the Gini coefficient among income earners in greater Buenos Aires rose from about 0.36 over 1974–76 to somewhere within the range 0.41–0.46 from 1978 on.[21] It is plausible, given the prominence of wage goods among Argentina's exports, that an increase in the real exchange rate (through devaluation, for example) would, *ceteris paribus*, lead to a decrease in the real wage rate and a worsening of the distribution of income. And in fact this rate (Argentine currency per dollar) does bear a short-run inverse relationship, over 1970–87 at least, with both the real wage and the ratio of the real wage to per capita income.[22] But it is clear that the longer-run worsening of the income distribution cannot be fully explained by this link with the real exchange rate, since significant net worsening occurred over periods when there was no net increase in the real exchange rate.

Possibly, structural changes wrought by the change in trade policy worsened inequality; a liberalization episode (1976–82) led not only to a fall of 11 per cent in manufacturing output, but also to an employment reduction of 37 per cent, as output per worker rose by a striking 41 per cent.[23] Many small and medium firms exited, while many large firms cut employment, increased capital stock and improved technology. Changes in labour policy almost certainly played a significant role as well; the bulk of the increase in inequality occurred between 1976 and 1978, when the new military government fixed wages, repressed trade unions, eliminated collective bargaining and the right to strike and reformed the labour code to the detriment of workers.[24]

Though the tearing down of labour market institutions would not perhaps be an obvious source of worsening in countries with small 'protected' segments of the labour force and large unprotected ones, in relatively advanced and highly urbanized countries such as Chile and Argentina such an effect is quite plausible. It might be especially strong in an economy where large rents come from a high productivity mining sector (Chile) or agricultural sector (Argentina) and where the public sector and other service activities have been living off those rents. When the public sector shrinks and wages are more closely linked to the marginal product of labour in the private sector, one might expect wages to fall more than in many other types of economy.

Uruguay

In Uruguay protectionism and monetary mismanagement have prevailed over most of the post-war period, and average growth has been very slow. Economic stagnation and high inflation gradually engendered social and political instability in the 1960s, leading eventually to a military coup in 1973. The new economic team installed in 1974 introduced a programme of price stability, relaxed some of the existing controls on foreign trade and capital movements and liberalized labour markets.[25] Neither the union movement nor collective bargaining played any visible role for the next 10 years. Average growth over 1974–78 of about 4 per cent per year was led by export-oriented industrial activities and the investment rate rose sharply, but the government deficit remained high due to increased spending on the military and on public investment projects.

Most of the evidence for the 1970s, when the key policy changes were introduced, points to a substantial increase in inequality, including a sharp fall in wages and an apparently sharp widening in the earnings differentials across educational levels. Favaro and Bension[26] suggest that the opening of the economy, the reduction in the relative size of the government and the prohibition of labour union activity all contributed to increasing inequality. They believe that the behaviour of the labour market during previous decades was greatly influenced both by the unions and by the state's participation in the wage boards, in the determination of wage levels and as employer of a significant share of the labour force. These factors, they feel, weighed in favour of a more uniform wage structure than would have resulted from market forces, created disincentives for more skilled workers and led to considerable emigration by this group.

Since the military handed the reins back to the civil society in the early 1980s, the new union movement has proved about as militant as the old. A couple of years of fast recovery were once again followed by stagflation. Williamson[27] cites the lack of deregulation in the labour market, where firing was again almost impossible, payroll taxes heavy and trade unions still strong, as a possible source of the still sluggish growth performance.

Mexico

Mexico grew rapidly during the 1970s (second only to Brazil among major LAC countries), but then ran foul of its debt build-up and has achieved an average growth of only about 2 per cent since 1980, with the 1990s performance little better than that of the previous decade in spite of the major policy reforms of the late 1980s. Over the long period of rapid growth up to the debt crisis in the early 1980s, it appears that most wages rose substantially[28] and that inequality either fell, as argued by Hernández-Laos and Cordoba,[29] or stayed about constant. Since 1984, however, it has risen significantly. Alarcón and McKinley[30] report that the Gini coefficient of total household income (grouped data) rose from 0.430 in 1984 to 0.475 in 1992, most of the increase having occurred by 1989. The main winners were the top decile, whose share in total household distribution rose from 32.8 per cent in 1984 to 37.9 per cent in 1989.[31] What is unusual about the Mexican case is the dramatically increased concentration among wage and salary earners, whose Gini coefficient rose moderately from 0.419 in 1984 to 0.443 in 1989, then leapt to 0.519 in 1992,[32] probably one of the highest Gini coefficients of wage income observed anywhere. The variance within virtually all groups exploded over 1989–92,[33] but most especially at higher levels of education, in the border states, in urban areas, in export manufacturing industries and, surprisingly, among union workers. While there was no increase in income variance among 'poor' workers, including those in domestic service, helpers and unskilled labourers in industry, street vendors and urban agricultural workers,[34] for the 'elite' occupations (such as professionals, managers and supervisors) at the other extreme the Theil L indexes of variance more than doubled. The group most clearly achieving a relative gain over the two periods was that with higher education.[35]

Colombia

Colombia and Ecuador are among the relative late-comers to the market-friendly policy package, pushing it vigorously only in the early 1990s. Since the late 1960s, Colombia's macroeconomic performance has also been among the best in the region, and the economy was least affected by the debt crisis and accompanying recession. This creditable performance, which dates from the late 1960s, has been based on generally good exchange rate management since the switch to a flexible rate in 1967, a trade regime offering incentives both for import substitutes and for exports and a relatively prudent fiscal and monetary policy, under which fiscal deficits never reached the unsustainable levels of a number of other LAC countries and monetary growth was accordingly more modest.

Colombia was perhaps the only Latin country to adopt the market-friendly policy package when not under severe pressure of circumstance to do so. Its adoption coincided with the sharp reversal of a previous (and perhaps unique) equalizing trend in the urban distribution of income between the early 1970s and the 1980s.[36] An important part of that earlier story was the unusually marked decline in earnings differentials across educational levels and between genders.[37] Inequality bottomed out in 1990, after which it has increased sharply; this reversal mainly reflects the increasing concentration of business income and coincided with both the main phase of import liberalization and with a significant labour market reform.[38]

Ecuador

Ecuador experienced rapid economic growth during the 1970s, when the country became an oil exporter. During the late 1970s, as those exports stagnated, growth was achieved at the cost of foreign borrowing, but as the external situation deteriorated, this growth strategy became unsustainable. Adjustment was pursued haltingly in the 1980s and the export quantum grew at a creditable 6.3 per cent per year between 1980 and 1993, but two natural disasters and a sharp decline in the terms of trade slowed economic growth. The implementation of structural adjustment policies from 1981 onwards was gradual, slow, selective and conflictive. A stable political consensus on economic policies was never reached, and social conflict resulted in frequent setbacks. In spite of its lacklustre performance, however, the country did not experience hyperinflation of over 100 per cent (though prices did rise by 60 per cent or more at the peak), a dramatic income decline, or violent social unrest, as in the cases of Peru, Bolivia and other countries of the region.

The implementation of structural adjustment speeded up and became more consistent from 1988 onwards. Although trade barriers were reduced from 1984 on, the most important step was adopted in 1990, when most import tariffs were reduced to somewhere within the range of 5 per cent to 30 per cent. Labour deregulation was pursued continuously during the period; real minimum wages declined and labour legislation was reformed to 'increase flexibility and eliminate rigidities unattractive to foreign investors'.[39] The reduction of the state apparatus was also pursued throughout the 1980s (except for a right-wing 'populist experience' between 1986 and 1988) and speeded up in the early 1990s. Public expenditure plunged dramatically from 21.6 per cent of GDP (current prices) in 1981 to 11 per cent in 1992.[40]

The evolution of functional income distribution[41] points strongly toward increases in inequality over 1980–84 and over 1987–91.[42] After 1980 the (paid) wage share of value added fell dramatically from about 30 per cent to less than 15 per cent. Between 1982 and 1992, the total wage bill declined by 43.4 per cent in real terms while net business income rose by 53 per cent. Urban household survey data available since 1987 also point to a sharp increase around 1990 in income concentration, both among earners and among households; the Gini coefficient among earners jumped from an average of 0.431 in 1988–90 to an average of 0.483 in 1992–93.[43] There was a severe deterioration for the poorest half of the population, exceeding 25 per cent for the bottom quintile, an unstable or slightly declining situation for the next 45 per cent, and a sharp improvement (of 25 per cent) for the richest 5 per cent.[44]

Costa Rica

On the evidence available to date, Costa Rica appears to be the only LAC country to undertake significant market-friendly reforms without suffering a large widening of income differentials – an increase in the Gini coefficient of say five percentage points or more. This nation brought a tradition of social and political stability to the trials of the 1980s, and came off a strong post-war economic performance in which average GDP growth exceeded 6 per cent over 1950–80. A good social service system gave it the highest life expectancy in Latin America, with the exception of Cuba, and the absence of an army allowed it to allocate more resources to civilian uses.

The second oil price hike, rising interest rates and the world recession brought a sharp 14 per cent decline in GDP over 1980–82, accompanied by a 23 per cent fall in income per capita and a 25 per cent cut in real wages. Over the next few years an adjustment programme was put in place, including tax increases, weakening of the power of unions (union strength had lain mainly in the public sector) privatization and new incentives for exports, especially non-traditional ones. It has been relatively successful in re-establishing a decent growth performance, about 4.5 per cent per year (through 1994) after returning to its pre-crisis GDP level in 1985. Policy changes were less extreme, more gradual and less erratic than in Chile. Real wages did not long remain low, as the indexing mechanism which linked nominal wage increases to past inflation was left in place with only mild modification so that when tightened monetary and fiscal policy brought inflation quickly to heel, real wages moved back to or near their previous peak in only three or four years.

Though some qualifications are necessitated by the uncertain quality of the Costa Rican data, the best guess at this time is that there was no significant, lasting negative impact of the post-1986 reforms on the level of inequality in Costa Rica.[45]

III. Lessons and Implications for Poverty Alleviation

Distribution has worsened significantly, if not dramatically, in most countries undertaking market-friendly economic reforms. The country experiences reviewed above suggest that the 'normal' observed increase in inequality accompanying reforms is 5–10 percentage points as measured by the Gini coefficient of primary income (Table 6.1). This increase is frequently associated with a jump in the share of the top decile, most of this accruing to the top 5 per cent or perhaps even the top 1 per cent (as in the cases of Colombia and Ecuador households) while most of the bottom deciles lose. In the three Colombian cities analysed by Berry and Tenjo, the ratio of the income of the top 5 per cent of households to the bottom decile rose from 13-fold to 20-fold, and the income share of the latter decile fell from 1.74 per cent to 1.45 per cent.[46] At a moderate GDP per capita growth rate of 2 per cent per year, it would require nearly 10 years of distribution-neutral growth to recover the 'lost ground' implicit in this drop in the income share of the bottom decile. If per capita income growth could be accelerated to, say, 5 per cent, the recovery period would be only four years. In Ecuador, where the percentage decline for the bottom decile was sharper (from 2.2 per cent in 1988–89 to 1.5 per cent in 1993),[47] nearly twenty years of distribution-neutral growth at 2 per cent per year per capita would be needed and about eight years at 5 per cent.

The possibility that the market-friendly economic reforms have caused the accentuation of inequality warrants serious concern. No definitive conclusions on the origins of the observed increases in inequality can be derived from the comparison of country experiences and the limited microeconomic evidence on the various elements of the reform package. We tentatively suggest that technological change, more open trade regimes, the dismantling of labour institutions and the 'socialization' of debts (whereby the state makes itself responsible for certain private debts which might otherwise threaten macroeconomic or financial stability) have all had negative impacts on distribution. The effect of the scaling down of the public sector (directly and via the privatization of public enterprise) is less likely to have been negative. Increasing foreign investment has also been proposed as a source of worsening (in Mexico, for example), but judgement should probably be reserved on this point also. Many questions remain with respect to how these various factors interact among themselves and/or complement one another, both in terms of their growth effects and their implications for income distribution.

Trade and labour market reforms have been consistent elements of the reform packages instituted in the LAC countries where distribution has worsened significantly. In each case it is easy to see mechanisms whereby their effects on distribution might be negative, and in each case there is at least some empirical evidence suggesting that those mechanisms are at work. It seems unlikely that the comparative advantage of the region lies in unskilled labour-intensive products and it appears that import liberalization shifts the price vector in favour of better-off families. Recent evidence contradicts the hope that agricultural workers would be significant beneficiaries. Meanwhile, labour market reforms appear to open the way for wider wage and salary differentials among individuals. A tentative guess would be that these two elements of reform packages may underlie most of the observed negative trends in distribution.

The 'socialization' of international and other debts in order to save teetering financial and other enterprises has doubtless had a significantly negative impact on distribution, as shown in the case of Chile by Meller.[48] This was, however, a crisis-response policy, less germane to our present concerns than the now ongoing financial liberalizations (assuming that such liberalizations do not henceforth lead to financial crises as they sometimes did during the 1970s and 1980s, as shown by Diaz-Alejandro, 1985). Solid evidence has yet to come in as to their distribution impacts, but there are plenty of reasons to suspect that these could be negative[49], and that the supporters of reform will here, as in the area of trade policy, prove to have been excessively optimistic.

The possible role of technological change in the increasing inequality observed is hard to assess since it is very difficult to get a quantitative reading of its speed and the extent to which it has been labour saving. Technology affects, through the shape of the demand curve(s) for labour, both the amount of productive employment and the distribution of income between labour and capital. For any given total capital stock in the economy, the demand for labour also depends on the distribution of capital, an outcome related to the fact that technology choice depends on the size of the productive unit, with smaller units typically being more labour intensive. When the bulk of the capital stock is in the hands of large firms while many small firms get by with meagre amounts of capital, total output is likely to be less than if capital were more equally distributed and the equilibrium wage is likely to be relatively low since it is determined by the firms which have little capital and hence low labour productivity. Given the generally significant level of technological change in the last couple of decades and the concentration of technological catching-up in the post-crisis period, it would not be surprising if this factor has played a significant role in the observed deterioration.

IV. Policy Responses

Some priority policy areas seem clear: education/training systems, clearly important in light of the danger that low-skilled persons are being left behind; small and medium enterprise policy, important given the major role this sector plays in the creation of productive employment; and poverty redressal, whether through better targeting or otherwise, in light of evidence that considerable social spending has not in the past been very efficiently carried out and the fact that under conditions of rapid economic change such systems must be unusually adept in order to do their job well. While the general importance of these measures may be easily accepted, the precise policy formula most likely to bear fruit in each of these areas is much less clear. Designing it has high priority. Better information and more analysis of the determinants of income distribution will be needed for policy to become more professional in this area.

Education and Training

There are both positive and negative reasons to put much weight on improving the distribution of education and human capital. On the positive side, it appears that the character and rapidity of technological change have raised the payoff to skills, or perhaps better put, have changed the set of skills on which the economic payoff is high and increased the advantages of training-for-flexibility and general training. On the negative side, there is evidence from several LAC countries (for example Mexico, Chile at times) that earnings differentials by level of education have widened in recent years, often in the wake of changed economic policies or greater outward orientation. Since unequal distribution of human capital is now perhaps the main single source of inequality in LAC countries, it is obviously important to avoid outcomes in which either earnings differentials by level of human capital become even wider or the distribution of that capital becomes even more unequal. The most straightforward way to avoid such outcomes is to diminish the inequality of such capital. In the context of most of the poorer LAC countries, this means ensuring that as few people as possible are stuck with low levels of education or poor quality education. In some countries, making sure that everyone completes primary school may be the highest priority aspect of this response; in others the quality of primary school, especially in rural and poorer urban areas, is central. Adult education may also be very important in some cases. The objective of such policy is to diminish the size of the lower tail of the income distribution when the factor underlying the low incomes of the people found there is their lack of human capital.

Technological Change

Technological change may have been a significant factor in the recent increases in inequality in LAC countries. And it is probable that the speed and character of technological change will directly and indirectly be a major, and perhaps the dominant, determinant of the evolution of productive employment and income distribution in the LAC countries over the coming decades. While bringing benefits in the form of growth, such change also holds the threat of increased income inequality. At present governments tend to have little understanding and even less access to policy instruments that could give them some direct control over the process and the effects of technological change. Support for small farms and for microenterprises and small and medium enterprises (SME), discussed in the next section, can influence these outcomes indirectly, since these units tend to choose less capital-intensive technologies than do larger ones. And one of the issues in the assessment of the relative merits of alternative trade policies is the way they affect the evolution of technology.

The relationship between technology and labour demand/income distribution involves at least three aspects:

(i)   the changing range of available technologies and the appropriate role of the LAC countries in building up their own capacity to develop and adapt new technology;
(ii) choice of technology and the problem of inappropriate technology resulting from distorted factor prices; and
(iii) the role of the size distribution of enterprises as a determinant of technology choice and factor proportions.

Technological change has long been suspect as a key factor in the inability of Latin America's growth to generate enough increase in the demand for labour to lead to an improvement in income distribution. The main argument was that technology developed in developed countries was not suited to the factor proportions of the region, and that it tended to be transferred with little adaptation. Tokman[50] suggests that the prevalence of foreign technology may have played a role in falling real wages of unskilled workers in a number of LAC countries, though others feel that this view is too pessimistic. The 'appropriate technology' question is an especially tricky one for LAC, since the region is less labour abundant than the Asian countries, so its comparative advantage in labour is less obvious. Technological change is essential but if it is either too fast[51] or of the wrong type, its distributional effects are likely to be negative and even its growth effects uncertain. It is this 'double-edged sword' character which makes the policy decisions around technology so tricky.[52] We are still searching for adequate inducement mechanisms to generate the 'right' rate. When well complemented by a high investment rate, a strong human capital formation policy and a strong SME technology policy, the risks associated with fast technological adoption may be reduced. It is likely that exchange rate and trade policies have impacts on the pattern (as well as the rate) of technology change, but these have not been well identified thus far. But logic dictates that Northern technology will sometimes be inappropriate. Empirically, about all that can be said so far is that if the extensive technological contact with the North over the post-war period as a whole has had negative effects on employment and distribution, these were not strong enough to produce a generalized worsening in the region prior to the crisis. It is possible that the transfer occurring after the crisis has played a role in the observed worsening of distribution in many of the more developed countries of the region, since the more liberalized trade and investment arrangements permit a freer flow of Northern technology.

Small and Medium Enterprises (SME)

Few informed observers doubt that SME has a major role to play in a healthy development process and that this role has been grievously neglected in the past. Neither macroeconomic nor microeconomic policies have taken this sector's needs and potential into account. The export and import competing potential of SME is an increasingly important issue as the LAC economies turn outward. In Colombia the share of manufactured exports coming from SME has risen significantly over the 1980s, for reasons still not established.[53] Although many SMEs face serious problems in breaking into export markets, these problems are now somewhat better understood and it is not unreasonable to believe that well-designed policies could appear in some LAC countries over the course of the next five years. However, though many SMEs can be significantly affected by macroeconomic, trade and exchange rate policy, in most countries the sector has virtually no voice in the making of such policy, and policy-makers typically know almost nothing about the sector and its needs. The increasing dominance of policy by macro specialists unfamiliar with the economics of major sectors of the economy (agriculture and SME come immediately to mind) has created the danger that the criteria for policy-making will be unduly simplistic.

The experience of many countries, including Japan and some of its Asian neighbours, illustrates the potential importance of linkages between efficient modern industry and smaller firms. Though the evidence is scanty from Latin America, it suggests that such mutually beneficial synergies are significantly less frequent, a situation attributed by some to the ISI history, the lack of competition in local markets and the daunting initial gap between the large and the small in productivity, technology and even culture. The contribution of effective linkages of this sort is likely to be more important in the open economy than in the closed one. Where it is the larger firms which do most of the exporting (as in Brazil, for example), export success may bring little productive employment in its wake unless smaller subcontractors are hooked into the process.

Labour Market Institutions and Policies

Labour market functioning may be particularly important to overall economic performance in situations of macroeconomic stress and of major structural or policy change requiring the shifting of labour sectors, decreases in labour costs or changes in relative wages. Just how much it matters and exactly how the outcomes are related to labour market functioning and to labour market policy is less clear. Labour resistance to mobility or to reduced wages may have different impacts according to what adjustments are needed to improve economic functioning. Sometimes, considerable shifting of output composition occurs with very little labour movement, as noted in the cases of Costa Rica[54] or Colombia.[55] Of particular importance to poverty issues is the extent to which wages will fall when not 'protected' by such institutions as the minimum wage and the welfare costs of job insecurity.

Among the labour market institutions under serious debate (and frequently attack) in the current labour market 'reform' processes are the level of job security built into the labour codes, the high level of non-wage costs, the mobility-reducing non-transferability of some pension plans/systems and the management of the minimum wage (including the way it is indexed for inflation). The appropriate role and structure of the unions and of union bargaining naturally lie behind these more specific concerns, with the distinction frequently made between public and private sector unions.

Given the inequalities so manifestly present in most LAC countries, the important potential role of unions as a defence of the worker is obvious, and their contribution along these lines may have been considerable. As in many other developing countries, however, the unions and much of the labour legislation have been criticized as protecting the interests of a labour elite at the expense of both the capitalist class and the rest of the workers, contributing to microeconomic inefficiency and macroeconomic instability and, of particular relevance here, pushing down the earnings of the poorer, unprotected workers by reducing labour demand in the formal sector of the economy.

The authors of the World Bank's 'Labour Markets in an Era of Adjustment' studies of the experiences in Argentina and Brazil conclude that the unions impeded adjustment and labour mobility, while the author of the Chile study concludes that they contributed to the painful nature of the recession and the ensuing high unemployment.[56] In Costa Rica the institutions remained more or less in place without apparent damage and in Bolivia were dismantled without apparent positive effect thus far.[57] Private sector unions in Costa Rica are relatively weak, especially since the collapse of the banana union after a major strike in the early 1980s. Labour legislation, however, is quite detailed and appears to be systematically implemented. An interesting hypothesis is that this combination played a role in Costa Rica's relatively successful passage through the 1980s crisis.

Less analysis has focused on the income distribution implications of labour legislation and union power. It has been widely noted that some of the more egalitarian countries of the developing world are found in East Asia where unions and labour legislation are less powerful than in LAC. Within Latin America, however, there appears to have been a positive association between equality and the strength of labour legislation and unions; Argentina had both the lowest level of inequality (prior to the late 1970s) and the strongest legislation/unions.

The traditionally strong barriers to firing in the medium and large private firms in most LAC countries and in the public sector were a natural outcome of labour's bargaining demands in a situation in which (i) there was no general unemployment insurance system to act as a safety net against the welfare losses associated with loss of job and (ii) because of labour market segmentation, the earnings associated with a 'protected' modern sector job were likely to be well above what one would expect to get in an alternative job. The widespread presence of severance payments developed as a partial substitute from the worker's perspective for the existence of a publicly funded unemployment insurance scheme. But it is clear that strong regulations against worker dismissal contribute to the reluctance of firms to expand employment, and lie behind some firms' deliberate rotation of workers after they have completed the probation period after which employment becomes permanent; such rotation may impede the accumulation of human capital. When actually applied with some rigour, these rules are seen to be particularly prejudicial to many SMEs, which are likely to need to vary their labour forces according to their market situations.[58] Riveros[59] concludes that Latin America got into a vicious circle of policies and pressures around labour issues and ended up with a highly inefficient and in many ways counter-productive system.[60]

Most countries have recently introduced or are introducing major labour market reforms. Though many of the criticisms levelled at the previous set of institutions are likely to be valid, at least up to a point, it must be noted that there is little persuasive empirical evidence to help guide the policy-maker as to how the reforms have affected or will affect performance. It is hard to sort out any growth effects from those of other factors at work at the same time, including the other components of the reform packages. And it has not been possible to demonstrate convincingly that they have led to raised 'productive mobility' of labour, reduced firms' reticence to hire or raised human capital accumulation. If they have had an impact on distribution, it has almost certainly been negative.

The impact of minimum wages on employment, wages and income distribution also remains controversial in the LAC countries, partly because enforcement is variable and not always well known, and partly because the effects are neither easily predictable nor detectable even when enforcement is systematic.

Riveros[61] has established that non-wage costs have been very high relative to wage costs in most countries of LAC (often in the range 60–80 per cent), much higher, for example than those observed in most Asian countries (more often 20–30 per cent or so). He believes that such non-wage benefits unrelated to productivity considerations may be dangerous to the success of export drives. Though there seems to have been little analysis of the degree to which the presence of such mandated costs raises total labour costs, it probably has some effect in this direction. It also clearly stretches out the time profile of expenditures on the labour whose product occurs at any given point of time (since some of these costs, for example the severance payment, accrue later); this might be of benefit to a young struggling firm, but it would also reduce the firm's flexibility to lower labour costs at a time of crisis.

Given the major dislocations in the labour market due to the crises and structural adjustment programmes, the value of effective labour adjustment support programmes has not been lost on the LAC governments. Some have initiated new schemes, some of them adaptations of systems in use in developed countries. They have shown reasonable promise and deserve to be retained as one instrument in the tool kit.[62] A number of LAC countries, including Brazil, Bolivia, Chile and Peru, have introduced emergency employment policies in response to the labour market crises of the 1970s and 1980s. They appear to have been effective for these emergency situations, can be implemented quickly and at low cost, and can be quite selective and hence help the poorest. Their impact is more on raising income of lower income families than on lowering unemployment; 70–90 per cent of the beneficiaries were women.[63] To avoid mismatches, it is important to take account of the characteristics of the persons to be helped and take this into account in the sort of jobs provided.

It is easy to conclude both from microeconomic theory and from observation of distortions and some of their direct costs that the reforms pursued have been and are important to the labour regulatory systems of many LAC countries. But research has not gone far in clarifying the details of a really good system or of how to proceed from an inferior to a better one. Chile has had the most complete reform; there the question is whether/how much the changes adopted contributed to the long and costly adjustment, whether they continue to have a negative impact on income distribution and whether they have contributed to the strong growth since the mid-1980s. Horton *et al.*[64] deduce from the comparison of the experiences of Bolivia and Costa Rica that the wholesale dismantling of labour institutions is neither necessary nor sufficient to economic success. But they suggest, and in this we concur, that strong unions are likely to be associated with labour market inefficiencies (though the causation may go in both directions). In East Asia strong growth and equity have been associated with weak unions.

Labour market regulation is a different story; some common instruments seem innocuous and basically positive, while others do not. There appears to be little serious evidence that minimum wages have been *per se* a cause of significant distortion, even when a system (for example that of Costa Rica) seems cumbersome and complicated; the experience of that country suggests that together with the benefits that minimum wages are expected to provide in the form of control of monopsonistic behaviour by employers, the institution probably helped the country through its macroeconomic crisis by providing reasonable stability of the wage relative to other prices. While the costs of job security regulations may be high, the benefits may also be significant (although less evidence is available on this). However, it is clear that the criticism of this institution has some substance.

V. Summary and Conclusions

The macroeconomic context must be taken into account in the design and implementation of poverty policies, partly because that context is a major determinant of the size of the poverty challenge (healthy equitable growth can by itself reduce poverty considerably) and partly because it defines where direct anti-poverty efforts need to be focused. Though economic growth is in most cases essential to long-run poverty alleviation, it does not automatically lead to a satisfactory growth of productive, stable and increasingly well remunerated employment – the direct source of most poverty alleviation. In particular, when labour displacing technological change is an important source of growth, the expansion of productive employment may be significantly less than that of output. Where operative, the link between growth and poverty reduction may occur primarily through creation of productive employment (especially when the labour market has an overabundance of low-skill workers and the task is just to get them employed) or through wage increases at the lower end of the earnings spectrum.

While the region's modest growth rate has provided some grounds for optimism, the frequency of increases in inequality around the time of the reforms is quite worrisome. The poverty challenge associated with the combination of modest growth and increased inequality is a serious one. In some cases other factors have no doubt been involved but only infrequently do they appear to explain the bulk of the increase in inequality. We tentatively suggest that technological change and economic downturns have played a role, along with more open trade regimes, the dismantling of labour institutions and the 'socialization' of debts. The effects of the scaling down of the public sector (directly and via the privatisation of public enterprise) and of increasing foreign investment are less clear.

Under the conditions described, it is urgent to achieve better combinations of growth and distribution than those of the last two decades. The experiences of Chile, Colombia and Costa Rica are perhaps the most interesting from the perspective of learning how to guide policy more effectively in the future. Costa Rica is one country which seems to have emerged from the reform process without a major deterioration of distribution. Colombia appears to have achieved the most significant pre-reform improvement in distribution, at least in the urban areas. And Chile undertook the reforms earliest, suffered high social costs thereafter, but eventually achieved a high growth path and also pioneered a number of policy experiments of relevance to other countries.

Growth rates may be expected to increase as more countries put the crisis and adjustment problems behind them, though the setbacks suffered to date carry the clear message that this cannot be taken for granted. Regional growth will likely settle somewhere between 4 per cent and 7 per cent per year, possibly not far from the middle of this range,[65] that is about the same as before the crisis. Recovering the pre-crisis rate of poverty reduction will require a combination of growth somewhat above the lower limit of the range just cited, together with little if any deterioration in the distribution of income. The challenges to be met under the new more market-friendly model of development will be somewhat different from those of the earlier ISI phase of development, and countries which do not learn to deal effectively with them may on balance be losers from the policy shift.

Notes

1. This chapter was written in 1996 as part of the UNDP project 'Poverty Alleviation and Social Development'.
2. The growth vs. equity debate which peaked a couple of decades ago involved *inter alia* the idea that new modern technologies were more efficient than traditional ones and that, since they were characterized by either capital intensity or skill-intensity or both, their use would imply a relatively concentrated distribution of income at least at the outset. This growth-equity 'trade-off' issue was discussed widely before much evidence from the contemporary experience of the developing world came in. In the event, no such pessimistic conclusion could be drawn, since (i) smaller, more labour-intensive units were often as or more efficient than their larger, more capital-intensive counterparts and (ii) several of the very fastest growing economies, most notably Taiwan, were also characterized by high levels of equity.
3. The labour surplus 'model' was put forward by W. Arthur Lewis, 'Development with unlimited supplies of labour', *Manchester School of Economics and Social Studies* 22, 2 (1954) and further developed by John C.H. Fei and Gustav Ranis, *Development of the Labour Surplus Economy* (Homewood, Illinois: Irwin, 1964).

4. It is useful to distinguish between 'primary income' – that income received by persons or families as a result of their participation in economic activity, whether as workers getting a wage, landowners getting rent or capital holders getting profits, and 'secondary income', which takes the form of transfers (gifts, pensions, etc.) from other people or the state. The figures used in most of the discussion are something of a mix between the two, but mainly reflect primary income.

5. Poverty can be measured in a variety of ways. The main alternative to the use of a measure of income (or consumption) involves focusing on the extent to which basic needs have been met.

6. Peru was an exception in pursuing a more outward looking strategy into the 1960s, but was less successful in relation to the goals of growth and equity – see Shane J. Hunt, 'Distribution, Growth and Economic Behaviour in Peru', in *Government and Economic Development*, ed. Gustav Ranis (New Haven: Yale University Press, 1971).

7. Enrique A. Gelbard, 'Changes in Industrial Structure and Performance Under Trade Liberalization: The Case of Argentina' (PhD diss., University of Toronto, 1990), p. 46.

8. See Anne O. Krueger, Hal B. Gary, Terry Monson, and Narongchai Akrasanee *Trade and Employment in the Developing Countries: 1, Individual Studies* (Chicago: University of Chicago Press, 1984).

9. See Carlos F. Díaz-Alejandro, 'Trade and the Import Control System in Colombia: Some Quantifiable Features', in *Essays on Industrialisation in Colombia*, ed. Albert Berry (Tempe, Arizona: Arizona State University Press, 1983) for Columbia; Timothy H. Gindling and Albert Berry, 'The Performance of the Labor Market During Recession and Structural Adjustment: Costa Rica in the 1980s', *World Development* 20, 11(November 1992) for Costa Rica.

10. A long-term trend toward capabilities to export manufactures beyond the region is noticeable – even in product lines involving fairly advanced stages of value added, skills and technology. See Simón Teitel, *Towards a New Development Strategy for Latin America* (Washington, DC: Interamerican Development Bank, 1992). These exports have two basic origins: the processing of agricultural and other raw materials (which accounts for the bulk of Chile's manufactured exports in recent years) and goods originally produced for the domestic market under the ISI policies, including intermediate products (steel, petrochemicals, metalworking products, industrial machinery, and so on) – this category currently being quite important in Brazil, Argentina, Mexico and Venezuela. Traditional labour-intensive products such as textiles, clothing and footwear are also important (especially for Colombia and several smaller countries of the region), though less so than at a similar point in the development of the NICs of East Asia.

11. Martín Rama, 'The labor market and trade reform in manufacturing', in *Essays of the Effects of Protectionism on a Small Country: The Case of Uruguay*, ed. Jaime de Melo and M. Connolly (The World Bank, 1994).

12. A significant feature of the 1984–89 period in Mexico was the contribution of a widening gap between urban and rural incomes to the overall increase in inequality, and of the sharp decline in income from agriculture and livestock as a share of rural income, Alarcón (1994): pp. 139, 148. In Colombia an unprecedented increase in the gap between urban and rural

incomes has appeared within the last two years, coincident with the process of liberalization.

13. This section draws on Albert Berry, 'The Effects of Stabilization and Adjustment on Poverty and Income Distribution: Aspects of the Latin American Experience', mimeo (Toronto, 1990) which presents background details and discussion.

14. Preliminary analysis for Jamaica indicates that expenditure distribution improved over 1991–93 as major trade liberalization was being initiated, so it may enter the categories of 'exceptions' as well. Several other countries have not undertaken the reform package far enough back in time to generate useful data by now, and for others the data are of too questionable quality.

15. As noted above, Brazil and Colombia had already taken serious steps to encourage exports by the late 1960s, but had not (at this time) undertaken an important liberalisation of imports, nor imposed changes on the institutions governing the labour and financial markets.

16. Over that period average private consumption per person fell by about 13 per cent and the share of the bottom quintile by 32%.

17. Meller reports an increase in poverty incidence from 17% in 1970 to 45% in 1985 with poverty lines not more than 6% apart. Patricio Meller, *Adjustment and equity in Chile* (OECD Development Centre, 1992): 23. This may somewhat exaggerate the trend. The high incidence of television sets (over 70%), refrigerators (49%), radios (83%) and bathrooms (74%) even in the lowest quintile throws some question on the 45% figure. Some of these items probably became much more prevalent due to the low prices which came with the import liberalization around 1980.

18. Meller (1992): 27.

19. Economic Commission for Latin America and the Caribbean, *Economic Survey of Latin America and the Caribbean: 1993* (Santiago, Chile: United Nations): 42.

20. Donald J. Robbins, 'Relative Wage Structure in Chile, 1957–1992: Changes in the Structure of Demand for Schooling', draft version (Harvard University, 1994).

21. Adriana Marshall, 'The Labour Market and Income Distribution in Argentina,' in *Poverty, Economic Reform, and Income Distribution in Latin America*, ed. Albert Berry (1998): Tables 4A and 4B.

22. Berry (1990): 31.

23. Gelbard, 'Changes in Industrial Structure' p. 54.

24. Cortés, Rosalía and Adriana Marshall, 'State Social Intervention and Labour Regulation: the case of the Argentine', *Cambridge Journal of Economics* 17, 4 (1993).

25. Steven G. Allen and Gaston J. Labadie, 'Labor Market Flexibility and Economic Performance in Uruguay and Chile.' Report to the Tinker Foundation, 1994: 10.

26. Edgardo Favaro and Alberto Bension, 'Uruguay,' in *The Political Economy of Poverty, Equity and Growth: Costa Rica and Uruguay*, ed. Simon Tottenberg (Johns Hopkins University Press, for the World Bank, 1993):276.

27. John Williamson, *Latin American Adjustment: How Much Has Happened?* (Washington: Institute for International Economics, 1990).

28. Peter Gregory, *The Myth of Market Failure: Employment and the Labor Market in Mexico* (Baltimore: Johns Hopkins University Press, 1986).

29. Enrique Hernández-Laos and Jorge Cordoba, *La distribución del ingreso en México* (México: Centro de Investigación para la Integración Social, 1982).
30. Diana Alarcón and Terry McKinley, 'Widening Wage Dispersion Under Structural Adjustment in Mexico,' paper presented at the symposium, 'El impacto del ajuste estructural en los mercados de trabajo y en la distribución del ingreso en America Latina', San Jose, Costa Rica, 1994.
31. Diana Alarcón, *Changes in the Distribution of Income in Mexico and Trade Liberalisation* (Tijuana, México: El Colegio de la Frontera Norte, 1994): 87.
32. Alarcón and McKinley (1994): Table 4.
33. *Ibid.,*: Table 3.
34. *Ibid.,*: 18.
35. *Ibid.,*: Table 6.
36. Juan Luis Londoño, 'Income Distribution in Colombia 1971–88: Basic Estimation,' report to the World Bank, 1989.
37. Jaime Tenjo, 'Evolución de los retornos a la inversión en educación 1976–89,' in *Educación, Mercado de Trabajo y Desarrollo en Colombia*, special issue of *Planeación y Desarrollo* (Bogotá: Departamento Nacional de Planeación, 1993).
38. The economy had earlier gone through a brief episode of liberalization (early 1980s), then a sharp reduction in openness followed by a gradual re-opening through the rest of the 1980s and the abrupt aperture of the early 1990s. Labour market reforms, oriented mainly towards reducing worker security and diminishing the cost to firms of firing workers, occurred mainly around 1990, though union power was already weakened by the recession of the early 1980s.
39. Alain de Janvry, Elisabeth Sadoulet and André Fargeix, *The Political Feasibility of Adjustment in Ecuador and Venezuela* (Paris: OECD, 1993): 79.
40. Carlos Larrea, 'Structural Adjustment, Income Distribution and Employment in Ecuador,' in *Poverty, Economic Reform, and Income Distribution in Latin America*, ed. Albert Berry (1998): Table 6.
41. The functional distribution of income refers to the division of income among the factors of production – land, labour and capital, or subfactors (for example categories of workers), rather than among families or individuals.
42. Larrea (1995): Table 9.
43. *Ibid.,*: Tables 10 and 11.
44. *Ibid.,*: Table 10.
45. Trejos and Sauma report Ginis of essentially the same magnitude in 1993 as in 1980. Juan Diego Trejos and Pablo Sauma, 'Pobreza y distribución del ingreso en el era del ajuste: Costa Rica 1980–1992,' paper presented at symposium, El Impacto del Ajuste Estructural en los Mercados de Trabajo y en la Distribución del Ingreso en America Latina, 1994, at San Jose, Costa Rica.
46. Albert Berry, Maria Teresa Mendez and Jaime Tenjo, 'Growth, Macroeconomic Stability and Employment Expansion in Latin America,' paper prepared under the ILO/UNDP project Economic Policy and Employment (Geneva: International Labour Office, 1994): Table 3B.
47. Based on calculations undertaken by Carlos Larrea as part of Larrea (1995).
48. Meller (1992).
49. The reforms tend to diminish the role of the institutions whose main role is to provide credit to the smaller firms, and may also tend to decrease pressure on

private and other banks to allocate loans in that direction. In many countries a significant share of the private part of the system is made up of banks which are part of large conglomerates and whose main function is to service the non-financial members of those conglomerates. Although there is also hope that, since the reforms discourage subsidization of credit, this may improve the access of smaller firms otherwise viewed with disfavour by the banks, the strength of this effect remains to be seen. Financial markets are notorious for their degree of oligopoly, making it very hard to judge the outcome of the reforms now under way.

50. Victor E. Tokman, 'Urban employment problems: research and policy in Latin America,' in *Fighting Urban Unemployment in Developing Countries*, ed. Bernard Salom (Paris: OECD Development Centre, 1989).
51. There is some danger of inducing overly capital-intensive technologies by either or both a low or negative interest rate or an overvalued exchange rate. Large firms have been the usual beneficiaries of low interest rates and of cheap rationed foreign exchange when the exchange rate is overvalued. The continuing very high level of income inequality in Brazil and other LAC countries, while it does not demonstrate that these phenomena have played a significant role, is consistent with that conclusion.
52. While the recent export performance testifies to the competitive potential of industries fostered under the old policy regime, Teitel (1992, 374) notes that a substantial technological discontinuity seems to have occurred in LAC around 1975–80; for the industrial applications required in the new fields, the learning embodied in the stock of human capital acquired during ISI is of limited use. He feels that to boost the region out of its current stagnation an enhanced role on the part of the public sector may be needed.
53. Albert Berry and José Escandón, 'Colombia's Small and Medium-size Enterprises and Their Support Systems,' Policy Research Working Paper 1401 (Washington, DC: World Bank, 1994).
54. Gindling and Berry, (1992).
55. Díaz-Alejandro, in Berry (ed.), *Essays on Industrialisation in Colombia* (1983).
56. Susan Horton, Ravi Kanbur and Dipak Mazumdar, *Labor Markets in an Era of Adjustment: An Overview* (Economic Development Institute, 1991): 39.
57. *Ibid*, 40.
58. Mariluz Cortés, Albert Berry and Ashfaq Ishaq, *Success in Small and Medium-scale Enterprises: The Evidence from Colombia* (Oxford: Oxford University Press, 1987) report that in a sample of SMEs firm-level employment showed much fluctuation over the histories of the firms.
59. Luis Riveros, 'Labor Markets, Economic Restructuring and Human Resource Development in Latin America', (Working Paper, 1992):19.
60. Panama and Peru were examples of very strict security regulations and labour market segmentation has been quite important. Job security legislation was earlier an important obstacle to mobility in Brazil but the creation in 1964 of a fund to provide severance pay eased the problem (Horton *et al.*, 1991, 40). In Bolivia (latter 1980s) job tenure was ended and job security reduced, and the government stepped out of the previously centralized bargaining. In Chile the public sector labour force was reduced by a third and regulations greatly simplified; that country now has a particularly liberal labour market regime.

61. Riveros (1992).
62. Experience in Mexico and Chile indicates that training courses of 2–3 months duration and costing about $600 per trainee can contribute to worker re-employment; greater success is expected when the programme is closely tied to the private sector, with intermittent periods of on-the-job training. See William Cline, *Facilitating Labor Adjustment in Latin America*, Working Paper (IDB, Economic and Social Development Department, 1992):17. Mexico's Labour Retraining Program began in 1984, enrolment peaking at 546,000 in 1984.
63. Tokman (1989): 168.
64. Horton *et al.* (1991):42.

References

Alarcón, Diana (1994) *Changes in the Distribution of Income in Mexico and Trade Liberalisation* (Tijuana, México: El Colegio de la Frontera Norte).

Alarcón, Diana and Terry McKinley (1994) 'Widening Wage Dispersion Under Structural Adjustment in Mexico'. Paper presented at the symposium, El impacto del ajuste estructural en los mercados de trabajo y en la distribución del ingreso en America Latina, San Jose, Costa Rica.

Allen, Steven G. and Gaston J. Labadie (1994) *Labor Market Flexibility and Economic Performance in Uruguay and Chile*. Report to the Tinker Foundation.

Berry, Albert (1990) 'The Effects of Stabilization and Adjustment on Poverty and Income Distribution: Aspects of the Latin American Experience' (Mimeo). (Toronto).

Berry, Albert and José Escandón (1994) 'Colombia's Small and Medium-size Enterprises and Their Support Systems', Policy Research Working Paper 1401 (Washington, DC: World Bank).

Berry, Albert, Maria Teresa Mendez and Jaime Tenjo (1994) 'Growth, Macro-economic Stability and Employment Expansion in Latin America'. Paper prepared under the ILO/UNDP project Economic Policy and Employment (Geneva, International Labour Office).

Cline, William (1992) *Facilitating Labor Adjustment in Latin America* (Working Paper). IDB, Economic and Social Development Department.

Cortés, Mariluz, Albert Berry and Ashfaq Ishaq (1987) *Success in Small and Medium-scale Enterprises: The Evidence from Colombia* (Oxford: Oxford University Press).

Cortés, Rosalía and Adriana Marshall (1993) 'State Social Intervention and Labour Regulation: The Case of the Argentine'. *Cambridge Journal of Economics* 17, 4.

De Janvry, Alain, Elisabeth Sadoulet and André Fargeix (1993) *The Political Feasibility of Adjustment in Ecuador and Venezuela* (Paris: OECD).

Díaz-Alejandro, Carlos F. (1983) 'Trade and the Import Control System in Colombia: Some Quantifiable Features'. In *Essays on Industrialization in Colombia*, ed. Albert Berry (Tempe, Arizona: Arizona State University Press).

Economic Commission for Latin America and the Caribbean (1993) *Economic Survey of Latin America and the Caribbean: 1993* (Santiago, Chile: United Nations).

Favaro, Edgardo, and Alberto Bension (1993) Uruguay. In *The Political Economy of Poverty, Equity and Growth: Costa Rica and Uruguay*, ed. Simon Tottenberg (Johns Hopkins University Press, for the World Bank).

Fei, John C.H. and Gustav Ranis (1964) *Development of the Labour Surplus Economy* (Homewood, Illinois: Irwin).

Ffrench-Davis, Ricardo (1992) 'Economic Development and Equity in Chile: Legacies and Challenges in the Return to Democracy'. Paper presented at conference, The New Europe and the New World (Latin America and Europe 1992, September, at Oxford University).

Gelbard, Enrique A. (1990) 'Changes in Industrial Structure and Performance Under Trade Liberalization: The Case of Argentina'. (Ph. D diss., University of Toronto).

Gindling, Timothy H., and Albert Berry (1992) 'The Performance of the Labor Market During Recession and Structural Adjustment: Costa Rica in the 1980s'. *World Development* 20, 11, (November).

Gregory, Peter (1986) *The Myth of Market Failure: Employment and the Labor Market in Mexico* (Baltimore: Johns Hopkins University Press).

Hernández-Laos, Enrique and Jorge Cordoba (1982) *La distribución del ingreso en México* (México: Centro de Investigación para la Integración Social).

Horton, Susan, Ravi Kanbur and Dipak Mazumdar (1991) *Labor Markets in an Era of Adjustment: An Overview*. Economic Development Institute.

Hunt, Shane J. (1971) 'Distribution, Growth and Economic Behaviour in Peru'. In *Government and Economic Development*, ed. Gustav Ranis (New Haven: Yale University Press).

Krueger, Anne O., Hal B. Gary, Terry Monson, and Narongchai Akrasanee (1984) *Trade and Employment in the Developing Countries: 1, individual studies* (Chicago: University of Chicago Press).

Larrea, Carlos (1998) 'Structural Adjustment, Income Distribution and Employment in Ecuador'. In *Poverty, Economic Reform, and Income Distribution in Latin America*, ed. Albert Berry (Boulder: Westview Press).

Lewis, W. Arthur (1954) 'Development with Unlimited Supplies of Labour'. *Manchester School of Economics and Social Studies* 22, 2.

Londoño, Juan Luis (1989) 'Income Distribution in Colombia 1971–88: Basic Estimation'. Report to the World Bank.

Marshall, Adriana (1998) 'The Labour Market and Income Distribution in Argentina'. In *Poverty, Economic Reform, and Income Distribution in Latin America*, ed. Albert Berry (Boulder: Westview Press).

Meller, Patricio (1992) *Adjustment and Equity in Chile*. OECD Development Centre.

Rama, Martín (1994) 'The Labor Market and Trade Reform in Manufacturing'. In *Essays of the Effects of Protectionism on a Small Country: The Case of Uruguay*, ed. Jaime de Melo and M. Connolly: The World Bank.

Riveros, Luis (1992) *Labor Markets, Economic Restructuring and Human Resource Development in Latin America* (Working Paper).

Robbins, Donald J. (1994) 'Relative Wage Structure in Chile, 1957–1992: Changes in the Structure of Demand for Schooling' (Draft Version) (Harvard University).

Tenjo, Jaime (1993) 'Evolución de los retornos a la inversión en educación 1976–89.' In *Educación, Mercado de Trabajo y Desarrollo en Colombia*, special issue of *Planeación y Desarrollo* (Bogotá: Departamento Nacional de Planeación).

Teitel, Simón (1992) *Towards a New Development Strategy for Latin America* (Washington, DC: Interamerican Development Bank).

Tokman, Victor E. (1989) 'Urban Employment Problems: Research and Policy in Latin America'. In *Fighting Urban Unemployment in Developing Countries*, ed. Bernard Salom (Paris: OECD Development Centre).

Trejos, Juan Diego and Pablo Sauma (1994) 'Pobreza y distribución del ingreso en el era del ajuste: Costa Rica 1980–1992'. Paper presented at symposium, El Impacto del Ajuste Estructural en los Mercados de Trabajo y en la Distribución del Ingreso en America Latina at San Jose, Costa Rica.

Williamson, John (1990) *Latin American Adjustment: How Much Has Happened?* (Washington: Institute for International Economics).

7 National Poverty-Reduction Strategies of Chile, Costa Rica and Mexico: Summary of Findings

Diana Alarcón

I. Introduction

This chapter summarizes findings with regard to macroeconomic policies and poverty reduction in three Latin American countries: Chile, Costa Rica and Mexico.[1] One of the central points of the chapter is that macroeconomic policies should be consistent with poverty-reduction programmes and this involves examining the inter-relations among three types of interventions: the basic strategy of development adopted by a country; the macroeconomic policies that it adopts – which often follow from its basic strategy – and the targeted programmes that are designed to deal directly with poverty.

A country's strategy of development and its associated macroeconomic policies can have as much impact on poverty as, if not more than, targeted interventions. For example, a country might engage in a long-term strategy of industrialization through protecting the domestic market and substituting for imports, or through opening up the economy and promoting exports. The policy it follows will have a substantial impact on the allocation of resources in the economy and the distribution of income and, therefore, on the extent of poverty. It is often assumed, for example, that liberalizing trade and devaluing the currency will benefit the poor through fostering the export of agricultural goods and employment-intensive manufactures.

The nature of macroeconomic policy, which is concerned with the management of economic activity at the aggregate and sectoral levels, can be influenced by a country's development strategy. Import-substitution industrialization is usually based, for instance, on turning the domestic terms of trade against agriculture. Overvaluing the currency is used to facilitate the import of intermediate and capital goods, but it penalizes exportables such as agricultural goods.

Macroeconomic policy affects not only the rate of growth of the economy but also the distribution of the benefits of growth across economic sectors and social groups. Its distributional effect depends, of course, on the initial conditions and structure of the economy. To return to our point above, devaluing the currency to promote exports could benefit the poor if the exporting sectors generate employment and income for them. But if, for instance, agricultural exports are grown on large landholdings and manufactured exports are produced by capital-intensive industrial firms, large landowners and industrialists might benefit at the expense of the poor.

While determining the basic direction of many macroeconomic policies, a country's strategy of development is often shaped in turn by the evolution of macroeconomic policies, which frequently are focused on the instabilities and imbalances that arise in the economy. Macro-economic policies maintain balance in any economy as well as influence the direction and character of its development. A major lesson of experience in Latin America, and elsewhere, is that if a country's basic development strategy and its associated macroeconomic policies constantly reproduce poverty, there is little that targeted interventions against poverty can achieve, except as short-term palliatives mitigating the worst aspects of deprivation.

Patterns of Development

Most of the remarks below with regard to Chile, Costa Rica and Mexico concentrate on a country's development strategy and its impact on poverty. Within this context, particular macroeconomic policies and poverty-reduction interventions are evaluated.

Although all three countries implemented policies of import-substitution industrialization during the post-war period, there are important differences in the degree of implementation and the timing of the re-orientation to a more open economy. See Table 7.1 for changes in their macroeconomic indicators from 1975 to 1993.

Since Costa Rica is a relatively small country, it is more reliant on external trade and thus has maintained a relatively open economy. Although it provided protection to domestic industrial producers, the revenue generated by the export of primary commodities provided a large part of its total income. What has been distinctive – and well known – about Costa Rica is that since the democratic revolution of 1948, the public sector has spent extensively on human development. As a consequence, the country ranks relatively high in terms of human development indicators. (Table 7.2).

Table 7.1 Macroeconomic Indicators

	Growth of GDP/Capita	Domestic Investment (% GDP)	Domestic Savings (% GDP)	Exports to GDP (%)	Annual Rate of Inflation (%)	Total External Debt (% GDP)	Debt Service/ Exports Ratio
			1975–1980				
Chile	5.77	19.45	17.42	24.26	82.47	52.38	14.50
Costa Rica	2.2	24.2	15.1	24.2	8.2	48.6	28.8
Mexico	4.03	23.18	21.05	11.01	21.36	28.70	36.79
			1981–1985				
Chile	-0.50	15.76	14.10	27.88	21.49	87.30	44.25
Costa Rica	-2.5	25.3	13.6	30.4	37.4	139.6	36.5
Mexico	-0.33	22.44	27.42	15.15	62.38	49.96	37.85
			1986–1993				
Chile	-5.42	24.47	27.46	33.86	18.38	71.72	17.73
Costa Rica	2.4	26.8	23.4	26.7	18.2	86.6	22.4
Mexico	-0.45	21.09	20.64	19.92	53.35	51.47	30.29

Source: World Bank Database 1995.

Table 7.2 Indicators of Human Development

	HDI Rank	HDI 1994	GDP/Capita PPP$ 1994	Life Expectancy at Birth 1994	Adult Literacy Rate (%) 1994
Chile	30	0.891	9,129	75.1	95.0
Costa Rica	33	0.889	5,919	76.6	94.7
Mexico	50	0.853	7,384	72.0	89.2

Source: Human Development Report 1997.

In the 1970s, Chile had a relatively high level of human development, based upon a comprehensive system of social security, operational since the 1920s. Like many other Latin American countries, Chile followed a development strategy of import substitution. But its pattern of development underwent an abrupt change of direction in the mid-1970s when a military government instituted a radical programme of reform that emphasized the rapid liberalization of trade and deregulation of the economy. Economic reform led to high social costs as the traditional system of social security was dismantled and employment and incomes drastically declined.

In 1986, Chile's economic recovery coincided with an increasing regulatory role of the government, and in the 1990s, a democratic regime implemented a more interventionist role in social policy. In evaluating the performance of Chile with regard to poverty reduction, it is useful to make the distinction between the military government that took power in 1973 and the democratic regime of the 1990s because of their differing sets of policies.

In Mexico, import substitution industrialization was very successful in generating rapid economic growth and substantial progress in human development. However, the discovery of large oil reserves at a time of high oil prices in the late 1970s led to an over-expansion of the economy largely financed with external credits. When oil prices decreased and international interest rates increased, growth in the economy became unsustainable. In 1982, in order to comply with its external obligations, the Mexican government adopted a radical stabilization programme and later initiated a more comprehensive programme of structural adjustment that included rapid trade liberalization and privatisation of state enterprises. These policies have been unable so far to restore the conditions for long-term growth in the economy and the social costs of reform have been large.

The Evolution of Poverty

With respect to the reduction of poverty, the record of the three countries has been mixed. Long periods of recession have naturally worsened poverty. Even during periods of growth, poverty has remained substantial.

The incidence of poverty in Costa Rica increased sharply during the years of recession in the early 1980s.[2] Poverty started to decrease when growth in the economy was restored, but controversy remains with respect to the impact of recovery on poverty reduction. Some studies report progress in the reduction of poverty – to a level much lower than that which prevailed in the early 1980s – while others contend that the incidence of poverty in 1992 was still higher than it had been in 1980. Most studies agree, however, that there was a substantial decline in rural poverty, particularly among producers of non-traditional agricultural products.

Poverty increased dramatically in Chile during the economic reforms of the 1970s and 1980s.[3] High and persistent unemployment and the deterioration of wages led to a severe decline in the standards of living of large segments of the population. A deterioration in the distribution of expenditures also adversely affected the poor. During military rule, targeted programmes to generate temporary employment and provide basic health services helped prevent a sharper deterioration in the standards of living of the extremely poor. But such strict targeting within the context of overall reduced government spending and economic recession worsened the quality and coverage of basic services and heightened the vulnerability of large segments of the population to economic fluctuations.

The resumption of rapid growth in the late 1980s led to a substantial decline in the incidence of both overall and extreme poverty – although the gains merely moved the country back to the lower levels of poverty that it had already achieved in the 1970s. In the 1990s, elected governments emphasized the need to enhance the complementarities between economic growth and poverty reduction programmes. Resources for social expenditures were increased and new programmes of poverty reduction were implemented to enlarge the group of beneficiaries beyond the extremely poor.

The evolution of poverty in Mexico during the period of adjustment of the 1980s and early 1990s remains a controversial topic. Most studies report an increase in the incidence of poverty during the period 1984–1994, which includes sub-periods of deep recession in the early 1980s and the resumption of moderate growth in the late 1980s.[4] Official estimates report a slight decrease of extreme poverty between 1989 and 1992 when the economy was growing. Despite these differences, one may safely argue that little occurred in Mexico, either in terms of more rapid growth or an improved distribution of income, that would lead to any significant decrease in poverty. By all accounts, poverty remained substantial throughout the period, and at best was roughly the same in 1994 as it was in 1984. Although data are not yet available to the author at the time of writing this chapter, poverty undoubtedly increased in the wake of the economic crisis of 1994.

Where economic growth has been substantial, poverty has been reduced. On this point, there is little controversy. What is most relevant for this discussion is the character of growth – namely, whether growth translates into increasing income and well-being for the poor.

II. Economic Growth and Poverty Reduction

For growth to substantially reduce poverty, it should be broad-based and of direct benefit to the poor. A pro-poor character of growth would imply that certain conditions are present.

Sectoral Growth

First, since the sectoral composition of growth directly affects the distribution of resources throughout the economy, sectors in which the poor are concentrated need to grow – either out of their own dynamics or through linkages with other growing sectors of the economy. Particularly important is the distribution of resources between rural and urban areas, since in many developing countries – and in Latin America also – poverty is concentrated in rural areas. Thus, creating conditions for the growth of agricultural and rural production is usually a crucial component of a strategy of poverty reduction.

By the 1990s, Costa Rica had successfully changed the composition of its output towards sectors that had a larger beneficial impact on the poor. Rapid growth of non-traditional agricultural exports helped decrease rural poverty. The rapid growth of tourism and manufactured exports also contributed to generate urban employment, especially for low-skilled workers.[5]

In Chile, growth in the economy has been based on relatively labour-intensive activities that have generated a substantial expansion of employment, particularly in manufacturing. Policies to promote the growth of exporting sectors placed special emphasis on the creation of backward and forward linkages to expand the multiplier effects throughout the economy and reach the poor.[6]

In the case of Mexico, the conditions for sustainable, broad-based growth have not yet been laid. The country has been heavily reliant on external capital, with little or no growth in agriculture and low employment creation in manufacturing. Thus any gains in reducing poverty have been limited or short-lived.

An important issue highlighted by these country experiences is that greater export orientation benefits the poor when it stimulates the creation of employment and income in sectors in which the poor earn their livelihood or in sectors with which their livelihood is connected.

Macroeconomic policies that promote greater export orientation, such as exchange rate policy, are likely to increase the income of the poor when export crops are produced on small-scale land units, as the case of Costa Rica illustrates, or when manufactured exports are relatively labour intensive, as in the case of Chile and, to some extent, the *maquiladora* sector in northern Mexico.

More generally, the poor are likely to benefit when exporting sectors are closely linked to the rest of the economy and are thus a source of demand and employment creation elsewhere. Among the three countries, only Chile adopted explicit policies to foster the inter-industry linkages of exporting sectors that could produce notable employment-multiplier effects. The liberalization of trade may have very small effects – or possibly even negative effects – on poverty reduction if exporting sectors are concentrated in relatively capital-intensive activities with few strong links with the rest of the economy – as seems to be the case with many of the sectors exporting manufactures in Mexico.

The Enabling Environment

For economic growth to contribute effectively to poverty reduction, a second condition that needs to exist is an enabling environment that enhances the economic opportunities of the poor, in the form of paid employment or self-employment. The greater the employment-intensity of growth, the more likely it is to benefit the poor. But more beneficial still is the expansion of the kind of jobs that the poor are most likely to fill. In Chile, poverty reduction was aided by the adoption of explicit policies to promote the growth of labour-intensive sectors. But the expansion of economic opportunities for the poor should encompass more than employment: it should also include increasing access to productive assets and an expansion of support services for the poor who are self-employed. In Costa Rica, investment in infrastructure and promotion of access to external markets for the export of traditional and non-traditional crops produced on small farms was an important factor in reducing rural poverty.

The experience of these countries and others in Latin America indicates that promoting access to productive assets is only part of the enabling environment. The other major part is helping increase the economic returns to those assets and this entails accompanying investments in physical infrastructure, such as rural roads and irrigation works, ready access to credit and extensive technical assistance to raise productivity levels in agriculture and other rural economic activities.

Human Capabilities

The third condition contributing to poverty reduction is the development of the basic human capabilities of the poor. This includes providing public services for health, education, nutrition and family planning. Through such public services, the poor are able to take advantage of expanding economic opportunities. The expansion of capabilities among the poor, in turn, creates opportunities for further development in the sense that it elicits new economic activities that can utilize the productive capabilities of the poor – much in the same way that the public provision of physical infrastructure opens up new investment opportunities for business by making transport, communication or utilities more readily available and cheaper.

Successful cases of poverty reduction have substantially reallocated resources to primary education and preventive health services. The improvement in overall human development in Chile and Costa Rica, even before the 1980s, was based on the long tradition of universal coverage of basic social services – dating back to the 1920s in the case of Chile and to the democratic revolution of 1948 in the case of Costa Rica. Universal coverage guarantees coverage of the poor. During the period of economic reform, total expenditures on health and education declined in both countries but the provision of basic services was maintained through the reallocation of resources to primary education and health. In Costa Rica there has been a continuous emphasis on the provision of universal programmes of basic health and education. Particularly in the area of health, Costa Rica has achieved virtually universal coverage with a fairly progressive distribution of expenditures that has benefited the poorest sectors. In the area of education, however, a recent evaluation of the distribution of resources by income class found that there is still a significant concentration of expenditures among higher income families. In Mexico, although there has been a recent change in priorities, expenditures on health and education remain largely biased towards higher education and curative health, with benefits accruing disproportionately to higher income groups.

One of the paradoxes of the process of reform in Chile was the continuous improvement of human development indicators during the military government despite the contraction of public expenditures. Such an improvement is attributable in part to the adoption of specific programmes of health and nutrition targeted to the extremely poor. The success of such targeted social programmes has also been due to the pre-existing universal coverage of programmes of basic services.

It should also be noted that despite progress made in the redistribution of resources to achieve full coverage – the kind of social services that benefit the poor – problems of regional inequalities in the coverage and quality of services remain. Poor regions are still at a disadvantage in all three countries. The provision of basic services is more difficult in rural areas, where the dispersion of the population in small, sometimes isolated, communities, requires a large commitment of resource. The quality of services has also varied across regions in all three countries. This problem was exacerbated in Chile during the military government because of the decentralization of basic services. Responsibilities for the provision of basic health and education were transferred to local governments without a corresponding increase in financial resources and managerial skills to administer the programmes. Large municipalities were able to generate enough resources to sustain and even improve the quality of basic services but the capacity of small municipalities, where the cost of providing social services is often higher than in large ones, was more restricted.

Decentralization to the local level may play a significant role in improving the management of basic services because local governments should be more accountable to their communities and have better knowledge about their particular needs. But for decentralization to be effective, adequate resources must become available at the local level in order to ensure quality standards. Unfortunately, high rates of coverage can mask poor quality of services at the local level.

External Conditions

The need for economic reforms in Latin America in the 1980s was brought about in part by the deterioration of the position of the region within the global economy. The sharp decline in the terms of trade that characterized the late 1970s, the slow growth of markets in industrialized countries and the financial burden imposed by a large external debt were factors leading to the adoption of harsh programmes of stabilization and structural adjustment. These programmes led to substantial changes in poverty.

The condition of the poor is not only determined by the nature of economic growth, broad- based investment in human development and expansion of economic opportunities, but also by external conditions and how countries try to insert themselves in the global economy.

This issue is well illustrated by the experience of Costa Rica, which suffered a sharp contraction of its economy in the early 1980s, but contrary to the experience of other countries, recovered relatively rapidly. One of the reasons was the firm stance that the government took with respect to its external debt, which included a non-confrontational moratorium on its commercial debt. Associated with the geopolitical role that Costa Rica played in the Central American conflict, the country also benefited from a continuous inflow of external assistance that eased its transition to a more open, less regulated economy.

The successful experience of Costa Rica highlights two issues, one concerning internal consistency of its policies and the other concerning external consistency. The first is concerned with consistency between macroeconomic restructuring and poverty reduction. This involves promoting those economic sectors in which the poor are concentrated or with which their livelihoods are connected, increasing investment in human development and expanding the access of the poor to productive assets. But the second form of consistency is between domestic economic restructuring and an enabling international environment. As the case of Mexico illustrates, a process of domestic restructuring is particularly difficult and the social costs high in countries with onerous financial commitments to foreign financial institutions or in which flows of external resources fluctuate dramatically on a short-term basis.

Income Distribution and Poverty

Traditionally, Latin American countries have been characterized by high levels of inequality in the distribution of income and wealth. Recent studies indicate that in the 1990s this region had the most unequal distribution of income of any region of the world.[7] In the three countries analysed in this chapter, income inequality has tended to increase during the process of adjustment.[8] The exception may be Costa Rica, where income distribution may have deteriorated only modestly.

The Latin American experience illustrates that even in some of the more successful cases of adjustment, which have led to a reduction in poverty, income distribution has deteriorated. This indicates that although the poor in those countries may have benefited from growth, the higher-income groups gained more. With a more equal distribution of income, economic growth would have been translated into a more substantial reduction in poverty.

Increasing inequality in the distribution of income in countries in which poverty declined – such as in Chile and Costa Rica – suggests that the two phenomena can move in opposite directions. It is possible for poverty to decline when income distribution worsens but economic growth has to be more rapid to compensate for this worsening or the regressive distribution of income must occur somewhere in the distribution other than in the lower end, where the poor are located. It is preferable, of course, that a pattern of growth be promoted that lowers income inequality, or at least maintains it at low levels.

The experience of even the most successful cases of poverty reduction in Latin America highlights the importance of adopting both objectives simultaneously: decreasing poverty and improving the distribution of income. Not only does increasing inequality reduce the efficiency of economic growth as a means to reduce poverty (resulting in a low output elasticity of poverty reduction),[9] but also it may impede economic growth. Recent evidence suggests that low inequality might in fact be conducive to growth.[10]

III. Poverty-reduction Programmes

The success of poverty-reduction programmes in the three countries has been mixed. Costa Rica has implemented several projects for poverty reduction targeted at specific groups, such as female heads of households, low-income schoolchildren and traditional-crop producers but it has also provided a broad base of support through comprehensive provision of social services such as health and education.

Poverty-reduction programmes in Chile have differed according to whether they were implemented during the period of the military government or afterwards. During most of the period of military government, strictly targeted programmes to restore minimum levels of employment, health and nutrition among the extremely poor proved effective in counteracting the most negative effects of recession but were accompanied by a significant increase in overall poverty and the deterioration of basic services for large segments of the population. With the return of democratic governments, resources for social expenditures increased. The new poverty reduction strategy was based on three factors: increasing the complementarities between economic growth and poverty reduction; promoting further decentralization of the provision of social services, mainly by increasing the participation of civil society organizations; and increasing the productivity of the poor through more investment in human capital, generating productive projects for the poor and improving their level of organization and participation in society. A major lesson of this experience is that targeted programmes have contributed to reducing poverty when they have incorporated the poor into growing sectors of the economy.

In Mexico, the implementation of large and expensive programmes of poverty reduction have not been able to counteract the adverse effects on poverty from economic fluctuations and the contraction of sectors from which the poor principally derive their incomes. The basic development strategy has appeared to work against poverty reduction.

In Latin America in general, programmes of poverty reduction have been most successful when they have been able to enhance economic opportunities of the poor within the context of broad-based growth of the economy. Targeted programmes are rarely successful on their own. The experiences of Chile and Costa Rica also illustrate that even under conditions of recession, the basis for future growth and poverty reduction can be protected through continuing investment in human capital and rural infrastructure.

Targeting

Any discussion of the effectiveness of poverty-reduction programmes must invariably address the pros and cons of targeted programmes versus programmes of universal coverage. The experience of the three countries discussed in this chapter – as well as of other countries, such as Malaysia and Indonesia, that have successfully reduced poverty – indicate that the most effective impact on poverty reduction takes place when poverty programmes (whether they are identified as such or not) start with a reallocation of resources towards providing universal coverage of basic social services: education, health, family planning and nutrition. Universal coverage of basic services can be growth-enhancing by expanding people's human capital and is guaranteed, by its very nature, to reach the poor. Even during the extreme economic conditions of Chile under the military government, the effectiveness of strictly targeted programmes for the poor was based, it has been argued, on the network of broad-based social services created in previous decades.

There are various ways of targeting the poor and debate continues on the most effective means to do so. A common method that is often successful is self-targeting. This method was used by the military government in Chile in low-wage public-works employment programmes that helped mitigate the high rates of unemployment during economic reforms. The wages paid in these programmes were so low that only extremely poor workers were attracted to them.

A second form of targeting involves 'demand-driven' programmes, in which the nature of activities are determined by the communities involved instead of the government. Mexico implemented this form of targeting by promoting community organizations that would define their own priorities and articulate their own demands for the provision of infrastructure and services. The problems associated with this form of targeting have raised concerns about the capacity of poor communities to voice their demands. Since the poorest segments of the population are usually the least organized and vocal, there tend to be large leakages of resources to the non-poor and substantial expenditures on non-priority programmes and projects.[11] More recent demand-driven programmes in Chile are attempting to resolve these problems by training community organizations in how to apply for resources and administer them properly. The evaluation of the success of these programmes is still pending.

A third form of targeting that has proved successful in such countries as Malaysia and Indonesia is the targeting of resources to economic groups and/or specific economic activities. An example in Costa Rica was the explicit support given to the production of non-traditional export crops, which had a significant impact on reducing rural poverty. In a similar way, the promotion of labour-intensive manufactures for exports in Chile contributed to increasing urban employment for the poor.

A fourth targeting method is the more traditional top-down determination by government of poor groups. The targeting of health and nutrition programmes to the extremely poor by the military government in Chile is an example of this approach. Obviously, much depends on the success in distinguishing the poor from the non-poor. By their very nature, these kinds of programmes are likely to be based on arbitrary decisions by the targeters. In the context of fiscal reductions, strict targeting adversely affected the quality and extent of coverage of basic services and augmented the vulnerability of large segments of the population.

The Chilean experience and the experiences of other countries indicate that social policy is most effective when it is implemented in three stages: starting with universal coverage of basic health and education, followed by targeting specific programmes to the remaining pockets of the poor, and concluding with an emphasis on boosting the quality and equitable distribution of basic services.

Poverty is multidimensional and so there is always a compelling argument for the design of multi-purpose programmes. However, these are often plagued by serious problems. As the experience of Mexico suggests, and also more recently that of Chile attests, there are frequent problems in co-ordinating diverse programmes. Trying to implement various programmes with multiple objectives often leads to the diversion of resources to non-priority programmes. Of serious concern are the large leakages to the non-poor, the frequent duplication of programmes and high administrative costs. Such programmes need to be continuously evaluated and adjusted to have a significant impact on poverty.

A sustainable impact on poverty often depends on whether programmes are designed to increase the economic opportunities of the poor or merely to transfer resources to them. The latter type of programme may temporarily alleviate poverty but is not likely to lead to a more permanent reduction in poverty and certainly cannot compensate for the lack of pro-poor growth. Even in periods of growth, income transfers cannot be regarded as a mechanism to enable the poor to participate in the growth process and benefit from it. More likely to do so are programmes, such as those in Costa Rica and Chile, that invested in the poor's human development and/or improved their enabling environment.

Notes

1. See Diana Alarcón, 'National Poverty Reduction Strategies: Case Study of Chile,' paper commissioned as part of the project Evaluation of Poverty Alleviation Programmes (New York: UNDP, 1997a); Diana Alarcón, 'National Poverty Reduction Strategies: Case Study of Costa Rica,' paper commissioned as part of the project Evaluation of Poverty Alleviation Programmes (New York: UNDP, 1997b); Diana Alarcón, 'Macroeconomic Policies and Poverty Reduction in Mexico,' paper commissioned as part of the project Evaluation of Poverty Alleviaiton Programmes (New York: UNDP, 1998). These are the three original case studies upon which this summary chapter is based.
2. See José A. Mejía and Rob Vos, 'Poverty in Latin America and the Caribbean: An Inventory, 1980–1995', Manuscript (Inter-American Institute for Social Development. Washington, DC: Interamerican Development Bank, 1997) and Samuel Morley and Carola Alvarez, *Poverty and Adjustment in Costa Rica*. Working Paper Series #123 (Washington, DC: Interamerican Development Bank, 1992).
3. See Dagmar Raczynski, 'Programs, Institutions and Resources: Chile,' in *Strategies to Combat Poverty in Latin America*, ed. Dagmar Raczynski (Washington DC: Interamerican Development Bank, 1995).
4. Diana Alarcón, *Changes in the Distribution of Income in Mexico and Trade Liberalization* (Tijuana, Mexico: El Colegio de la Frontera Norte, 1994).
5. See T.H. Gindling and Albert Berry, 1994. 'Costa Rica,' in *Labor Markets in an Era of Adjustment* Vol. 2 Case Studies, ed. Susan Horton, Ravi Kanbur and Dipak Mazumdar (Washington, DC: Economic Development Institute of the World Bank, 1994).
6. See Patricio Meller, 'Chilean Export Growth, 1970–90: An Assessment,' in *Manufacturing Exports in the Developing World, Problems and Possibilities*, ed. G. Helleiner (London: Routledge, 1995).
7. Londoño, Juan Luis and Miguel Székely, 'Sorpresas distributivas después de una década de reformas: América Latina en la década de 1990'. Paper presented at the seminar 'Latin America after a decade of reform: what are the next steps?' March 1997 Banco Interamericano de Desarrollo.
8. Although data restrictions do not allow for proper measurement of family income in Costa Rica available estimates show no improvement and perhaps a slight deterioration in the distribution of income.

9. The proportion by which poverty decreases when the economy grows is low.
10. See the chapter in this volume by Keith Griffin and Amy Ickowitz, 'The Distribution of Wealth and the Pace of Development'.
11. For evaluations of Mexico's poverty programme, see Cristina Laurell, 'La Cuestión Social Mexicana y el Viraje en la Política Social,' *Coyuntura*, no. 44/45 (1994) México, D.F.; Horcasistas Molinar, Juan and Jeffrey Weldon. 'Electoral Determinants and Consequences of National Solidarity,' in *Transforming State-Society Relations in Mexico: The National Solidarity Strategy*, ed. Wayne Cornelius, Ann Craig and Jonathan Fox (San Diego, USA: Center for US-Mexican Studies, 1995); Eduardo Zepeda, 'El Gasto Social en México: De la Establización Ortodoxa al Neoliberalismo Social,' *Frontera Norte*, no. 1 (1994), Número Especial. Tijuana, Mexico: El Colegio de la Frontera Norte; Eduardo Zepeda and David Castro, 'Solidaridad: Combatiendo la Pobreza Extreme?' Ponencia presentada en el Congreso Nacional de Ciencia Política. 25–28 September 1996, Mexico City.

References

Alarcón, Diana (1994) *Changes in the Distribution of Income in Mexico and Trade Liberalisation* (Tijuana, Mexico: El Colegio de la Frontera Norte).

Alarcón, Diana (1997a) 'National Poverty Reduction Strategies: Case Study of Chile'. Paper commissioned as part of the project 'Evaluation of Poverty Alleviation Programmes'. (New York: UNDP).

Alarcón, Diana (1997b) 'National Poverty Reduction Strategies: Case Study of Costa Rica'. Paper commissioned as part of the project 'Evaluation of Poverty Alleviation Programmes'. New York: UNDP.

Alarcón, Diana (1998) 'Macroeconomic Policies and Poverty Reduction in Mexico'. Paper commissioned as part of the project 'Evaluation of Poverty Alleviation Programmes'. New York: UNDP.

Gindling, T.H. and Albert Berry (1994) 'Costa Rica'. In Susan Horton, Ravi Kanbur and Dipak Mazumdar (eds). *Labor Markets in an Era of Adjustment*. Vol. 2, Case Studies. Washington, DC: Economic Development Institute of the World Bank.

Laurell, Cristina (1994) 'La Cuestión Social Mexicana y el Viraje en la Política Social'. *Coyuntura*, No. 44/45 México, D.F.

Londoño, Juan Luis and Miguel Székely, 'Sorpresas distributivas después de una decada de reformas: América Latina en la década de 1990'. Paper presented at the seminar 'Latin America after a decade of reform: What are the next steps?' March 1997 Banco Interamericano de Desarrollo.

Mejía, José A. and Rob Vos (1997) 'Poverty in Latin America and the Caribbean: An Inventory, 1980–1995'. Manuscript. Inter-American Institute for Social Development. Washington, DC: Interamerican Development Bank.

Meller, Patricio (1995) 'Chilean Export Growth, 1970–90: An Assessment'. In G. Helleiner (ed). *Manufacturing Exports in the Developing World, Problems and Possibilities*. London: Routledge.

Molinar, Horcasistas, Juan and Jeffrey Weldon (1995) 'Electoral Determinants and Consequences of National Solidarity'. In Wayne Cornelius, Ann Craig and Jonathan Fox (ed). (1995). *Transforming State-Society Relations in Mexico: The National Solidarity Strategy*. San Diego, USA: Center for US-Mexican Studies.

Morley, Samuel and Carola Alvarez (1992) *Poverty and Adjustment in Costa Rica*. Working Paper Series #123. Washington, DC: Interamerican Development Bank.

Raczynski, Dagmar (1995) 'Programs, Institutions and Resources: Chile'. In Dagmar Raczynski (ed). *Strategies to Combat Poverty in Latin America.* Washington DC: Interamerican Development Bank.

Zepeda, Eduardo (1994) 'El Gasto Social en México: De la Establización Ortodoxa al Neoliberalismo Social'. *Frontera Norte* No. 1, Número Especial. Tijuana, Mexico: El Colegio de la Frontera Norte.

Zepeda, Eduardo and David Castro (1996) 'Solidaridad: Combatiendo la Pobreza Extreme? Ponencia presentada en el Congreso Nacional de Ciencia Política'. 25–28 September 1996. Mexico City.

8 The Macroeconomic Implications of Focusing on Poverty Reduction

Terry McKinley

I. Introduction

The prevailing opinion in the economics profession is that macroeconomic policy should not be used for redistributive purposes. The 'macroeconomics of populism' is a term coined to refer to recurrent populist economic policies that advocate policies of growth and redistribution which do not respect fiscal and foreign exchange constraints and foster unsustainable deficit financing and high rates of inflation.[1] Ultimately, it is claimed, such policies end in failure, hurting most the intended beneficiaries of redistributive policies.

The implication is that macroeconomic policies should be focused most on maintaining internal and external balances and achieving output and price stability. Since it is supposed that de-stabilization of an economy affects the poor most adversely, the logic of economic reform dictates that when an economy is out of balance, stabilization policies take precedence in the short term, to be followed later by growth-stimulating policies, and only then after growth has resumed should the issue of the redistribution of the benefits of growth be directly addressed. Admittedly a stylization of the logic, this argument for policy sequencing nonetheless captures the essence of much of the thinking on economic reform and the interconnection between stabilization and structural adjustment.

There are several problems with this logic:

(1) it tends to reduce macroeconomic policies to short-term policies focused on stabilization of the economy,
(2) such policies of stabilization often undercut the long-term basis for economic growth,
(3) the logic ignores the fact that practically all macroeconomic policies have redistributive effects, and

(4)   the populist policies of redistribution that are criticized often were
      not targeted to the poor. The Latin American version of economic
      populism, for example, advanced policies – such as minimum wage
      legislation and social security programmes – that mainly benefited
      formal-sector workers and the middle class instead of the rural and
      urban poor.[2]

If macroeconomic policies have inevitable redistributive effects – such
as contributing to depress wages and raise profits or lower the returns to
productive investment and boost the returns to speculation – should they
be judged on this basis as well as on whether they foster stability and
efficiency of resource use? Some would argue, for example, that standard
policies of structural adjustment for developing countries have occasioned a number of regressive shifts in the distribution of income:

- from workers to owners of business,
- from petty producers and small businesspeople to owners of large
  businesses,
- from domestically owned businesses to foreign-owned enterprises, and
- from businesses engaged in productive activity to financial interests.[3]

The shortcomings of the conventional approach to macroeconomic
policies have several implications. One is that macroeconomic policy
needs to be refocused more on the long term, that is on the basic
determinants of long-term economic growth. A second implication is that
policies of stabilization need to be evaluated within the context of growth
policies. And third, growth policies need to be evaluated in terms of the
efficiency with which they promote human development – and, in
particular, reduce poverty. This chapter attempts to shift attention to the
search for redistributive policies that i) improve the access of the poor to
productive assets and opportunities and ii) are growth-enhancing or at
least growth-compatible. This also involves evaluating whether macroeconomic policies are supportive of such objectives. Turning the question
the other way around, the chapter is seeking to determine how shaping
the character of growth can serve to channel a disproportionate share of
resources to the poor, and what role macroeconomic policy can play in
this regard.

   This is not a novel endeavour. There has been progress already along a
number of the above directions. New Growth Theory has helped refocus
attention on the long-term determinants of growth. Criticism of
stabilization policies for their recession-inducing effects are already well

advanced. Most recently, new historical evidence is accumulating that certain forms of redistribution may stimulate growth rather than retard it. And among some circles, the character of growth as a contributor to poverty reduction is becoming as much a focus as the pace of growth. This has served to re-stimulate discussion on the basic issue of a country's development strategy as a determinant of how successful it is in reducing poverty. We start the discussion with a focus on macroeconomics itself.

II. What is Macroeconomics?

Macroeconomics is concerned with the theory of how income is determined, based on the level of utilization of resources and the rate of growth of these resources. Since the adoption of Keynesian policies in the post-war era, macroeconomics has become most preoccupied with fluctuations in the utilization of resources and in matching aggregate demand with aggregate supply to overcome these fluctuations. Only recently has it renewed its interest in the determinants of the growth of resources. In the short run, the objective of macroeconomic policy is to achieve full employment of resources with stable prices. In the long run, the objective broadens to include the increase in the total stock of resources and the efficiency with which this stock is used within the constraints imposed by the growth of population and the limited supply of natural resources.

Macroeconomics deals with economic aggregates provided by a system of national income and wealth accounting. Within this system, much can be revealed by examining:

(i)   the composition of both the resources and the output produced by those resources and
(ii) how resources are distributed among the population.

The structure of demand in an economy will determine what is produced and therefore largely condition what resources are used. In turn, the distribution of resources will determine how income is distributed and therefore how demand is structured. For our purposes, we are interested in whether the poor have access to productive resources and whether the goods and services that satisfy their needs are being produced in sufficient quantities and at affordable prices.

The system of national income and wealth accounting is necessarily incomplete, of course, being based as it is on economic valuation – on explicit or imputed prices. Much of what we value – such as the environment or human development itself – transcends a money metric. What this recognition implies is the subject of widening policy discussion and debate.

III. A Broader Context

What is implied for our present discussion – which seeks to trace out the macroeconomic implications of making poverty reduction a central concern of economic policy and development strategy – is that the objectives of macroeconomics have to be placed within the broader context of promoting sustainable human development.

Linking macroeconomic policy ultimately to goals of sustainable human development may appear at first to be an ill-advised endeavour. Macroeconomics does not, for example, even explicitly encompass a concern with equity, which has been delegated to the other major sub-division of economic theory, microeconomics. Traditionally, microeconomics has been preoccupied with how the behaviour of economic agents, transacting with one another through markets, has affected the efficiency with which resources are utilized. Microeconomics has recognized that equity is an objective separate from efficiency, but the desired degree of equity has been regarded as a normative judgement best left to the decisions of policymakers and the functionings of the political processes. Where it has made pronouncements is on how equity decisions can affect the degree of resource efficiency.

The major point to highlight is that for most recent conventional economic theory, equity considerations are treated as a subset of efficiency considerations. Moreover, a judgement is customarily made about what the optimal degree of equity is with respect to promoting efficiency. It is assumed that, at least beyond a certain point, there is a trade-off between equity and efficiency – and that some degree of inequality is preferable as a spur to increase efficiency of resource use.

IV. What Trade-off?

A re-evaluation is underway on this supposed trade-off, and it has focused on human capital. There is growing consensus that as a general rule human capital is the decisive productive input. Rough estimates of the contribution of the major forms of capital to economic growth have shown that human capital accounts for about two-thirds of the total, with natural and human-made capital together accounting for the other third.[4] Most importantly, there is growing evidence that the distribution of human capital makes a difference to growth. Most empirical studies have shown, for example, that the rates of return to primary education in developing countries exceed those to higher levels of education.

In a decisive shift of emphasis, some recent studies have suggested that the rapid economic growth of the East Asian 'miracle' economies has been powered in part by a relatively equal distribution of productive assets, notably of human capital.[5] An additional point is that a relatively equal distribution of productive assets, such as land, facilitates access to credit, and thus helps to boost investment.[6] With collateral from owning land, for example, the poor are better able to borrow for investment in their own health and education.

Corroborating evidence with regard to Latin America's economic performance since the 1970s suggests that its anaemic growth rates are related not so much to lack of accumulation of productive assets as to inequalities in their distribution, and of human capital in particular.[7] The over-emphasis on economic growth as the main determinant of poverty reduction has neglected the constraining role that inequality has played, both directly on achieving poverty reduction and indirectly through dampening growth itself.

If the historical relationship between equality and growth sketched above is generally true, this has far-reaching consequences – for growth theory and macroeconomics in general and for the relationship between growth and poverty reduction.

Much of New Growth Theory has given back-handed support to a human development perspective. In seeking to identify the determinants of technological progress (that is the increase in the efficiency with which resources are used), recent studies have highlighted the positive externalities associated with the accumulation of human capital. Most people possess an asset, namely their ability to labour, whose productive power can be augmented through experience, training and education. Not everyone, however, has access to natural capital or physical capital. In many countries land ownership remains concentrated, and in many industries large enterprises owned by a privileged few continue to dominate. By its very nature, however, human capital has more 'democratic' potential. The one potential asset, it is often argued, that the poor have in ready supply is their labour power.

V. Investment in the Poor

There is no argument that investment is the driving force of economic growth, whether it be investment, broadly speaking, that increases productive assets or enhances their efficiency. Where to direct investment is a question more germane to our immediate purposes. A central issue is whether investment in the poor – or giving the poor the opportunity to invest in themselves – is indeed growth-enhancing. If certain kinds of such investment were growth-enhancing, this would close one-half of the loop between sound macroeconomic policies and poverty-reduction policies.

This is obviously a question that requires more research. In the past, this has not been a major research area because of the presumption that diverting resources to the poor would tend to lower economic growth. Part of the problem has been the emphasis on providing the poor with transfers and safety nets, that is with maintaining their level of expenditures or raising it above a monetary-based poverty line.

Consequently, poverty-reduction efforts have often been associated with raising people's current level of consumption at the expense of investment and therefore of growth. Investments in the poor need not however confront the same type of trade-off. In many cases, the poor have suffered from development strategies that have subjected them to an involuntary generation of surplus to finance the accumulation of other people's productive assets – usually industrial assets. This has been the case when peasant agriculture has been compelled to bear adverse terms of trade with industry.[8]

Very closely related to the question of investment in the poor and by the poor is the issue of savings. Without an enlarged pool of domestic savings, it is difficult to sustain higher rates of domestic investment – unless there is increased reliance on foreign capital. Conventional development economists have often assumed that the most effective way to boost savings is to channel income to those who are relatively rich, since they have higher marginal propensities to save than low-income groups. But the savings rates of the poor often tend to be higher than is generally assumed, and moreover, a more equal distribution of assets that provides the poor with greater access to assets can have substantial positive effects on their savings rates. Higher savings rates are usually tied to greater investment opportunities, and such opportunities most commonly arise from the possession of assets that can be built up over time. Those without assets and little prospect of obtaining them understandably have a dampened incentive to save.

A renewed emphasis on providing the poor with productive assets has centred on human capital. New Growth Theory has provided contra-dictory support to such policies. It has endorsed the proposition that the accumulation of human capital tends to raise the level of efficiency in an economy, but this could well imply investment in more advanced forms of human capital. One strand of New Growth Theory has focused its attention, for example, on the positive externalities associated with Research and Development, which could imply a disproportionate demand for specialized, advanced skills usually obtained in tertiary educational institutions. Investing in the skills or productive assets of the poor would by implication tend to slow the rate of economic growth.

It is important to recognize that the choice of the form of investment can have opportunity costs. Building up one form of capital can imply, for instance, the depletion of other forms of capital. This becomes clearer when using a broad inventory of capital stock that includes human capital and natural capital as well as the traditional category of physical or human-made capital. Investing in certain forms of human-made capital (for example an extensive system of irrigation pumps) could well deplete natural capital (for example available water supplies). A capital-intensive manufacturing sector could contribute to high rates of unemployment and thereby the loss of manufacturing skills of an idled workforce. Investing disproportionately in higher education could lower the relative numbers of workers with the basic education needed for most industrial jobs.

Emphasizing such trade-offs helps to reassert the importance of human capital and natural capital, both of which have been neglected until recently in economic valuation. It also helps to illuminate how an economy is functioning below its production possibility frontier because of the idled capacity or inefficient capacity utilization of the productive assets that could be employed by the poor – their unskilled labour being the primary asset. But these are still economic calculations that weigh the desirability of poverty reduction on the scales of resource efficiency and growth.

VI. Human Development Efficiency

The question of whether an equitable distribution of productive assets – and in particular a distribution that favours the poor – can be efficiency-enhancing is a testable hypothesis within the conventional parameters of growth theory. If such an asset distribution were not as efficiency-enhancing as other more unequal distributions, then what would be the judgement? On a narrow economic rate-of-return basis, inequality would be preferable. However, on a broader human-development basis, an equitable distribution could well be optimal.

In order to address these issues, we attempt to close the other 'half of the loop' between growth and human development. In strictly economic terms, efficiency is gauged in terms of the magnitude of output of goods and services produced on the basis of a given application of inputs. From a human development perspective, however, this output is not an end in itself. The question then becomes whether these produced commodities enhance human well-being.

There is thus a second, broader sense of efficiency – call it 'human-development efficiency' if you will – that is concerned with how the production of goods and services is translated into human development. This perspective immediately raises questions about what is produced and for whom. Is diamond jewellery being produced, for instance, instead of milk and bread? Are the mass consumption needs of the poor being met, or the luxury demands of the rich? As a reflection of human-development efficiency, the basic level of human development, such as is measured by the Human Development Index or the Capability Poverty Measure, could be relatively high or low for the same aggregate level of output, such as the GNP per capita of a country. The implication is that for a given supply of national resources, more or less human development than average could be achieved.

What this also implies is that from a human development perspective, macroeconomic policy should be emphasizing the issue of the composition of output, not just whether output is high or low. In other words, the questions are: what is being produced and for whom is it being produced, and most importantly, is human development being advanced?

It has long been recognized that growth is not equivalent to development. In the 1970s, strategies of growth with equity were devised in recognition that rapid growth in many developing countries had failed to make any substantial dent in reducing unemployment and under-employment, inequality and poverty. It is now increasingly acknow-ledged that economic growth can occur alongside persistent shortfalls in people's health, nutritional status and educational attainment, pollution and degradation of their environment, and erosion of their vital social institutions.

For example, recent macroeconomic reforms that have been intended to stimulate growth have in fact widened the gap between the rich and the poor, strengthened the political structures and social relations that generate poverty in many developing countries, and intensified a downward spiral of increased poverty and heightened environmental degradation. The most vulnerable groups in society have been compelled to pursue unsustainable survival tactics based on the consumption of natural resources.[9] The poor have become trapped in a situation in which they are unable to employ their labour power either in rural or urban settings and therefore have had to intensify the depletion of environmental assets – such as cultivating marginally productive soils or clearing forest cover – just in order to survive. According to conventional criteria, some countries that have undertaken macroeconomic reforms have been successful, that is they have stabilized their economies and registered improvements in growth; but in the process, they have sacrificed both social equity and environmental integrity, and thereby have also undermined their prospects for long-term and sustainable economic growth.

It is difficult to provide a meaningful evaluation of growth as an end in itself, other than to assume naively that more is better than less – that a larger pile of commodities is preferable to a smaller pile. Of course, more is not always better than less; it depends on what is being produced and its effects on human well-being, the environment and social cohesion.

Some aspects of human development are not easily measurable in the standard money-metric terms. Non-monetary indicators are available, however, that can reflect the expansion of human capabilities. The Human Development Index contains, for instance, life expectancy and adult literacy. The Capability Poverty Measure contains the percentage of children under five years of age who are underweight. Other capability-focused indicators are the percentage of low-birth babies, children who are stunted or wasted, mortality rates and the incidence of diseases. Even net enrolment ratios, school completion rates and immunization rates are good proxies for reflecting capabilities.

Such human development indicators should be used – alongside indicators of the stock and quality of environmental resources – to supplement the usual macroeconomic indicators of growth of aggregate output and inflation. Some macroeconomic policies that stimulate growth and stabilize prices may not significantly advance human development or reduce capability poverty. Much will depend on the character of growth – on the composition of output and the kind of demand that it satisfies.

This proposal is not suggesting that standard macroeconomic indicators be replaced, or by implication that such a macro balance as that between aggregate demand and aggregate supply or between exports and imports be ignored in the name of achieving 'higher ends'. It is suggesting that a 'first-order' evaluation of the efficiency with which economic inputs are converted into outputs be supplemented with a 'second-order' evaluation of the efficiency with which the use of inputs and the production of outputs are translated into human development.

VII. Pro-poor Growth

When poverty is measured in income terms, there is in general a positive relationship between the rise in mean per capita income and the percentage of people lifted above an absolute poverty line. In some cases, growth may in fact be 'immiserising', implying that the absolute condition of the poor has worsened; or growth may simply 'bypass' the poor, whose condition remains largely unchanged. More likely to be a problem is that the mean per capita income of the poor may not be rising as much as the mean per capita income of the whole population. In this case, the poor would not be sharing equitably in the benefits of growth. This would be reflected in a low growth elasticity of poverty reduction – in which the percentage reduction in the headcount index, for instance, is lower than the percentage increase in average per capita income. In terms of the objective of poverty reduction, this would imply that growth is inefficient. A greater degree of inefficiency may well be registered if poverty is measured by lack of basic capabilities – such as is done by the Capability Poverty Measure – and not merely by lack of income.

Pakistan provides an example of how rapid growth and poverty reduction can move in opposite directions. During a period of rapid growth in the 1960s, the incidence of rural poverty and overall poverty increased, whereas during the slower growth between 1969 and 1977 poverty declined noticeably. Poverty increased in the 1960s despite rapid economic growth because of the increasing inequality in the distribution of landholdings; it decreased during the 1970s despite slower growth due in part to the dramatic rise in remittances from workers abroad.

As an earlier historical illustration, during the period of industrialization in the United States and United Kingdom in the nineteenth century, economic growth appeared to have little success in substantially reducing poverty. An examination of this period identified four factors that could have explained the lack of progress.[10] All of them could have relevance for the pattern of growth being undertaken by developing countries today. The first is that technical change that saved on unskilled labour led to a lag in earnings of the working poor. Secondly, the relative cost of living facing the poor markedly rose because of a lack of technical change in the production of food and housing, the two biggest expenditure items of the poor. Thirdly, industrialization undermined many cottage, or domestic, industries, on which poor households relied for supplemental income, especially from the labour of women, children and the elderly. Lastly, modern economic growth eroded 'non-market entitlements' or traditional support systems of the poor.

There is no argument that, all other things being equal, rapid economic growth more effectively reduces poverty than slow economic growth. What is at issue is the character of economic growth, which is determined in part by the structure of the economy and by government policy. A pattern of growth that is pro-poor would lead to a more-than-proportionate improvement in the condition of the poor – whether measured in terms of income or capabilities. A growth elasticity measure could help gauge this performance. Such a condition could imply that the growth of output is concentrated in the economic sectors in which the bulk of the poor labour and this output generates income for the factors of production possessed by the poor, for example unskilled labour, land growing food crops and capital for small trade and service enterprises. Alternatively, there could be strong linkages between the sectors where the poor are concentrated and the more dynamic sectors of the economy, or the poor could be drawn in large numbers into the latter. The sectoral concentration of economic growth has very distinct distributional effects. The composition of growth is itself a distributional issue.

Whether a pattern of growth is pro-poor or not follows from the fundamental nature of a country's development strategy and whether this is consistent with its initial endowment of resources. Is the development strategy, for example, one that is agriculture-led? This would imply a disproportionate allocation of resources to the agricultural sector. Or is it a development strategy based on import-substitution industrialization, in which resources are taken out of agriculture and channelled into industry producing for the domestic market? Or is the development strategy based on labour-intensive exports or on natural-resource-intensive exports? This would lead to a flow of resources into export sectors and out of sectors producing for the home market, or more generally into the production of tradable goods and out of non-tradable goods.

The experience of the People's Republic of China in being able to reduce poverty illustrates how important a country's basic development strategy can be. Because of the emphasis on rural development in the early 1980s, poverty rapidly declined. In this period the personal income of the rural population grew rapidly on the basis of a high rate of growth of agriculture and a marked improvement in agriculture's terms of trade. After 1985, China's development strategy moved away from an emphasis on rural development: the growth rate of agriculture declined, its terms of trade deteriorated, inequality increased significantly in both rural and urban areas and growth became concentrated in the relatively rich coastal and eastern provinces. As a consequence, by the early 1990s, the reduction in the proportion of the poor came to a halt, and the number of poor increased.

The experience of Nepal provides similar evidence of the link between a country's development strategy and its success in poverty reduction. Economic growth in Nepal during the period 1977–1992 (the period during which four poverty estimates were made) would have been sufficient to at least prevent a rise in the incidence of poverty, but it was concentrated in non-agricultural and non-rural activities. The growth of agriculture declined sharply during this period, which slowed the growth of rural incomes, and inequality rose in both rural and urban areas. As a result, the incidence of poverty did not decline, but steadily rose.

Just as important as the sectoral composition of growth is the issue of whether a country's development strategy leads to the construction of an enabling environment that will allow the poor to have access to resources and to use them efficiently. Do the rural poor, for example, have access to land and are they supported by an adequate infrastructure, for example water supply, electricity, roads? Lastly, are they empowered to take advantage of the resources available to them? This involves questions of basic empowerment, such as whether they are healthy, well-fed and educated, and of political participation, such as whether they have any influence on important economic and social decisions.

The countries in East Asia that have been the most successful in combining rapid growth with an equitable distribution of the benefits of growth have focused to some degree on improving the enabling environment of the poor and invested heavily in their basic education and health. Indonesia followed, for a while, an integrated policy of support to agricultural development that, combined with a relatively equal distribution of land, had a notable impact on the capacity of the poor to generate higher income levels. Malaysia followed a much more explicit policy of redistributing productive assets and creating new assets for the poor. The allocation of land to the poor was accompanied by technical support, credit, subsidized inputs and infrastructural development. In addition, rapid expansion of the educational system at the primary and secondary level contributed to generating a fairly equal distribution of earnings among workers.

VIII. The Structure of Incentives

Every economy is structured by a system of incentives, which is based on relative prices in different sectors, on the structure of markets and on the degree of access that people have to markets. What is produced, how much is produced and what methods of production are utilized are questions largely determined by the activities encouraged or discouraged by the prevailing set of incentives.[11]

The structure of incentives cannot simply be reduced to the set of relative prices; if the structure is distorted, it cannot be corrected by merely 'getting the prices right'. Equally important are barriers that exclude people from participating in some markets, or features that restrict their ease of access, or overt discrimination that bars them from market opportunities. In some cases, markets are missing, so that output is not explicitly valued and therefore the labour that produces it is not recognized; this is the case with much of the household labour of women.

Distortions in the structure of incentives or inadequacies of market mechanisms can lead to inefficiencies in the allocation of resources. They can lead to an artificially high capital intensity of industrial production, as resulted, for example, from the incentives built into the strategy of import-substitution industrialization. They can lead to an unusually rapid depletion of natural resources, especially when negative externalities are not internalized by private economic activity. They can also occasion under-investment in human capital because of the inability of private firms to reap all the benefits of financing more education and training of their employees. A country's basic development strategy can have a big impact on determining the structure of incentives in the economy and therefore on directing the allocation of resources.

The structure of incentives largely determines whether resources in the aggregate flow to the poor or away from them. If resources are flowing away from the poor, the first step in any strategy focused on poverty reduction is to attempt a restructuring of the set of incentives causing this outflow. The state has a role to play in altering the system of economic incentives – for the purposes of generating greater growth or reducing poverty. The customary programmes of 'structural adjustment' involve a fundamental re-alignment of the system of incentives. However, such programmes usually assume that the state has a distorting impact on economic incentives and that the allocation of resources is best determined by the unfettered play of market forces.

The most efficient allocation of resources, it is often argued, is brought about by a 'neutral' system of incentives, in which resources flow into sectors in accordance with relative rates of return, not in accordance with artificial price setting by the government that favours some sectors over others. The provocative question to pose is then whether a 'neutral' set of incentives is the most conducive to poverty reduction. The standard answer would be that such a structure of incentives leads to the most efficient allocation of resources, which stimulates the most rapid rate of economic growth and therefore the quickest reduction of poverty.

What this logic fails to address is that nothing guarantees that economic growth would not be accompanied by widening income inequality that could leave substantial numbers of poor people unaffected by the general trend of economic progress. Resources may well flow to the sectors where productive assets are concentrated – where capital intensity is high, where human capital is abundant, where technology is advanced and economic infrastructure well developed. This could well imply, for example, that resources would by-pass the agricultural sector, where in many countries the poor are concentrated.

The controversial point is whether resources should be deliberately directed to sectors where the poor are heavily concentrated and to factors of production – such as unskilled labour, small farms for food production and small-scale enterprises for trade and services – on which the poor are heavily reliant. Such a flow of resources would raise the returns to these factors of production, and the direction of this flow could be affected by macroeconomic policy.

The other half of the picture is making sure that the poor possess factors of production with which they can take advantage of economic growth. This would imply a redistribution of assets to the poor – such as through land reform, ample credit to small enterprises and adequate training and education. The sooner the redistribution the better: the poor would then be more likely to benefit from future growth. Also, with greater human capital, the poor would be able to move into the higher-productivity sectors of the economy.

If the structure of the economy is biased against sectors in which the poor are concentrated and against factors of production on which the poor rely, then directing state transfers to the poor will not substantially improve their condition. Relying on a social safety net would invariably become very expensive since the country's basic development strategy would continuously throw people on to the net. The character of economic growth in this case would regenerate poverty, not reduce it.

IX. The Global Economy

There is also a system of incentives built into the structure of the global economy. And this structure can cause resources to flow out of developing countries instead of into them. Factors that could cause such an outflow include declining terms of trade, the volatile reaction of speculative capital to economic setbacks, capital flight occasioned by higher rates of return in more developed economies, the increasing human-capital intensity and technology-intensity of global production and traded goods. Those countries with an advantage in accumulated productive assets – human capital, physical capital, infrastructure and technology – may attract further resources, and those countries with a distinct disadvantage may experience an outflow of even their own financial resources.

If the international structure of incentives turns dramatically against developing countries, and they are unable to re-align their domestic structure of incentives accordingly, they will begin to suffer unsustainable current account deficits – which was the case for many of them during the 1970s. The second oil shock and the contractionary macroeconomic policies of industrialized countries in the late 1970s, which depressed demand for developing-country exports, led quickly to their large trade deficits. These factors combined with a curtailment of credit and a sharp rise in its cost to severely restrict their growth prospects.[12]

In the 1990s, world trade outpaced world output, and there is general optimism, issuing in part from the Uruguay Round of trade talks, that developing countries can quickly develop their economies through greater integration with the world economy. The conventional development paradigm assumes that rapid economic growth based on integration with the global economy will be the principal force in reducing poverty in developing countries. This conventional wisdom is based on a number of key assumptions, a few of which are:

- the prior protectionist strategy in most countries, that of import substitution, was biased toward capital, toward the production of nontradables, and toward urban areas,
- the prior path of state-led development was inefficient,
- privatization, deregulation and liberalization will lead to the efficient functioning of markets and therefore to rapid growth, and
- export promotion will create a high rate of employment throughout the economy because it is intensive in the utilization of labour.

The picture may, however, be more mixed than the above scenario suggests. Not all international markets are open to developing countries – not all product markets, and certainly not labour markets. Moreover, much of the growth from greater integration with the global economy is expected in middle-income developing countries. Even if growth is stimulated in low-income countries, it may not easily translate into greater poverty reduction. Increased integration may in fact lead to higher relative returns to scarce and internationally tradable assets (for example physical capital, human capital and financial capital), which are held mainly by the non-poor, and lower the relative returns to abundant, non-tradable assets (for example, unskilled labour and land) held by the poor.[13]

In low-income developing countries, boosting income in the agricultural sector is critical to reducing both rural and urban poverty. But agricultural producers in these countries stand to gain little in the medium term from globalization and recent trade liberalization. It is difficult for them to respond to a changing pattern of incentives, either by becoming more competitive with imports or becoming more export-oriented, because of their low supply elasticity based on a lack of capital, credit, current inputs and land.

Even if agriculture in these countries were to become more competitive, it is unlikely to do so without becoming more technology- and capital-intensive and thus creating more surplus labour.[14] Since in low-income countries agriculture still employs the bulk of the labour force, these trends will have serious consequences for rural poverty and will also likely lead to a sharp rise in urban poverty through migration. The large influx of labour into the urban informal sector caused by the liberalization of agriculture will likely drive down income levels even if there is renewed growth in the relatively small sectors of the economy providing formal employment. This is a problem even for such large countries as India and China where industry has generated considerable employment in urban areas; the picture is bleaker for smaller low-income countries, especially in sub-Saharan Africa, where the industrial sector is small and stagnant.

The prevailing opinion is that rapid economic growth of developing countries is contingent on achieving openness to, and close integration with, the world economy. However, the experience of countries that are held up as models in this regard appears to run counter to such advice.[15] Based on the successes of Japan, the Republic of Korea, Taiwan Province, and later on of Malaysia and Indonesia, some analysts have argued that developing countries should seek 'strategic' rather than 'close' integration with the global economy. Closely related to this view and based on the same historical experience is the position that the state must play an active economic role and pursue a 'dynamic industrial policy' in order to achieve rapid growth.

All governments intervene to one degree or another in the operation of their country's industries; having an 'industrial policy' implies that state interventions are co-ordinated and coherent and are based on some strategic view of the direction forward for industrial development. In pursuit of such development, both Japan and the Republic of Korea maintained import barriers, subsidized exports and regulated foreign direct investment. They integrated with the global economy only to the extent that their interests of national economic growth and industrial development were served. In other words, for them the 'optimal' degree of integration was not close and indiscriminate, but selective and strategically determined.

X. Macroeconomic Stability

One of the chief points of controversy in the current debate between a people-centred strategy of development and a growth-centred strategy is the evaluation of policies of structural adjustment. This relates to the role of macroeconomic policies in helping to promote human development, but it also raises the larger question of what kind of development strategy should be followed. The policies of structural adjustment have become more clearly delineated as a development strategy, configured around the objective of rapid economic growth based on macroeconomic stability, close integration with the global economy and liberalization of the domestic economy.

Within this conventional strategy, macroeconomic policy has been focused on achieving stability, that is correcting the imbalances between public expenditures and public revenue, money supply and money demand, imports and exports, investment and savings, and, more generally, aggregate expenditures and Gross National Product. In all these cases, imbalance has been typified by the excess of the former over the latter and is assumed to adversely affect economic growth.

In an accounting sense, macroeconomics operates on the assumption that aggregate supply (GNP) equals aggregate demand (total expenditures on goods and services, including net expenditures on foreign goods and services). This can be expressed as follows: $GNP = E + (X - IM)$, where E signifies total domestic expenditures (for example on private and public consumption and on private and public investment), X signifies expenditures on exports and IM expenditures on imports.

The equation can be re-arranged to express the following: $(GNP - E) = (X - IM)$. Since these are accounting identities, a trade deficit, that is $(X - IM) < 0$, corresponds to an excess of total domestic expenditures over GNP, that is $(GNP - E) < 0$. These macro imbalances can be addressed in various ways. Domestic expenditures have to be reduced relative to output, but such reduction should not be indiscriminate and need not result in recession. Expenditure reductions need to be focused on tradable goods –

in order to reduce expenditures on imports and release goods and services for export. At the same time, resources need to be re-allocated to the production of tradable goods. But it is difficult to carry through such a re-allocation when aggregate demand for goods and services – including tradable goods and services – is depressed. This implies that structural adjustment should be carried out gradually and is most successful under conditions of economic growth, rather than recession. The excess of domestic expenditures over output need not be removed exclusively by reducing expenditures: it can also be removed by increasing output – namely, in the tradable goods sector.

XI. Restructuring through Growth

There are examples of countries that have adjusted their economies on the basis of maintaining a significantly positive rate of economic growth. Indonesia has been cited as one example, at least during the 1980s. Its success was based on emphasizing switching policies, such as substantial real depreciation of the exchange rate, which facilitated the transfer of resources from the production of non-tradable goods to tradable goods. But this transfer was made possible by 1) maintaining growth and 2) eliciting a strong supply response from agriculture and manufacturing, which was based on earlier investment in rural infrastructure and human capital.[16] The poor were able to benefit, it has been argued, in part because land was not very unequally distributed and opportunities for employment in labour-intensive manufacturing were available.

There is now much more acceptance of the approach that bases economic restructuring on expansionary macroeconomic policies. What needs to be further researched is whether these expansionary policies can be targeted more at the poor themselves. The objective would be to boost investment in infrastructure that directly benefits the poor and to facilitate investment by the poor in building up their own assets, for example land, human capital and microenterprises.

When a trade imbalance exists, it has to be financed – either by drawing down a country's own international savings, namely, its reserves of gold or accepted international currencies, or by borrowing from the rest of the world. Restructuring contributes to a country's ability to reduce an external imbalance by improving its access to foreign financing. By the early 1980s, many developing countries were running substantial trade deficits, had depleted their reserves, could not service the international debt that they had already incurred (due in large part to rising real interest rates) and could not obtain new international financing. They experienced a huge and abrupt swing from a net inflow of resources to a large net outflow. If real interest rates had not risen to historically high levels and if some means of financing their deficits had continued, a rapid and wrenching adjustment would not have been necessary. However, based principally on the advice of the multilateral financial institutions, international creditors made debt relief conditional on accepting orthodox policies of stabilization and structural adjustment.

Macroeconomic policy became narrowly identified with policies of stabilization and structural adjustment and with rectifying imbalances in the economy. The standard policy recommendation was to lower total domestic expenditures relative to output (*E* relative to *GNP*) and imports relative to exports (*IM* relative to *E*). The initial contractionary effects occasioned by cutbacks in public expenditures advocated by stabilization policies had alarmingly negative effects on the poor. The balance between *GNP* and *E* was not achieved in the short run because contraction resulted in insufficient aggregate demand, and *GNP* therefore fell precipitously, necessitating even further reductions in *E*. A similar story occurred with regard to the external imbalance between imports and exports. The lowering of barriers by policies of trade liberalization occasioned an influx of imports, and devaluation alone could not boost the competitiveness of domestic industries producing import substitutes nor dramatically improve the ability of domestic firms to export.

XII. Investment and Growth

The transfer of resources – from the public sector to the private sector or from the production of non-tradables to the production of tradables – takes time and does not respond to price changes alone. Time is required because investment is needed in new sectors and in new forms of capital; moreover, investment does not often rise significantly in periods of general economic contraction, nor even during periods of slow and uncertain growth.

Initial structural adjustment policies were based on the facile assumption that privatisation, deregulation and liberalization could bring about a fairly rapid re-allocation of resources without a significantly large or sustained loss of output. What in fact occurred in many developing countries was not 'structural adjustment through reallocation', as sketched out by standard modelling, but 'structural adjustment through contraction'.[17] Resources were drained out of previously unprofitable sectors, triggering a contraction of economic activity in general, but output stagnated in the potentially profitable sectors to which the resources were intended. The resulting economic contraction led to high unemployment and massive poverty. Macroeconomic policies served to exacerbate poverty not only in the short term, but also in the long term because of the adverse effects on the underlying determinants of growth.

This implies that macroeconomic policies for economic restructuring need to be re-oriented towards promoting growth. To do so, they need to be focused on investment, the driving force of growth. This implies abandoning the premise of the smooth re-allocation of pre-existing resources, many of which may be suited to the particular economic activities in which they are engaged but are not necessarily easily adaptable to the new activities being projected. More realistic is the re-allocation of resources through the medium of the growth of resources. Adjustment based on contraction of an economy leads to a fall in income, which in turn causes a fall in aggregate savings. Without domestic savings, investment cannot be financed and economic growth cannot be increased. Greater reliance on foreign savings is induced. However, foreign private savings are not likely to be attracted – nor is domestic savings likely to be generated – in the absence of investment opportunities.

Part of the predisposition against carrying out structural adjustment based on growth is the widely held belief that only a recession can effectively remove an external imbalance. But adjustment need not be based on reducing growth, but rather on stimulating growth in the tradable-goods sectors of the economy.

Also contributing to the predisposition against growth-induced adjustment is the inordinate fear of inflation. But again, the experience of developing countries with structural adjustment has demonstrated that moderate inflation – up to about 25 per cent a year – is not detrimental to economic growth.[18] Attempting to reduce inflation to zero would be counter-productive because it would strangle any prospects for growth. With a zero inflation rate, relative prices would have difficulty in adjusting to re-allocate resources.

Since inflation is often regarded as being due to an excess of money supply in relation to the output of goods and services, reducing output may only exacerbate the problem. Some would argue that recession is in fact an avoidable cost of stabilization.[19] If the greatest restriction in the economy is an external imbalance, structural adjustment may indeed precede stabilization, as happened in Brazil in the early 1980s. Inflation can be tolerated for a while as long as resources are being effectively transferred from the production of non-tradable goods to that of tradable goods. In fact, the devaluation of the exchange rate that would facilitate such a transfer may well increase inflation in the short term. Under such circumstances, it is better to tolerate moderate inflation to allow the adjustment of relative prices and re-allocation of resources. This also implies that the government should be able to run a modest fiscal deficit (allowing for an excess of aggregate demand over aggregate supply) if it can manage increased domestic borrowing and can use this financing for public investment that stimulates growth.[20] A similar logic would apply to financing increased investment by the poor.

XIII. The Role of the State

This approach implies that the state has a key role to play in mobilizing domestic savings and inducing investment to flow into certain activities. Many of the East Asian economies – such as the People's Republic of China, the Republic of Korea, and Taiwan (Province of China) – provide successful examples of this role.[21] The state's own expenditures should be shifted as much as possible towards investment in human, physical and natural capital. By building up human capital (through investment in education, training, health and nutrition) and physical infrastructure (through investment in rural roads, electricity, water supplies, irrigation works and sewerage facilities), the state can directly promote economic growth and indirectly stimulate it by fostering greater private investment. Under such conditions, public and private investment are complementary.

Beyond providing social and physical infrastructure, does the state have a role to play in directing investment into certain sectors or activities? This question relates to the debate on the advisability of industrial policy. A recent interpretation of the East Asian experience points, for example, to the primary importance of an investment boom, not an export boom, in such economies as the Republic of Korea and Taiwan. This investment boom was engineered through active intervention by the state, which utilized such policy instruments as credit subsidies, tax incentives and public investment to stimulate industrial growth. Such intervention was necessary because market prices could not reflect the future profitability that would ensue from a large-scale re-allocation of resources within an economy.[22]

The focus of this discussion is still on whether resources can be effectively channelled into industries with the greatest growth potential. For our present discussion, the more relevant question is whether the state should help redirect investment to the poor. In other words, how can macroeconomic policy be directed toward the central objective of poverty-reducing growth while maintaining vital balances in the economy, for example between savings and investment and between expenditures and output? The blockage of resources flowing to the poor could be attributable to a 'co-ordination failure', that is the inability of the market mechanism to reflect the future rates of return resulting from a major re-allocation of resources to the poor.

The first place that the state can start in re-allocating resources is in structuring its own expenditures. The focus should shift more to promoting investment for the poor and by the poor. There has been growing consensus on the core list of public investment projects, for example rural roads, health clinics, primary schools, water supplies and sanitation facilities. A larger and more controversial question is whether the state should attempt to alter the general structure of incentives in the economy in order to direct resources to the sectors where the poor are heavily concentrated.

XIV. Are Neutral Incentives Preferable?

The conventional development paradigm assumes that correcting the widespread bias against the production of tradable goods will do much to generate growth, provide employment and reduce poverty. A large part of the standard package of structural adjustment policies involves instituting a more 'neutral' set of incentives that will redress the imbalance between the production of tradables and the production of non-tradables. The prevailing assumption is that increased export orientation and production of tradables will help reduce poverty because 1) agriculture – where many of the poor are concentrated – produces tradables and 2) greater employment for the poor will be provided by a concentration on manufactured exports because their production is more labour-intensive than that of non-tradables. However, in many countries the poor are concentrated, not in export cash crops, but in subsistence food production; whether they would be able to shift their meagre resources into the production of cash crops is problematic. Also, most of the urban poor are not concentrated in formal-sector employment in manufacturing exports; they work predominantly in informal-sector activities – in small-scale manufacturing, services and trade. For the poor, the economic links between the urban formal sector and the urban informal sector are tenuous, as are the links between cash crop production and subsistence food production.

What this implies is that a 'neutral' set of incentives may not lead to a substantial reduction of poverty. The economic linkages to the sectors where the poor are concentrated need to be strengthened. To some degree, resources should be directly channelled to the poor who are engaged in subsistence food production and urban and rural informal-sector activities (where the goods and services being produced are in practice non-tradables). It is unrealistic to assume that growth that is concentrated in the exporting sectors of agriculture and manufacturing will substantially reduce poverty. Much will depend on the linkages between these growth sectors and the sectors in which the poor labour. The benefits of such growth for the poor are not likely to materialize without resources for investment being directed to the poor themselves (for example promoting primary education or providing ample credit to microenterprises). Part of a sound anti-poverty strategy involves channelling resources to the poor to help them build up their economic assets in the relatively low-productivity activities in which they may be engaged; the longer-term solution is to enhance their ability to move into the higher-productivity growth sectors of the economy.

Relying on establishing a 'neutral' set of incentives assumes that the functioning of market mechanisms, undistorted by governmental intervention, will substantially reduce poverty. However, there is reason to believe that macroeconomic policies should not remain 'neutral' in terms of how they affect the allocation of resources. The question of the redistribution of assets is in a sense independent of macroeconomic policy. Land reform is not *per se* a question of macroeconomic policy, for example. But if land reform is carried out in order to give the poor greater access to productive assets, macroeconomic policy should be reformulated to support such redistribution, for example by discouraging capital flight from agriculture or improving the terms of trade between agriculture and industry. Such actions would serve to raise the returns to the assets that have been redistributed. The larger question, and the more controversial one, is whether macroeconomic policy instruments – fiscal, monetary and exchange-rate reforms – should be utilized to alter the structure of incentives in the economy so as to re-direct the allocation of resources to the poor.

Notes

1. Rudiger Dornbusch and Sebastian Edwards, 'The Macroeconomics of Populism', in *The Macroeconomics of Populism in Latin America*, ed. Rudiger Dornbusch and Sebastian Edwards (Chicago: University of Chicago Press, 1991).
2. Eliana Cardoso and Ann Helwege, 'Populism, Profligacy, and Redistribution', in *The Macroeconomics of Populism in Latin America*, ed. Dornbusch and Edwards, 1991.
3. Prabhat Patnaik, 'A Note on the Redistributive Implications of Macroeconomic Policy', paper prepared for UNDP, Jawaharlal Nehru University (March 1997).

4. United Nations Development Programme (UNDP), *Human Development Report 1996* (Oxford University Press: New York, 1996): Ch 2.
5. Nancy Birdsall, David Ross and Richard Sabot, 'Inequality as a Constraint on Growth in Latin America, mimeo, Inter-American Development Bank, (December 1994); Nancy Birdsall, David Ross and Richard Sabot, 'Inequality and Growth Reconsidered: Lessons from East Asia', *The World Bank Economic Review* 9, 3 (September 1995); Klaus Deininger and Lyn Squire, 'New Ways of Looking at Old Issues: Inequality and Growth', 1998; Klaus Deininger and Lyn Squire, 'Does Inequality Matter? Re-examining the Links between Growth and Inequality', mimeo, World Bank (July 1996).
6. Deininger and Squire (1996, 1998).
7. Nancy Birdsall and Juan Luis Londoño, 'Asset Inequality Does Matter,' paper prepared for the session, 'Applied Economics in Action': The World Bank at the American Economic Association Meeting, 4–6 January, 1997 in New Orleans.
8. Azizur Rahman Khan, 'Macroeconomic Policies and Poverty: An Analysis of the Experience in Ten Asian Countries', synthesis paper prepared for the Regional Poverty Alleviation Programme for Asia and the Pacific, 1997, included in Chapter 5 of this volume.
9. David Reed and Fulai Sheng, 'Macroeconomic Policies, Poverty and the Environment', paper prepared for Social Development and Poverty Elimination Division, UNDP by the Macroeconomics Program Office of the World Wide Fund for Nature, May 1997 in Washington, DC.
10. Ben Polak and Jeffrey G. Williamson, 'Poverty, Policy, and Industrialization in the Past', in *Including the Poor*, ed. Michael Lipton and Jacques van der Gaag (Washington DC: World Bank, 1993).
11. Keith Griffin and Terry McKinley, *Implementing a Human Development Strategy* (London: Macmillan, 1994).
12. Georges Chapelier and Hamid Tabatabai, *Development and Adjustment: Stabilization, Structural Adjustment and UNDP Policy* (UNDP Policy Discussion Paper, BPPE/UNDP, New York, 1989).
13. David Woodward, 'Effects of Globalization and Liberalization on Poverty: Concepts and Issues', in *Globalization and Liberalization: Effects of International Economic Relations on Poverty* (Geneva: United Nations Conference on Trade and Development, 1996).
14. Woodward (1996).
15. Ajit Singh, 'Openness and the Market Friendly Approach to Development: Learning the Right Lessons from Development Experience', *World Development* 22, 12 (1994): 1811–23.
16. Frances Stewart, *Adjustment and Poverty: Options and Choices* (Routledge: New York, 1995).
17. Keith Griffin, 'Macroeconomic Reform and Employment: An Investment-Led Strategy of Structural Adjustment in Sub-Saharan Africa', Department of Economics Working Paper, University of California, Riverside (October 1996), included in Chapter 2 of this volume.
18. I.M.D. Little, Richard Cooper, W. Max Corden and Sarath Rajapatirana, *Boom, Crisis, and Adjustment: The Macroeconomic Experience of Developing Countries* (New York: Oxford University Press, 1993).

19. Joseph Ramos, 'Macroeconomic Equilibria and Development', in *Development from Within: Towards a Neostructuralist Approach for Latin America*, ed. Osvaldo Sunkel (Boulder: Lynne Rienner Publishers, 1993).
20. Griffin (1996).
21. Dani Rodrik, 'Getting Interventions Right: How South Korea and Taiwan Grew Rich', mimeo (1996).
22. Rodrik (1996).

References

Birdsall, Nancy and Juan Luis Londoño (1997) 'Asset Inequality Does Matter'. Paper prepared for the session, 'Applied Economics in Action', The World Bank at the American Economic Association Meeting, 4–6 January, in New Orleans.

Birdsall, Nancy, David Ross and Richard Sabot (1994) 'Inequality as a Constraint on Growth in Latin America'. mimeo, Inter-American Development Bank (December).

Birdsall, Nancy, David Ross and Richard Sabot (1995) 'Inequality and Growth Reconsidered: Lessons from East Asia'. *The World Bank Economic Review* 9, 3 (September).

Cardoso, Eliana and Ann Helwege (1991) 'Populism, Profligacy, and Redistribution'. In *The Macroeconomics of Populism in Latin America*, ed. Rudiger Dornbusch and Sebastian Edwards (Chicago: University of Chicago Press).

Chapelier, Georges and Hamid Tabatabai (1989) *Development and Adjustment: Stabilization, Structural Adjustment and UNDP Policy*. UNDP Policy Discussion Paper, BPPE/UNDP, New York.

Deininger, Klaus and Lyn Squire (1998) 'New Ways of Looking at Old Issues: Inequality and Growth'. *Journal of Development Economics* 57: 2.

Deininger, Klaus and Lyn Squire (1996) 'Does Inequality Matter?: Re-examining the Links between Growth and Inequality'. Mimeo. World Bank (July).

Dornbusch, Rudiger and Sebastian Edwards (1991) 'The Macroeconomics of Populism'. In *The Macroeconomics of Populism in Latin America* ed. Rudiger Dornbusch and Sebastian Edwards (Chicago: University of Chicago Press).

Griffin, Keith (1996) 'Macroeconomic Reform and Employment: An Investment-Led Strategy of Structural Adjustment in Sub-Saharan Africa' (Department of Economics Working Paper, University of California, Riverside) (October).

Griffin, Keith and Terry McKinley (1994) *Implementing a Human Development Strategy* (London: Macmillan).

Khan, Azizur Rahman (1997) 'Macroeconomic Policies and Poverty: An Analysis of the Experience in Ten Asian Countries'. Synthesis paper prepared for the Regional Poverty Alleviation Programme for Asia and the Pacific funded by UNDP and implemented by the International Labour Organization's South Asia Multidisciplinary Advisory Team (February).

Little, I.M.D., Richard Cooper, W. Max Corden and Sarath Rajapatirana (1993) *Boom, Crisis, and Adjustment: The Macroeconomic Experience of Developing Countries* (New York: Oxford University Press).

Patnaik, Prabhat (1997) 'A Note on the Redistributive Implications of Macroeconomic Policy'. Paper prepared for Social Development and Poverty Elimination Division, UNDP, Jawaharlal Nehru University (March).

Polak, Ben and Jeffrey G. Williamson (1993) 'Poverty, Policy, and Industrialisation in the Past'. In *Including the Poor*, edited by Michael Lipton and Jacques van der Gaag (Washington, DC: World Bank).

Ramos, Joseph (1993) 'Macroeconomic Equilibria and Development'. In *Development from Within: Towards a Neostructuralist Approach for Latin America*, edited by Osvaldo Sunkel (Boulder: Lynne Rienner Publishers).

Reed, David and Fulai Sheng (1997) 'Macroeconomic Policies, Poverty and the Environment'. Paper prepared for Social Development and Poverty Elimination Division/UNDP by the Macroeconomics Program Office of the World Wide Fund for Nature, Washington, DC (May).

Rodrik, Dani (1996) 'Getting Interventions Right: How South Korea and Taiwan Grew Rich'. Mimeo. Columbia.

Singh, Ajit (1994) 'Openness and the Market Friendly Approach to Development: Learning the Right Lessons from Development Experience'. *World Development* 22, no. 12: 1811–23.

Stewart, Frances (1995) *Adjustment and Poverty: Options and Choices* (New York: Routledge).

United Nations Development Programme (1996) *Human Development Report 1996* (Oxford University Press: New York).

Woodward, David (1996) 'Effects of Globalization and Liberalization on Poverty: Concepts and Issues'. In *Globalization and Liberalization: Effects of International Economic Relations on Poverty* (Geneva: United Nations Conference on Trade and Development).

9 The Distribution of Wealth and the Pace of Development

Keith Griffin and Amy Ickowitz

Economists have long been interested in the relationship between the distribution of income and the rate of economic growth. Two propositions have tended to dominate the literature. The first, associated with the name of Simon Kuznets, asserts that the degree of inequality varies systematically with the level of income per head, initially increasing as incomes rise and then, beyond some point, decreasing with further increases in income per head.[1] The second proposition, often associated with Arthur Okun, asserts that there is a 'great trade-off' between equality and efficiency and hence policy interventions intended to reduce inequality have a high cost in terms of a lower average income.[2] Taken together, the two propositions have been used to argue against public policies intended to create a less unequal society, since the Kuznets proposition indicates that in the long run policy interventions are unnecessary and the Okun proposition indicates that in the short run they are harmful.

In this chapter we attempt to do three things. First, we reconsider the evidence behind the Kuznets and Okun propositions. Second, we explore the implications for development of shifting the focus of analysis from the distribution of income to the distribution of productive assets or wealth. Third, we consider where appropriate the implications for the analysis of substituting human development for an expansion of gross national product (GNP) as the objective of development policy. Our conclusion is that a more equal distribution of wealth is more likely to accelerate the pace of human development than retard it and hence the earlier view that emphasized a conflict between equality and development is seriously misleading.

The belief in a trade-off between equity and growth, in both developed and developing economies, is widely held. Recent evidence, however, indicates not only that the two are compatible but also that they are mutually reinforcing. Traditional analyses of the relationship between

227

inequality and growth have focused on the relationship between income inequality and the growth of GNP. In this chapter, in contrast, we will examine inequality not only in terms of income but also in terms of the distribution of productive assets, that is natural, physical and human capital. Furthermore, while all of the empirical testing thus far defines growth as an increase in GNP, the results will have to be carefully reinterpreted if one assumes that growth of GNP is not the ultimate goal of development but simply a means to the end of increasing human development. Economic growth may help to advance human development, and per capita income enters into the human development index, but the two are not synonymous.

In Section I of this chapter we examine the empirical evidence that has been gathered to date on the relationship between growth and inequality. We begin with a review of the evidence on income inequality and then discuss the evidence on inequality in the distribution of assets. In Section II we explore some of the current theories which try to explain why growth and inequality might be inversely related. In Section III we consider some of the evidence from individual countries. Finally, in Section IV we raise some of the policy implications that arise from this re-examination of the data, the theories and actual experience. Our ultimate objective is to show that a redistribution of productive assets could serve as a catalyst for growth, both in terms of an expansion of GNP and in terms of higher levels of human development.

I. Empirical Evidence

Discussion of the empirical evidence begins with the famous Kuznets hypothesis. We then consider more recent work on the distribution of income and its link to economic growth. Next, we consider the importance of natural capital, concentrating on the distribution of land ownership. Lastly, we consider human capital, taking as an example the distribution of education.

The Kuznets Hypothesis

For nearly four decades the Kuznets hypothesis was accepted as a stylized fact by most economists. The well-known inverted U-shaped relationship between income inequality and the level of income affected the way economists approached theory as well as policy. In the early 1990s, however, economists increasingly began to question the idea that there was a close relationship between the level of income per head and the degree of inequality. The need for a re-evaluation had been apparent for quite some time. The insights from human capital theory, the refinement of endogenous growth theory and apparent real world anomalies combined to encourage scholars to take a second look at the Kuznets hypothesis. Several papers were published in the early years of the decade which claimed that not only was there no inverse relationship between growth and income equality during the first stages of development but that, on the contrary, initial inequality in the distribution of income was inimical to growth.

Simon Kuznets, writing in the 1950s and 1960s, developed his hypothesis that income inequality tends first to rise and then fall with increases in real income per capita after examining the historical experience of the developed countries and a very small sample of developing countries for which data were available. He believed that the historical record showed that such a relationship existed, but he was very careful to point out that this did not mean that there was an inherent trade-off between growth and equality, as he is sometimes interpreted to have argued: 'All we can say is that the unequal distribution of income in the earlier decades in the presently developed countries did not prevent rapid economic growth. But our data do not reveal the specific social and economic circumstances, and we cannot say that a somewhat less (or more) unequal size distribution might not have contributed to even faster growth.'[3]

During the years after Kuznets first published his observations regarding the historical relationships between growth and income equality, several empirical studies were done using cross-sectional data to test whether this inverse relationship held, using the larger amount of data that had become available from the developing countries. In 1973, Felix Paukert, using cross-sectional data on 56 countries originally gathered by Adelman and Taft Morris,[4] concluded that 'the data ... support the hypothesis expressed but not fully tested by Kuznets that with economic development income inequality tends to increase, then becomes stable and then decreases'.[5] Perhaps the most well known of the empirical studies is that done by Ahluwalia[6] using cross-sectional data from 60 countries. He was convinced enough by the data of the existence of a U-shaped relationship between equality and growth to call it a 'stylized fact'. Sherman Robinson went even further and claimed that the U hypothesis 'has gathered the force of economic law'.[7]

Not all economists agreed that the empirical tests were convincing enough to elevate the status of the U hypothesis to 'stylized fact', let alone 'economic law'. In 1983, Ashwanti Saith criticized Paukert and Ahluwalia's use of cross-sectional data to test what is really a secular relationship. By using cross-sectional data they implicitly assumed that every country travelled along 'one well-trodden U-path'. They thus ignored the fundamental inter-country differences pointed out by Kuznets in 'size, historical heritage, and timing of their industrialization process'[8] among other things. Saith proceeded to question the robustness of Ahluwalia's results. He re-ran Ahluwalia's regression on his sample of developing countries, dropping those observations which he considered to be outliers and Spain since he believed that it could not really be called a developing country. He found that Ahluwalia's coefficients were no longer significant and concluded that 'Ahluwalia's quadratic fit, and hence the U-curve, are the products of a few outliers, and if these are excluded from the sample, the U-curve fades into insignificance.'[9]

Ahluwalia and the authors of later studies performed in the 1970s and 1980s relied on a data set assembled by Shail Jain.[10] Much of these data are of poor quality and therefore call the conclusions of these investigations into question. Deininger and Squire[11] have specified three basic criteria that data must meet in order for them to qualify as 'quality' data:

(1)   the data must come from nationally representative household surveys;
(2)   all sources of income (or uses of expenditure) must be included (and not, for example, only wage income);
(3)   the survey must be representative of the country's entire population and results must not be based on extrapolations from information gathered only from specific subgroups (for example it should not be a survey of only the urban population or only whites).

These appear to be reasonable criteria, but much of the data used in past empirical investigations of the relationship between inequality and growth have not met these basic standards. Only 61 of Jain's original 405 observations, for example, meet the minimum requirements set by Deininger and Squire.

The World Turned Upside Down

More recent empirical research not only questions the validity of the Kuznets hypothesis but seems to reverse the conclusions. Persson and Tabellini were perhaps the first to find econometric evidence that there might be a negative relationship between initial income inequality and the rate of growth. They used two sets of data, one based on historical data from 9 developed countries and the other cross-sectional data from 56 countries since the end of the Second World War. On their historical sample, they performed what has become a standard growth regression of GDP growth on various variables including the income share of the top 20 per cent of the population as a measure of inequality. In their sample for the post-war period, they focus on the median voter and therefore, rather unpersuasively, use the income share of the third quintile as their measure of inequality. They reported that 'a strong negative relation between income inequality at the start of the period and growth in the subsequent period is present in both samples'.[12] That is, high initial inequality is associated with slow growth of output and incomes.

Alesina and Rodrik perform similar regressions for two periods, namely, 1960–1985 and 1970–1985. In addition to using a Gini coefficient on income as a measure of inequality, however, they also include a Gini coefficient on land as one of their regressors. Their high quality data set uses Jain's data from the OECD countries and data from Fields[13] for 29 developing countries. 'The results indicate that income inequality is negatively correlated with subsequent growth.'[14] When they use the Gini coefficients for land and for income separately, they find both to be significant at the 5 per cent level or higher, depending on the sample. When they use them both together, however, the Gini coefficient for land stays significant at the 1 per cent level, but the significance of the Gini coefficient for income declines to 10 per cent for the sample from the longer period and to 5 per cent for the shorter period. George Clark runs similar regressions using various income inequality measures and then performs sensitivity analysis to test the robustness of the negative relationship between income inequality and growth. His results 'confirm a robust and negative relationship between inequality and growth'.[15]

It seems that the most recent work using more and better data comes to a different conclusion regarding the relationship between inequality and income growth from those studies done in the past. However even the data used in the most recent studies are still far from perfect. Deininger and Squire question the quality of Persson and Tabellini's data on quintile shares of income. Only 18 out of Persson and Tabellini's 56 data points meet their criteria for quality data. 'The negative relationship between income inequality and growth evaporates if, for example, we rerun the regressions by Persson and Tabellini using only the eighteen . . . high-quality observations contained in their sample.'[16]

Deininger and Squire are also critical of the data in Alesina and Rodrik as well as in unpublished work by Perotti. Both studies include observations for developed countries from Jain's data set. Some of the income figures for these countries are based on wage income, which can create the impression of high disparities in countries which may have low inequality of net household income. Also, a large number of observations from developed countries (36 out of the 69 in Alesina and Rodrik and 50 out of Perotti's 67) 'give rise to the suspicion that the statistical analysis captures structural differences between developed and developing countries more than regularities that are equally valid for both groups'.[17] Deaton also argues that 'Jain's figures are not a sound basis on which to make international comparisons, and results that rely on them should be viewed with great scepticism, although the lesson is widely ignored in the recent political economy literature, for example, Persson and Tabellini (1990) and Alesina and Perotti (1992).'[18]

Deininger and Squire use a new data set on income distribution to re-examine the relationship between growth and inequality. They collected as many observations of income distribution as they could from both primary and reliable secondary sources and obtained a total of 2,600. After applying their criteria for quality data outlined above, they were left with 682 high quality observations, which is substantially more than are contained in the data sets used in previous studies. Not only do they have more cross-sectional observations, they also have a significantly greater number of time series observations for each country. This is crucial because the empirical testing of the Kuznets hypothesis in the past used cross-sectional data to try to draw conclusions about what is, in reality, a longitudinal relationship. According to Deininger and Squire, 'Indeed, our data provide little support for an inverted-U relationship between levels of income and inequality when tested on a country-by-country basis, with no support for the existence of a Kuznets curve in about 90 per cent of the countries investigated.'[19]

When they run the standard growth regression used in the past but with their high quality data, Deininger and Squire's results appear at first to corroborate those of Persson and Tabellini, Alesina and Rodrik, and Perotti, in showing that initial inequality has a negative effect on future growth. This effect, however, is no longer significant when regional dummies are introduced into the regression. This suggests to them that 'a wide range of region-specific characteristics which may, but need not, include inequality, could be at the root of the relationship that has been observed in much of the literature'.[20] While their results do not confirm that there is an inverse relationship between initial income inequality and growth, they do confirm that initial income inequality is not positively correlated with growth. Thus the idea that income redistribution is incompatible with growth receives no support from the cross-section evidence and the view that inequality is a precondition for growth is increasingly untenable.

Even though Deininger and Squire do not find a significant correlation between aggregate growth and overall income inequality, they do find a significant and positive correlation between growth and increases in income of all but the top quintile. The relationship is strongest for the bottom quintile, implying that growth is associated with a reduction of poverty. They found that during decadal growth episodes, the incomes of the bottom quintile increased in more than 85 per cent of the cases they examined.[21]

What does this imply for human development? It is reasonable to suppose that an increase in income increases human capabilities but that it does so at a diminishing rate. That is, there are diminishing returns to income in terms of its ability to increase human development. This assumption, in fact, is incorporated into the construction of the human development index. It follows from this that, for any given increase in the average level of income, the more evenly distributed is the increase in income, the greater will be its contribution to raising human development. In other words, an egalitarian pattern of economic growth contributes more to human development than an inegalitarian pattern.[22]

The Distribution of Land

As we have seen, empirical testing of the relationship between inequality and growth has traditionally been done using data on the distribution of income. Like Alesina and Rodrik, however, Deininger and Squire have also used data on the distribution of land. They hoped to use these data as a proxy for the distribution of assets in general. Quite apart from the problem of using land as a proxy for productive assets as a whole, data on the distribution of land almost always understate the degree of inequality. There are several reasons for this.

First, measures of land concentration ignore those who own no land at all, namely landless agricultural wage labourers. That is, the data refer to the distribution of land among landowners and not among the entire rural population. Second, most of the data refer to the distribution of land holdings and not to units of ownership. Thus, for instance, an estate that is divided into ten tenant farms would be counted as ten holdings and not as one unit of ownership. This results in an underestimate of the degree of inequality since land holdings tend to be distributed more equally than landownership. Many owners of large farms prefer to rent out their land to tenants rather than cultivate the entire area themselves. Third, measures of land concentration ignore those who own more than one farm by counting each farm as a separate unit of ownership. This, too, results in an underestimate of the degree of inequality. Finally, land is treated as a homogeneous asset of uniform quality. That is, measures of land concentration are in practice measures of inequality in surface area and not measures of inequality in the value of land as a productive asset. If, as is often the case, most of the best land is owned by large landowners, the degree of inequality will be understated by most conventional measurements.

Despite these problems, Deininger and Squire are right to underline the importance of land inequality, particularly since the 'possession of land could be a major determinant of an individual's productive capacity and their ability to invest, especially in agrarian societies where land is a major asset'.[23] Using regression analysis, Deininger and Squire find that the relationship between the initial degree of inequality in the distribution of land and subsequent growth is negative, significant and robust. Greater land inequality leads to slower growth. When regional dummies are added to the regression, the significance of the coefficient on land distribution is reduced, but it remains statistically significant. Given the fact that the degree of inequality as measured by the Gini coefficient for land distribution is almost certainly understated, the true relationship would be even stronger than the estimated relationship.

The Distribution of Human Capital

While land is an important asset in most developing countries, human capital is perhaps an even more important determinant of a country's growth potential. Recent evidence suggests that the contribution of human capital to growth is higher than that of either natural or physical capital, and perhaps more than the two combined.[24] This is especially true if one reinterprets growth to mean an increase in human development, since improvements in health and education contribute directly to human development as well as indirectly through their effects on increasing the growth of output and incomes.

Using data on 98 countries from the period 1960–1985, Robert Barro finds that the growth rate of real GDP per capita is positively related to the initial stock of human capital as proxied by primary and secondary school enrolment rates.[25] Thus the more equitably distributed are educational opportunities, that is the higher the percentage of the population enrolled in primary and secondary schools, the higher the growth rate. The effects on raising human development would be stronger still, because of the direct contribution of education to human development.

The microeconomic evidence supports these findings. Rati Ram estimates that the returns to schooling are 13 per cent on average for all countries, with a higher return in developing countries compared to developed countries.[26] Evidence also indicates that the returns to primary and secondary education are higher than the returns to tertiary education. George Psàcharopoulos explains that 'for primary education, unit costs are small relative to the extra lifetime income or productivity associated with literacy. For university education, the opposite is true'.[27] Given that tertiary education usually favours the elite in developing countries – and even in developed countries the middle and upper classes are disproportionately represented – a more equal distribution of expenditures on education would increase efficiency and growth as well as equity. Indeed in another paper Psacharopoulos finds that in developing countries the rates of return on investments in primary education are more than 25 per cent, whereas they fall sharply at higher levels, namely, to 15–18 per cent in secondary education and to 13–16 per cent in tertiary education.[28]

A recent study by the Asian Development Bank enables one to estimate the contribution of various factors to the difference in the rate of growth of per capita income in East and Southeast Asia during the period 1965–1990, on the one hand, and three other regions during the same period, on the other hand. Consider, for example, sub-Saharan Africa. During the 25 years under examination, the rate of growth of output per head in sub-Saharan Africa was 4 percentage points a year slower than in East and Southeast Asia. This difference of 4 percentage points can be decomposed as follows: 2.3 percentage points are due to differences in human capital (namely, 'schooling' and 'demography'), 1 percentage point is due to differences in natural capital (namely, 'resources and geography') and 0.1 percentage points are due to differences in physical capital (specifically, 'government savings rate'). The remaining 0.6 points are attributed to other factors.[29] A broadly similar result was found in South Asia but not, curiously, in Latin America, where 'initial conditions' and 'openness' appear to have been much more important.

While such decomposition exercises must be treated with some scepticism, the Asian Development Bank study confirms the importance of human capital in accelerating economic growth and, in the cases of East and Southeast Asia and South Asia, suggests that human capital was more than twice as important as natural and physical capital combined in explaining differences in economic performance. These results are therefore consistent with other recent empirical findings.

II. Theoretical Explanations

Why might one expect that inequality in the distribution of income and wealth could harm development and that reduced inequality could accelerate it? Both political and economic explanations have been put forward. Let us begin with the insights of political theory and then turn our attention to possible economic reasons.

Political Insights

There are three separate strands of argument to the analysis which connects inequality in the distribution of income and wealth to political instability. First, it has been argued that inequality can result in redistributive taxation which is harmful to growth of output. Second, it has been argued that inequality can result in a change in the composition of public expenditure which increases unproductive outlays and in the process reduces both the rate of growth of output and human development. Third, it has been argued that inequality can result in class conflict and unco-operative behaviour which reduce technical and institutional change and the growth of output.

Several papers published in the early 1990s examined the possible link between inequality and growth through the channel of voting behaviour. Each of these papers involves the construction of a theoretical model designed to capture both the economic and the political choices of the members of an economy and a polity. All of the papers make use of the median voter theorem, which purports to demonstrate that when people vote on different possible tax rates, the tax rate preferred by the median voter will be the one chosen.

Persson and Tabellini were the first to set up such a model and used an overlapping generations framework in which different individuals are assumed to have different incomes. An individual acts as an economic agent as well as a voting citizen. It is assumed that the role of the government is to redistribute income from those who invest more than the average to those who invest less than the average. Agents work and invest in human capital. Individuals with more skills accumulate more capital. The government levies taxes at a rate proportional to income, while the revenues are redistributed in a lump sum manner to all agents so that poor agents benefit as much as rich ones but pay a relatively smaller amount in taxes.

The authors assume that the more of the returns on her investment that an individual can retain, the higher will be the growth rate. This is because investment (and hence growth) is sensitive to the after-tax rate of return. On this basis the authors conclude that inequality is harmful to growth and offer the following explanation:

> if the median voter coincides with the average investor, he prefers a nonredistributive policy, whereas he prefers a tax (a subsidy) on

investment if he is poorer (richer) than the average. More generally a median voter with higher individual skills . . . and therefore a higher k^m (median voter's capital accumulation) prefers more private appropriability. A higher average skill level . . . gives higher average accumulation and hence increases the cost of redistribution, so that the voter prefers a less interventionist policy.[30]

The chain of causality is thus: lower income inequality leads to less voter preference for redistributive tax intervention; less government intervention leads to more investment and hence to faster growth.

The idea behind Alesina and Rodrik's model is similar to that in Persson and Tabellini, but the technical details are slightly different. They use an endogenous growth model and instead of differentiating between individuals based on income, they focus on differences in the relative shares of labour and capital endowments. The government, in their model, uses proportional taxation of capital income to finance public investment. A large increase in taxation lowers the after-tax return on private capital investment and thus reduces the incentive for agents to invest and therefore reduces the growth rate of the economy. They too make use of the median voter theorem and argue that 'the higher the proportion of capital income to total income of the median voter, the lower the tax rate chosen by the voting process and the higher the rate of investment and growth. In terms of income distribution, the poorer the median voter in relation to the voter with average income, the higher the equilibrium tax rate and the lower the growth rate.'[31]

Like Alesina and Rodrik, Bertola[32] uses an endogenous growth model and focuses on relative capital and labour shares. The government's role in his model, however, is not public expenditure, but redistribution from capital to labour through a proportional tax on capital. The intuition of the results is similar to that in Alesina and Rodrik. The higher the level of taxation, the lower the after-tax return on capital, which results in a lower investment rate and a lower growth rate. The higher the ratio of profit income to wages for an individual, the less likely she is to vote for a high tax rate. Again, the median voter theorem suggests that the tax rate that will emerge will be inversely related to the profits–wages ratio of the median voter. An implication of both papers is that the more even is the initial distribution of profits, and hence of productive wealth, the more rapid is likely to be the rate of growth. This follows from an assumption that government interventions are harmful to growth, for example, that taxes reduce the return on private investment, that the return on public investment is lower than the return on private investment or that public investment is a very small share of total public expenditure on the margin.

A surprising implication of the idea that political behaviour is the crucial link between equality and growth is that this relationship is likely to be stronger in democracies than in authoritarian regimes since it is only in democracies that the median voter can vote on tax policies. Persson and Tabellini divided their sample into two groups – democratic and non-democratic – and found that indeed the positive relationship between equality and growth held only for their democratic sample. However, in performing a similar test with their data, Alesina and Rodrik found that the coefficient on the dummy variable for democracy in their regression 'is not statistically significant, rejecting the hypothesis that the relationship between inequality and growth is different in democracies and nondemocracies'.[33] While Deininger and Squire take this as incontrovertible evidence that the political instability argument fails to explain the reason for the inverse relationship between inequality and growth, Alesina and Rodrik offer an alternative interpretation of their result. They argue that it is possible that 'the pressure for redistribution coming from the majority is felt not only in democracies but also in other regimes ... some dictators are subject to political influences similar to those experienced by elected representatives.'[34]

Alesina and Rodrik are correct to point out that even a highly authoritarian regime is unlikely to be totalitarian and hence often will have to respond to political pressures in one way or another. In some cases the response may be accommodating, for example through adjustments of tax rates or the level of transfer payments. In other cases, however, the response may be increased repression, for example through higher spending on police, prisons, the judiciary, secret police and perhaps the armed forces. That is, the adjustment may occur not on the revenue side but via changes in government expenditure which reduce resources available for redistribution and accelerating growth. In this second case, 'inequality can be costly to maintain'.[35] Bowles and Gintis argue in a similar vein that one explanation for 'the sharply contrasting economic performances of the very unequal Latin American and less unequal East Asian economies over the 1980s and early 1990s is related to the high enforcement cost of economic inequality'.[36]

Moreover, countries with a highly unequal distribution of wealth are likely to be characterized by sharp class conflict and periodic civil violence. Quite apart from the costs of repression, such conflicted and polarized societies will find co-operation between workers and asset owners to be difficult, be the asset owners large landowners or urban capitalists. 'Each will be suspicious of the other; each will resist changes proposed by the other. The result will be greater risk, lower levels of investment, slower rates of technological and institutional change and a slower long term rate of growth.'[37]

Thus there are several political channels which can link inequality and growth. Statistical regularities that can be captured in a regression equation probably do not exist and if they do exist, they are likely to be hard to detect.

Insights from Economic Theory

Economic theory offers a number of insights that help one to understand why reduced inequality of income and wealth could increase the pace of development, whether measured in terms of growth of GNP or expansion of human capabilities. We shall concentrate on investment in human capital, asset distribution and the rate of savings, and employment and the distribution of physical assets.

Stiglitz and Weiss[38] have argued that because of imperfect information about the characteristics and future behaviour of borrowers, the loanable funds market does not produce a market clearing price in equilibrium but instead is characterized by credit rationing. One consequence of this is that agents (individuals and firms) are able to borrow only if they own an asset that can be used as collateral. This restricts the number of investors in general and in particular makes it difficult to finance human capital formation.

Investments in human capital are lumpy and usually require either accumulated savings or credit. If credit rationing limits access to funds, then those who have more initial wealth are better able to invest in human capital, partly because they have more of their own funds to use and partly because their wealth provides collateral which, in turn, gives them greater access to credit. The distribution of wealth will thus affect investments in human capital which, in turn, will affect output and growth.[39] 'A more unequal initial distribution of assets would then imply that, for any given level of per capita income, a greater number of people are credit constrained. In an economy where individuals make indivisible investments – in schooling and education for example – that have to be financed through credit, this would imply lower aggregate growth.'[40] This is even more true if by 'growth' one means human development since education contributes directly to enhanced capabilities. Hence if the poor were to own more assets that could be used as collateral, for example land, they could borrow money to invest in the human capital of their families and thereby become more educated, healthier and more prosperous citizens.

Deininger and Squire believe that credit market imperfections provide a stronger link between inequality and growth than do the political channels discussed above. They cite two pieces of evidence in support of this view. First, in the advanced economies where one would not expect land to be an important source of collateral, the initial distribution of land does not in fact appear to be a significant determinant of growth. Second, in the developing countries the initial degree of land inequality is significantly and negatively associated with the average educational attainment of the population. This lends credence to the proposition that assets such as land may make it easier for people in developing countries to obtain access to credit which can be used to finance education.

While a greater supply of educated workers may be necessary for a faster pace of development, it is not sufficient. The human development approach sometimes ignores the importance of demand for an educated labour force. From the human development perspective, the enhancement of human capital is of course a goal in itself, independent of its impact on accelerating the growth of output. However, the impact of improvements in human capital on human development would be magnified if human capital formation were also to accelerate growth of GNP since economic growth contributes to an enhancement of human development. If investment in people is to have the desired impact on growth, there must be a demand for the skills created. Increasing the number of taxi drivers with advanced degrees is unlikely to have a strong effect on the growth rate. Hence it is important to take into account the social rate of return on different types of human capital when allocating resources. It is equally important that macroeconomic and trade policies, that is the development strategy in general, be supportive of an employment-intensive pattern of growth.

In some developing countries enrolment ratios for women are still far below those of men. Enhancing the human capital of women through education bestows the same direct benefits on society as educating men in terms of having a more skilled and productive work force. Birdsall, Ross and Sabot have shown that 'substituting gender-specific primary-school enrolment rates into the original Barro model [produces] no significant difference between the coefficient values for males and females'.[41] There are, however, indirect effects or positive externalities of education associated with its effect on reducing fertility rates. It is widely known that rapid population growth rates have been an obstacle to development in many poor countries, even in those which have managed to achieve reasonable rates of growth of GNP. In all countries the education of women confers triple benefits: it raises human development directly, it contributes to a faster growth of output and, by reducing the fertility rate, it increases the rate of growth of per capita income.

Another possible link between asset inequality and growth arises from incentive compatibility problems which are common in highly unequal economies. Bowles and Gintis offer an example of how inefficient incentive structures can affect productivity and growth:

> Consider an agrarian economy of a hundred households in which most of the land is owned by a single landowner who hires labour and/or leases land under share-cropping tenancy. Both of these forms of employment have adverse incentive effects. Wage workers have little intrinsic work motivation, since they do not own the results of their work. As a result, the cost of supervising agricultural labour may be considerable. Share-croppers, too, have diluted incentives as they are only partial owners of their work. They will thus allocate less effort and care to their rented land than they would if they owned it themselves.[42]

A redistribution of land would clearly result in greater efficiency in the presence of these incentive and monitoring problems. One reason why this does not come about through the market mechanism is because of the credit market imperfections discussed above.

Let us turn now to the question of savings.

One theoretical justification for the Kuznets hypothesis was proposed by Nicholas Kaldor.[43] He made two crucial assumptions:

(i) that a high savings rate is essential for growth and
(ii) that rich people have a higher marginal propensity to save than poor people.

It follows from these assumptions that in order to ensure a high savings rate and hence rapid growth, income should be concentrated in the hands of the rich. We have already qualified the first of Kaldor's assumptions by arguing that the returns on human capital can be as high as the returns on saving and investing in physical capital. The second assumption also can be questioned, since it is not obvious that rich people always save proportionally more than the poor.

Particularly in developing countries, the amount an individual or household saves is likely to be strongly influenced by available investment opportunities.[44] The reason for this, as with investment in education, has much to do with the incomplete coverage and malfunctioning of capital markets. Because of the extreme credit market imperfections in most developing countries – in the rural sector and in the informal urban sector – most poor people have virtually no access to the formal credit market. They can neither save (deposit funds) through the banking system nor obtain loans (borrow funds) from formal sector commercial banks. In the developed countries, in contrast, the credit market intermediates between an investor and a saver, in principle (although not in practice) allowing all those with commercially viable projects to obtain finance capital.

In developing countries, for those who do not have access to the credit market, notably the poor, the investor and the saver must be the same individual, and the decision to save becomes identical to the decision to invest. In such cases an individual is likely to save only if she has a profitable investment opportunity within reach. A landless agricultural labourer, for example, has few investment opportunities and hence can be expected to save little whereas a small peasant landowner with a similar level of income can invest in the land and hence can be expected to save relatively more. The implication is that a more even distribution of assets could increase the overall savings rate by giving land or other productive assets to the currently assetless poor and thereby provide them with profitable outlets for their savings.

Some of the earlier literature suggests that this may be true. A study of rural savings rates in India, for example, showed that farmers with access to land ('cultivating families') saved on average 13 per cent of their income (not including direct investment of labour in their land, which would have raised the estimate to 20 per cent); landless households (or 'non-cultivating families'), in contrast, saved less than 4 per cent of their income, presumably for precautionary motives.[45] In other words, those who had an outlet for their savings actually saved three to five times more than those who did not. A study in then-undivided Pakistan showed that rural inequality and average incomes were lower in East Pakistan than in West Pakistan, but personal savings rates were higher in rural East Pakistan (12 per cent) than in rural West Pakistan (9 per cent).[46] That is, according to the conventional view, rural savings should have been higher in West Pakistan than in East Pakistan since the former was both less poor and had a greater concentration of income, but the opposite was the case.

Finally, there is some evidence that among those who do have land, there is no systematic tendency for large farmers to save more than small ones. A study of 72 holdings in Ludhiana District in the Punjab, in 1969–70, showed that net savings were highest on medium-sized farms (26.5 per cent of total income), followed by large farms (26.1 per cent) and then small (16.7 per cent). In the Hissar District of Haryana, a study of 108 holdings again showed that net savings were proportionately highest on medium-sized farms (35.5 per cent of total income), but small farms were a close second (34.2 per cent) followed by large farms (31.3 per cent). These data suggest that a redistribution of land among already existing landowners would not reduce the savings rate. These conjectures are supported by the redistributive land reforms in Taiwan province and mainland China, where if anything, savings rates increased after assets were redistributed.

It is reasonable to ask, however, whether arguments that apply to the distribution of land apply with equal force to the distribution of physical capital such as machinery and buildings. The empirical studies by Deininger and Squire use land as a proxy for all assets and find that there is a positive relationship between a more equal distribution of assets and growth. Furthermore, as argued above, the true relationship is likely to be even stronger than the estimated relationship since the measurements used for empirical testing understate the true degree of land inequality. One must be cautious, however, before making a leap from the distribution of land to the distribution of productive assets in general. It is conceivable that there are peculiar features of land that make its equitable distribution more favourable to growth than might be true of other productive assets. It is well established, for example, that 'output per hectare tends to be higher on small farms than on large, because small farmers use their land more intensively and utilize more labour-intensive techniques of production'.[47] It does not follow from this that small businesses tend to adopt more labour intensive techniques than large or obtain a higher output per unit of capital. That is something that needs to be established.

As far as we know, there has not been a systematic attempt to test empirically the relationship between the distribution of physical assets and growth. There are reasons to believe, however, that this relationship is positive as well. First, there is abundant case study evidence that indicates that small and medium enterprises create more employment per unit of capital than large enterprises. A smaller average size of enterprise is therefore likely to be associated with greater labour intensity, a higher productivity of capital and, of course, a more equal distribution of income. Second, in most developing countries – particularly those which followed an import-substituting pattern of industrialization – the industrial sector is dominated by large, monopolistic enterprises which are highly inefficient. A more equitable distribution of physical capital could lead to a more competitive market, greater efficiency and higher average incomes. Since most developing countries have a comparative advantage in relatively labour intensive processes and products, greater emphasis on small and medium-sized enterprises would enable them to exploit their resources more efficiently and, in addition, accentuate human development by increasing the demand for skilled labour, that is human capital.

Third, as argued above, if savings in developing countries are in part a function of investment opportunities, then policies which give the majority of people greater access to physical assets will simultaneously give them an important reason to save and invest. Even adequate shelter can provide an investment opportunity, since many poor families can use a room in their house to establish a business, for example a restaurant, bar or teahouse, a repair shop or a microenterprise.[48] Home based enterprises can be a stepping-stone to larger activities and they certainly are an advance over ambulatory vendors and sales by squatters on the sidewalk.

There are thus several advantages of basing industrial development on small and medium enterprises. The practical problems that have impeded the development of small scale, labour intensive enterprises in the past have been credit market imperfections discussed above, onerous government regulations, controls and licences, and policies that have favoured large enterprises, including protection from imports, subsidized bank credit and tax benefits. Taiwan is a counter-example. It avoided a heavy bias in favour of large, capital intensive enterprise and instead emphasized the expansion of small scale industry. The results, in terms of equity and growth, were remarkable.[49]

III. Evidence from Country Studies

While the theoretical insights and the econometric studies discussed above have been instrumental in encouraging a re-evaluation of the relationship between growth and inequality, perhaps the greatest blow to the Kuznets hypothesis and the Okun proposition came from the blatant anomalies represented by the experiences of several east Asian economies such as Japan, China, South Korea and Taiwan. A Southeast Asian country, namely Vietnam, probably should also be added to this list. These countries experienced outstanding achievements as measured by almost all indicators of development while they managed for long periods to maintain and even at times to improve their performance with respect to equality. Speaking specifically of South Korea and Taiwan, Tibor Scitovsky claims, rightly we believe, that 'by the double criterion of growth and equity, they have been the most successful of all the developing nations.'[50] During the 1980s in particular, their performance was in stark contrast to those countries in Latin America and sub-Saharan Africa that experienced both slow (and in some cases negative) growth rates and worsening inequality. Do any of the theories discussed in the previous section shed any light as to why the east Asian and, say, Latin American countries performed so differently with respect to growth and equality?

Those theories which focus on class conflict and political instability do not appear at first glance to be relevant in the east Asian context. While there were indeed redistributive measures in several countries of the region, they did not take the form of income redistribution as described in the models, nor were the redistributive measures the outcome of a voting process. If, however, one thinks of the models as metaphors that express the advantages of redistribution in a political economy context, then perhaps some insights can be gained. The east Asian governments did not redistribute income or use tax-financed transfer policies, they redistributed assets instead. Taiwan, South Korea, China and Japan all implemented major land reforms following the Second World War. These redistributions of wealth, however, were not a result of the voting process but of historical circumstances. Indeed the threat of communism, and the example of the land reform in China, provided strong political incentives to introduce land reforms first in Japan, then in Taiwan and last in South Korea.

In Latin America, in contrast, the elites were not as threatened by a communist revolution and could afford to disregard the alienation of the poor. Even so, the modest land redistribution in Mexico during the interwar period and the much more radical land reform in Bolivia in 1952 were warnings that social injustice could not be ignored completely. Pressure for land reform increased after the Cuban revolution, but only in Chile (during the Frei and Allende administrations) was there a significant redistribution of land, and even there land reform was reversed during the Pinochet dictatorship. Indeed, the usual response to inequality in Latin America was repression, unlike east Asia where several governments attempted to 'ensure that all groups in the population benefited visibly from growth'.[51]

More generally, east Asian governments were more vigorous in promoting agricultural and rural development, partly by encouraging technological change (the green revolution) and partly by creating a more appropriate policy environment. While the Latin American countries tended, for example, to overvalue their exchange rates to the detriment of the agricultural and export sectors, in east Asia the exchange rate was either kept close to its free market value or even in some cases undervalued. This benefited a large proportion of the working population, and particularly the poor, a majority of whom were employed in agriculture and the export sector.

Birdsall, Ross and Sabot emphasize human capital as providing the crucial link between development and equality when comparing the relative performances of east Asia and Latin America. After regressing primary and secondary school enrolment rates on income per capita for over 90 countries during the period 1965–1987, they found that 'countries in East Asia, with the exception of Thailand, had significantly higher primary and secondary enrolment rates than predicted by cross-country comparisons. The performance of Latin American countries is not nearly as strong as that of East Asia and is mixed relative to the international norms.'[52] Moreover, while enrolment rates in both regions increased over time, the quality of education in east Asia has continuously improved, while the quality of education in Latin America has declined, as evidenced by lower completion rates.

The difference in performance between the two regions does not seem to reflect differences in government commitment to education, at least as represented by differences in public expenditure on education as a percentage of GNP. In fact, the differences are not great. For example, in 1960 public expenditure on education as a percentage of GNP was 2.0 per cent in South Korea and 1.9 per cent in Brazil, while in 1992 the figures were 4.2 per cent in South Korea and even higher in Brazil, namely, 4.6 per cent.[53] The east Asian countries, however, enjoyed the benefits of both rapid growth and rapid declines in fertility rates. These two factors combined to ensure that absolute expenditure per child on education was much higher in east Asia than in Latin America.

Compared to east Asia, slow economic growth in Latin America and a much less rapid decline in fertility rates meant that resources for spending on education increased slowly while the size of the school age population expanded rapidly. Since fertility rates are inversely related to the level of education (particularly female education), there is a virtuous circle wherein increased education leads to lower fertility which in turn results in greater education expenditures per child, which lowers fertility further.[54] East Asia was involved in this virtuous circle whereas Latin America was not.

Latin America's relative disadvantage was exacerbated by differences in the composition of educational expenditure. Consider South Korea and Brazil again. In 1992, about 7 per cent of expenditure on education in

South Korea was allocated to higher education whereas in Brazil the share was 26 per cent. Yet we know that expenditures on primary and secondary education have a stronger impact on economic growth, human development and equality than expenditure on tertiary education. Brazil, in other words, chose her priorities within education unwisely. This does not necessarily mean that the priorities were irrational. Large investments in tertiary education usually subsidize the education of the elites, who are able to capture the resources of the state and use them to their advantage. It should not be surprising that in Latin America, where inequality is very great, the proportion of education expenditures allocated to tertiary education tends to be much higher than in east Asia.

Low enrolment rates are both a result of and a cause of inequality. Once again, there is cumulative causality. Williamson finds that much of the difference in secondary school enrolment rates between South Korea and Brazil can be explained by differences in inequality.[55] By educating only part of a population, the human capital of that group is enhanced and as a consequence that section of the population has an asset which gives them an advantage over those who remain uneducated, thus exacerbating inequality.

Birdsall, Ross and Sabot describe two virtuous circles in east Asia wherein 'education contributed to economic growth, which, in turn, stimulated investment in education' and then 'education contributed to low levels of income inequality which, in turn, stimulated investment in education.'[56] Latin America, alas, was caught in two vicious circles where poor educational performance and inappropriate development strategies combined to impede growth. Slow economic growth then contributed to relatively low investment in education. At the same time, poor educational performance contributed to high income inequality which in turn limited investments in education.

Not only did the east Asian countries do better than other developing countries in terms of improvements in the supply of education – both quantity and quality – they also stand out as examples of countries which created a strong demand for labour. By promoting their agricultural and export sectors through investment in infrastructure, by adopting favourable exchange rate policies and by reducing distortions in factor markets, the east Asian countries encouraged labour intensive methods of production. These policies not only helped to increase living standards in the agricultural sector, they also raised wages in the non-agricultural sector by raising the reservation wage. This was especially true in countries which had a redistributive land reform. That is, redistributive measures in agriculture also reduced inequality in the urban, industrial sectors of the economy.

The export sectors in most countries of east Asia initially relied on intensive use of low-skilled labour, but over time exporting became more and more skill intensive. The combination of expanding employment opportunities and increasing real wage rates ensured that the returns to education at the level of the individual remained high. In Latin America, on the other hand, the demand for labour remained weak. Many of the Latin American countries adopted an import-substituting industrialization strategy in the 1960s and 1970s which discriminated against agriculture. Industrial production was highly capital intensive and thus did not require large numbers of educated and skilled workers. As a result, the private returns to education were reduced and hence the incentives for individuals and families to invest in education were lower than they might have been had the development strategy been different. Birdsall, Ross and Sabot underscore the importance not only of enhancing human capital by increasing educational opportunities, but also of ensuring that there is a demand for the skills created. They argue that 'weak demand for educated labour may help to explain why countries such as Peru and Argentina, which like East Asia, had greater than predicted human capital endowments, nevertheless have tended to underperform, with respect to growth.'[57]

Finally, the extensive land reforms that took place in South Korea and Taiwan provided the majority of households with a valuable asset in which to invest. In addition, in Taiwan, the process of industrialization was not concentrated in urban areas as is usually the case, but encompassed the rural areas as well. Indeed Taiwan (like China and the Punjab of India) industrialized the countryside. This pattern of development gave farmers and their families an additional source of employment and income. In 1975, for instance, 53.7 per cent of farm incomes in Taiwan came from jobs off the farm.[58] The industrialization process in Taiwan also was unusual in that much of the growth in industry originated as a result of increases in the number of small firms. That is, industrialization in Taiwan was led by small and medium enterprises, not by large private oligopolies or state enterprises as in most developing countries. John Mellor notes that 'an extraordinarily high proportion of total non-agricultural output takes place in small firms. Indeed, 60 percent of all exports come from firms of less than 100 employees. Those firms are broadly distributed through the previously rural areas.'[59] Thus the combination of land reform and small enterprise development in the countryside meant that natural and physical capital and hence investment opportunities in Taiwan were widely distributed among households. In addition, the labour intensive pattern of growth ensured that human capital was a valuable asset and this, in turn, ensured that investment in education would enjoy a high rate of return.

IV. Policy Implications

The focus of attention in this chapter has been on the microeconomics of asset redistribution. A supportive general development strategy is, however, essential. Macroeconomic policy must ensure that the rate of inflation is not so high that the functioning of the price mechanism is impaired; and it must ensure that the pressure of demand is not so low that investment incentives and the overall level of employment are depressed. International trade policy must not be strongly biased either against exporting or import substitution. Most important, a high level of investment is desirable to give flexibility to the economy and to enable the structure of incentives to operate effectively in allocating resources. In such an environment the opportunities created by asset redistribution are most likely to be grasped.

Economic theory, econometric evidence and historical experience combine to produce an eloquent message: relative equality in the distribution of wealth contributes to faster economic growth and enhanced human development. It goes without saying that a redistribution of assets in favour of the poor would reduce poverty, both once-for-all and over time, because of its effect on the rate of economic growth. This would be true whether poverty is conceptualized as insufficient income or as a deficit in capabilities. The question of how best to achieve this more equitable distribution of productive assets still remains. The answer is bound to be affected by the characteristics of the three types of productive assets, namely natural capital, human capital and physical capital. In the abstract it appears that there are two possible paths which governments can take to redistribute wealth. One is the more direct route of an immediate, once-for-all redistribution of the stock of existing assets. The other involves a more circuitous path of redistributing the flow of investments so that on the margin new additions to the stock of assets are equitably distributed.

Of the three types of productive assets, only existing stocks of natural capital can be redistributed quickly and relatively easily. The class of natural capital, however, is large – including farm land, forests and plantations, pastures, water rights and fishing rights – and the importance of natural capital in the total stock of capital tends to vary inversely with the level of income per head. That is, the poorer the country, the more significant is natural capital likely to be in determining the overall distribution of wealth. At the other extreme, existing stocks of human capital evidently cannot be immediately redistributed since most human capital is embodied in human beings. An improvement in the distribution of human capital will consequently depend on reallocating and increasing expenditure on such things as education, training, health, nutrition programmes and family planning services. This redirection of the flow of investment in human capital, however, need not take long to have an impact on the composition of the stock of human capital. It takes less than a decade, for example, to provide primary and some secondary education to a child, and the provision of basic health services takes even less time. One should not imagine therefore that a redistribution of human capital is necessarily a long term objective; much can be achieved rather quickly.

A redistribution of the stock of physical capital is more complicated than a redistribution of natural capital. Direct investment by the state in the manufacturing sector once was common in developing countries. In addition, partial or complete nationalization of assets has been attempted in many countries and the consequences for distributive equity have depended on whether the value added of the nationalized enterprises rose or fell and on how the value added was distributed among the population. Many formerly socialist countries have pursued the opposite strategy, denationalizing or privatizing state-owned enterprises, but the experience so far is not particularly encouraging. Indeed in many formerly socialist countries privatisation has resulted in an extremely unequal distribution of productive wealth with no compensating pay-off in terms of a sharp acceleration in the pace of development.[60]

The most promising approach is to ensure that access to finance capital is widespread, that obstacles to the creation and growth of small and medium enterprises are removed, and that relative factor prices provide incentives to adopt employment intensive patterns of growth. Beyond this, it may be possible to help the poor accumulate assets, for example where appropriate, by turning the assets constructed on public works programmes over to a co-operative composed of those who laboured to build them.[61] Similarly, housing policy can be designed to promote widespread ownership of dwellings and a house plot, which can provide not only shelter but a place of business.

The argument that savings are a function of investment opportunities, and that a redistribution of productive assets would accelerate growth and human development and reduce poverty, rests on an assumption that there are slack resources in poor households which can be mobilized. There is surplus labour that can be used for investment. There is a margin of consumption above physical subsistence that can be squeezed if attractive investments are available. There is a potential for savings to rise if access to financial markets can be improved. In other words, the poor are quantity constrained rather than price constrained, and opportunities for employment, investment and borrowing are more influential in determining the pace of capital accumulation and savings by the poor than the wage rate, the profit rate and the real rate of interest. Asset redistribution, in effect, eases the quantity constraint and permits savings and the employment of labour to increase, thereby raising the level of investment.

It is sometimes argued that although a land reform would increase the rate of growth, a rise in aggregate investment would have an even greater effect, and if a land reform were to lead to social unrest and a decline in overall investment, a redistribution of assets might not be worthwhile.[62] However, a classic study of Latin America by William Cline comes to the opposite conclusion.[63] He argues that even if one makes pessimistic assumptions about the effect of redistribution on aggregate savings and investment, a redistribution of income in Argentina, Brazil and Mexico to roughly the then-British level of equality would benefit the poor. Assuming there is a fall in the annual growth rate by 0.66 per cent in Argentina and by approximately 1 per cent in Brazil and Mexico, the incomes of the bottom 70 per cent of the population nevertheless would rise considerably. In fact, for the poorest 70 per cent to reach the post-redistribution level of income with the undiminished pre-redistribution rate of growth would require 34 years in Argentina, 56 years in Brazil and 49 years in Mexico. By then, most of those originally poor would have died.

Moreover, theory and empirical evidence since the time Cline wrote suggest that a redistribution of productive assets could in some circumstances increase investment and accelerate the rate of growth. If correct, this strengthens the case for redistribution. Similarly, while redistribution of land and other assets, or the threat of redistribution, could lead to social unrest and lower investment, as Deininger and Squire suggest, the perpetuation of inequality also can be costly in terms of resource use and this can lower the level of investment and the rate of growth. At the very least, the case against a redistribution of wealth is much weaker than once thought and the case in favour of redistribution is much stronger. Finally, asset redistribution is occurring willy-nilly in the ex-socialist countries and in many others (particularly in Africa and Central America) racked by civil conflict. The redistribution of wealth in these cases is disorderly and arbitrary rather than purposive and an opportunity is being missed to redistribute on a more systematic basis to encourage equity and long term economic and human development. In economies entering a period of post-war reconstruction or a transition from central planning to a more market-oriented economic system, the fluidity of politics may provide a brief opening for imaginative policies which link the distribution of wealth to the pace of development.

Notes

1. Simon Kuznets, 'Economic Growth and Income Inequality', *American Economic Review* 45 (1955), 1–28.
2. Arthur Okun, *Equality and Efficiency: The Big Tradeoff* (Washington, DC: Brookings Institution, 1975).
3. Simon Kuznets, 'Quantitative Aspects of the Economic Growth of Nations: VIII. Distribution of Income by Size,' *Economic Development and Cultural Change* 11, 2 (1963), 69.
4. Irma Adelman and Cynthia Taft Morris, 'An Anatomy of Patterns of Income Distribution in Developing Nations. Part II of Final Report' (Grant AID/csd-2236: Northwestern University, 1971).
5. Felix Paukert, 'Income Distribution at Different Levels of Development: A Survey of Evidence', *International Labour Review* 108 (1973), 120.
6. Montek S. Ahluwalia, 'Inequality, Poverty, and Development', *Journal of Development Economics* 3 (1976), 307–342.
7. Sherman Robinson, 'A Note on the U-Hypothesis', *American Economic Review* 66, 3 (1976), 437.
8. Simon Kuznets, 'Underdeveloped Countries and the Pre-Industrial Phase in the Advanced Countries,' in *The Economics of Underdevelopment*, ed. by A.N. Agarwala and P.S. Singh (New York: Oxford University Press, 1967), p.153.
9. Ashwanti Saith, 'Development and Distribution: A Critique of the Cross-Country U-Hypothesis', *Journal of Development Economics* 13 (1983), 378.
10. Shail Jain, *Size Distribution of Income: A Compilation of Data* (World Bank, 1975).
11. Klaus Deininger and Lyn Squire, 'New Ways of Looking at Old Issues: Inequality and Growth', (1998).
12. Torsten Persson and Guido Tabellini 'Is Inequality Harmful for Growth?' *American Economic Review* 84: 3 (1994), 601.
13. Gary Fields, 'Changes in Poverty and Inequality in Developing Countries', *World Bank Research Observer* 4 (1989), pp. 167–86.
14. Alberto Alesina and Dani Rodrik, 'Distributive Politics and Economic Growth', *Quarterly Journal of Economics* 108 (1994), 481.
15. G.R.G. Clarke, 'More Evidence on Income Distribution and Growth,' *Journal of Development Economics* 47, 2 (1995), 422.
16. Klaus Deininger and Lyn Squire, 'A New Data Set Measuring Income Inequality,' *World Bank Economic Review* 10, 3 (1996), 573.
17. Deininger and Squire (1998), 7.
18. A. Deaton, 'Data and Econometric Tools for Development Analysis,' in *Handbook of Development Economics*, Vol. IIIA, ed. Jere Behrman and T.N. Srinivasan (New York: Elsevier Science B.V., 1995): 1803.

19. Deininger and Squire (1996), 573.
20. Deininger and Squire (1998), 13.
21. *Ibid.*, 7.
22. Keith Griffin, 'Culture, Human Development and Economic Growth,' UNRISD/UNESCO, Occasional Paper Series on Culture and Development, no. 3. (1997), 4.
23. Deininger and Squire (1998), 8.
24. See Griffin (1997), 3; United Nations Development Programme, *Human Development Report* (New York: Oxford University Press, 1996); Asian Development Bank, *Emerging Asia: Changes and Challenges* (Manila: Asian Development Bank, 1997).
25. Robert J. Barro, 'Economic Growth in a Cross Section of Countries,' *Quarterly Journal of Economics* 106 (May 1991), 407–43.
26. Rati Ram, 'Level of Development and Returns to Schooling: Some Estimates from Multicountry Data,' *Economic Development and Cultural Change* 44, 4 (1996), 848.
27. George Psacharopoulos, 'Education and Development. A Review,' *World Bank Research Observer* 3, 1 (1988), 101.
28. George Psacharopoulos, 'Returns to Investment in Education: A Global Update,' *World Development* 22 (1994), 1325–43.
29. Asian Development Bank (1997), 80.
30. Persson and Tabellini (1994), 604.
31. Alesina and Perotti (1994), 361.
32. Guiseppe Bertola, 'Factor Shares and Savings in Endogenous Growth,' *American Economic Review* 83, 5 (1993), 1184–98.
33. Alesina and Rodrik (1994), 481.
34. *Ibid.*, 483.
35. Keith Griffin, *Studies in Globalization and Economic Transitions* (London: Macmillan, 1996), p. 144.
36. Samuel Bowles and Herbert Gintis, 'Escaping the Efficiency-Equity Trade-off: Productivity-Enhancing Asset Redistributions,' in *Macroeconomic Policy After the Conservative Era*, ed. Gerald A. Epstein and Herbert M. Gintis (New York: Cambridge University Press, 1995), 411
37. Griffin (1996), p. 144.
38. Joseph Stiglitz and Andrew Weiss, 'Credit Rationing in Markets with Imperfect Information,' *American Economic Review* 71 (1981), 393–409.
39. G.C. Loury, 'Intergenerational Transfers and the Distribution of Earnings,' *Econometrica* 49 (1981), 843–67.
40. Deininger and Squire (1998), 10.
41. Nancy Birdsall, David Ross and Richard Sabot. 'Inequality as a Constraint on Growth in Latin America,' Inter-American Development Bank (1994), 10.
42. Bowles and Gintis (1995), 412.
43. Nicholas Kaldor, 'Capital Accumulation and Economic Growth,' in *Further Essays on Economic Theory*, ed. Nicholas Kaldor (New York: Holmes and Meier, 1978).
44. Keith Griffin, *The Political Economy of Agrarian Change* (London: Macmillan, 1974); Keith Griffin and Azizur Rahman Khan, *Growth and Inequality in Pakistan* (London: Macmillan, 1972).
45. P.G.K. Panikar, 'Rural Savings in India,' *Economic Development and Cultural Change* 10, 1 (1961).

46. A. Bergan, 'Personal Income Distribution and Personal Savings in Pakistan, 1963/64,' *Pakistan Development Review* 7, 2 (1967).
47. Keith Griffin and Terry McKinley, *Implementing a Human Development Strategy* (London: Macmillan, 1994), p. 81.
48. Keith Griffin and Mark Brenner, 'Domestic Resource Mobilization and Enterprise Development in Sub-Saharan Africa.' Department of Economics, University of California, Riverside, Working Paper 97–01 (1997), Chapter 4 in this volume.
49. John C.H. Fei, Gustav Ranis and Shirley W.Y. Kuo, *Growth and Equity: The Taiwan Case* (New York: Oxford University Press, 1979).
50. Tibor Scitovsky, 'Economic Development in Taiwan and South Korea,' *Food Research Institute Studies* 19, 4 (1985), 215–64.
51. Birdsall, Ross and Sabot (1994), 2.
52. *Ibid.*, 7.
53. UNDP (1990) and (1996).
54. Birdsall, Ross and Sabot (1994).
55. Jeffrey G. Williamson, 'Human Capital Deepening, Inequality, and Demographic Events along the Asia-Pacific Rim,' in *Human Resources in Development Along the Asia-Pacific Rim*, ed. Naohiro Agawa, Gavin W. Jones, and Jeffrey G. Williamson (New York: Oxford University Press, 1993).
56. Birdsall, Ross and Sabot (1995), 482.
57. Birdsall, Ross and Sabot (1994), 12.
58. Scitovsky (1985).
59. John Mellor, *Agriculture on the Road to Industrialization* (Baltimore: The Johns Hopkins University Press, 1995), p. 322.
60. Juha Honkkila, *Privatisation, Asset Distribution and Equity in Transitional Economies*, United Nations University, World Institute for Development Economics Research, Working Papers No. 125 (1997).
61. Griffin (1996), 140.
62. Deininger and Squire (1998), 25.
63. William R. Cline, *Potential Effects of Income Redistribution on Economic Growth: Latin American Cases* (New York: Praeger, 1972).

References

Adelman, Irma and Cynthia Taft Morris (1971) 'An Anatomy of Patterns of Income Distribution in Developing Nations'. Part II of Final Report. Grant AID/csd-2236: (Northwestern University).

Ahluwalia, Montek S. (1976) 'Inequality, Poverty, and Development'. *Journal of Development Economics* 3: 307–42.

Alesina, Alberto and Roberto Perotti (1994) 'The Political Economy of Growth: A Critical Survey of the Literature'. *The World Bank Economic Review* 8, 3: 351–71.

Alesina, Alberto and Dani Rodrik (1994) 'Distributive Politics and Economic Growth.' *Quarterly Journal of Economics* 108: 480–90.

Asian Development Bank (1997) *Emerging Asia: Changes and Challenges* (Manila: Asian Development Bank).

Barro, Robert J. (1991) 'Economic Growth in a Cross Section of Countries'. *Quarterly Journal of Economics* 106 (May): 407–43.

Bergan, A. (1967) 'Personal Income Distribution and Personal Savings in Pakistan, 1963/64'. *Pakistan Development Review* 7, 2.

Bertola, Giuseppe (1993) 'Factor Shares and Savings in Endogenous Growth'. *American Economic Review* 83, 5: 1184–98.

Birdsall, Nancy, David Ross, and Richard Sabot (1994) 'Inequality as a Constraint on Growth in Latin America', mimeo (Interamerican Development Bank).

Birdsall, Nancy, David Ross, and Richard Sabot (1995) 'Inequality and Growth Reconsidered: Lessons for East Asia'. *The World Bank Economic Review* 9, 3: 477–508.

Bowles, Samuel and Herbert Gintis (1995) 'Escaping the Efficiency-Equity Trade-off: Productivity-Enhancing Asset Redistributions'. In *Macroeconomic Policy After the Conservative Era*, ed. Gerald A. Epstein and Herbert M. Gintis (New York: Cambridge University Press).

Clarke, G.R.G. (1995) 'More Evidence on Income Distribution and Growth'. *Journal of Development Economics* 47, 2: 403–27.

Cline, William R. (1972) *Potential Effects of Income Redistribution on Economic Growth: Latin American Cases* (New York: Praeger).

Deaton, A. (1995) 'Data and Econometric Tools for Development Analysis'. In *Handbook of Development Economics*, ed. by Jere Behrman and T.N. Srinivasan. Vol. IIIA (New York: Elsevier Science B.V).

Deininger, Klaus and Lyn Squire (1998) 'New Ways of Looking at Old Issues: Inequality and Growth'. *Journal of Development Economics* 57: 2.

Deininger, Klaus and Lyn Squire (1996) 'A New Data Set Measuring Income Inequality'. *World Bank Economic Review* 10: 3: 565–91.

Fei, John C.H., Gustav Ranis and Shirley W.Y. Kuo (1979) *Growth and Equity: The Taiwan Case* (New York: Oxford University Press).

Fields, Gary (1989) 'Changes in Poverty and Inequality in Developing Countries'. *World Bank Research Observer* 4: 167–86.

Griffin, Keith (1974) *The Political Economy of Agrarian Change* (London: Macmillan).

Griffin, Keith (1996) *Studies in Globalization and Economic Transitions* (London: Macmillan).

Griffin, Keith (1997) 'Culture, Human Development and Economic Growth'. UNRISD/UNESCO, Occasional Paper Series on Culture and Development, No. 3.

Griffin, Keith and Mark Brenner (1997) 'Domestic Resource Mobilization and Enterprise Development in Sub-Saharan Africa'. Department of Economics, University of California, Riverside, Working Paper 97–01.

Griffin, Keith and Azizur Rahman Khan (1972) *Growth and Inequality in Pakistan* (London: Macmillan Press).

Griffin, Keith and Terry McKinley (1994) *Implementing a Human Development Strategy* (London: Macmillan).

Honkkila, Juha (1997) *Privatisation, Asset Distribution and Equity in Transitional Economies*. United Nations University, World Institute for Development Economics Research, Working Papers No. 125.

Jain, Shail (1975) *Size Distribution of Income: A Compilation of Data* (World Bank).

Kahlon, A.S. and Harbhajan Singh Bal. n.d. *Factors Associated with Farm and Farm Family Investment Pattern in Ludhiana (Punjab) and Hissar (Haryana) Districts: (1966–67 through 1969–70)*. (Department of Economics and Sociology, Punjab Agricultural University, Ludhiana).

Kaldor, Nicholas (1978) 'Capital Accumulation and Economic Growth'. In *Further Essays on Economic Theory*, ed. Nicholas Kaldor (New York: Holmes and Meier).

Kuznets, Simon (1955) 'Economic Growth and Income Inequality'. *American Economic Review* 45: 1–28.

Kuznets, Simon (1963) 'Quantitative Aspects of the Economic Growth of Nations: VIII. Distribution of Income by Size'. *Economic Development and Cultural Change* 11, 2: 1–80.

Kuznets, Simon (1967) 'Underdeveloped Countries and the Pre-Industrial Phase in the Advanced Countries'. In *The Economics of Underdevelopment*, ed. A.N. Agarwala and P.S. Singh (New York: Oxford University Press).

Loury, G.C. (1981) 'Intergenerational Transfers and the Distribution of Earnings'. *Econometrica* 49: 843–67.

Mellor, John (1995) *Agriculture on the Road to Industrialization* (Baltimore: The Johns Hopkins University Press).

Okun, Arthur (1975) *Equality and Efficiency: The Big Tradeoff* (Washington, DC: Brookings Institution).

Panikar, P.G.K. (1961) 'Rural Savings in India'. *Economic Development and Cultural Change* 10: 1.

Paukert, Felix (1973) 'Income Distribution at Different Levels of Development: A Survey of Evidence'. *International Labour Review* 108: 97–125.

Perotti, Roberto (1991) 'Income Distribution, Politics and Growth: Theory and Evidence'. (Columbia University. Mimeo).

Persson, Torsten and Guido Tabellini (1994) 'Is Inequality Harmful for Growth'. *American Economic Review* 84, 3: 600–21.

Psacharopoulos, George (1988) 'Education and Development. A Review'. *World Bank Research Observer* 3, 1: 99–116.

Psacharopoulos, George (1994) 'Returns to Investment in Education: A Global Update'. *World Development* 22: 1325–43.

Ram, Rati (1996) 'Level of Development and Returns to Schooling: Some Estimates from Multicountry Data'. *Economic Development and Cultural Change* 44, 4: 839–57.

Robinson, Sherman (1976) 'A Note on the U-Hypothesis'. *American Economic Review* 66, 3: 437–40.

Saith, Ashwanti (1983) 'Development and Distribution: A Critique of the Cross-Country U-Hypothesis'. *Journal of Development Economics* 13: 367–80.

Scitovsky, Tibor (1985) 'Economic Development in Taiwan and South Korea'. *Food Research Institute Studies* 19, 4: 215–64.

Stiglitz, Joseph and Andrew Weiss (1981) 'Credit Rationing in Markets with Imperfect Information'. *American Economic Review* 71: 393–409.

United Nations Development Programme (1990) *Human Development Report* (New York: Oxford University Press).

United Nations Development Programme (1996) *Human Development Report* (New York: Oxford University Press).

Williamson, Jeffrey G. (1993) 'Human Capital Deepening, Inequality, and Demographic Events along the Asia-Pacific Rim'. In *Human Resources in Development Along the Asia-Pacific Rim*, ed. Naohiro Agawa, Gavin W. Jones, and Jeffrey G. Williamson (New York: Oxford University Press).

Index